WOMEN IN THE
THIRD WORLD

A Reference Handbook

Other Titles in ABC-CLIO's
CONTEMPORARY WORLD ISSUES
Series

Books in the Contemporary World Issues series address vital issues in today's society such as terrorism, sexual harassment, homelessness, AIDS, gambling, animal rights, and air pollution. Written by professional writers, scholars, and nonacademic experts, these books are authoritative, clearly written, up-to-date, and objective. They provide a good starting point for research by high school and college students, scholars, and general readers, as well as by legislators, businesspeople, activists, and others.

Each book, carefully organized and easy to use, contains an overview of the subject; a detailed chronology; biographical sketches; facts and data and/or documents and other primary-source material; a directory of organizations and agencies; annotated lists of print and nonprint resources; a glossary; and an index.

Readers of books in the Contemporary World Issues series will find the information they need in order to better understand the social, political, environmental, and economic issues facing the world today.

WOMEN IN THE
THIRD WORLD

A Reference Handbook

Karen L. Kinnear

**CONTEMPORARY
WORLD ISSUES**

ABC-CLIO

Santa Barbara, California
Denver, Colorado
Oxford, England

Library of Congress Cataloging-in-Publication Data

Kinnear, Karen L.
    Women in the Third World : a reference handbook / Karen L. Kinnear.
        p.   cm. — (Contemporary world issues)
    Includes bibliographical references and index.
    ISBN 0-87436-922-3 (alk. paper)
        1. Women—Developing countries. 2. Women's rights—
Developing countries. I. Title. II. Series
HQ1870.9.K58   1997
30504'09172'4—dc21   97-17330

02 01 00 99 98 97 10 9 8 7 6 5 4 3 2 1

ABC-CLIO, Inc.
130 Cremona Drive, P.O. Box 1911
Santa Barbara, California 93116-1911 ∞ .

Manufactured in the United States of America

This book is printed on acid-free paper.

To the spirit of Western College, its faculty, staff, and students, for opening my eyes and heart to the people of different cultures;
to Nagu, Rama, and Bragadam, for befriending me while I was in India and for trying to explain Indian social customs to me;
to Moana and my Tongan family for patiently teaching me the customs and practices of their country and culture;
and to the countless other women and men I've met in my travels who have taught me about their cultures and about human nature and friendship.

Contents

Preface

The purpose of this book is to provide a survey of the available literature and other resources on the topic of women in the Third World and to provide sources for further research. The vast range of literature and resources available offers many opportunities to learn more about women in the Third World, their lives, and the challenges many of them face in their daily lives. A tremendous amount of growth in knowledge and research has occurred in this field in recent years, especially since the United Nations declared 1975 as International Women's Year and the years 1975 to 1985 as the International Decade for Women. This document provides a resource for students, writers, and researchers as well as professionals in the field.

While much progress has been made in alleviating many of the problems that women in the Third World face, many areas still exist in which improvements can be made. International laws, as well as many national laws, prohibit various forms of discrimination against women, but in reality, discrimination still exists. For example, although an amendment to the Childhood

Marriage Act in India in 1978 raised the minimum age at which a girl could be married to 18 years, in practice many girls younger than 15 are married. In 1951, the International Labour Organization adopted the Convention Concerning Equal Remuneration for Men and Women Workers for Work of Equal Value. This convention calls for equal pay for equal work for both men and women. But, today, women in most countries do not earn the same as men for similar work. Laws passed at the national or international level cannot always change well-established traditions or change the attitudes of many people.

The Fourth World Conference on Women held in Beijing in 1995 focused the attention of the world, for a short period of time, on the condition of women throughout the world. Thousands of women converged on Beijing, as well as on Huairou, where the nongovernmental organization (NGO) Forum on Women was held. Thousands more searched the media for news of the events and surfed the Internet to keep posted on the activities of the conference. Attention was focused on how many women, especially in developing countries, fight for survival on a daily basis, spending much of their time gathering food, hauling water, and maintaining a household, and on their resilience in the face of these challenges.

The growing number of NGOs signals greater interest in improving the lives of women and at the same time indicates the vast amount of work that still needs to be done to help women achieve equality in life. The fundamentalist movement is gaining ground in many Muslim countries, where hard-won rights for women are being rolled back. Countries ratify international conventions agreeing to adhere to the resulting provisions but do not change their national laws to comply. Work must continue for women to gain equal rights as human beings and to have a chance at improving their standard of living. This book reviews current knowledge and resources in order to help the reader understand the issues concerning this important and timely topic.

This book, like other books in the Contemporary World Issues series, provides a balanced survey of the resources available and a guide to further research on the topic of women in the Third World. Chapter 1 reviews the literature concerning women in the Third World, including aspects of education, health, the family, work, and politics. Chapter 2 provides a chronology of the significant events in the recent history of women in the Third World. Chapter 3 offers biographical sketches of women who have played or are currently playing key roles in some aspect of the field of women in the Third World. Chapter 4 provides statistical information on the status of women in the Third World and excerpts from key, relevant United Nations documents and other international legal documents concerning the treatment and status of women in the Third World. Chapter 5 provides a directory of representative private and public organizations, associations, and government agencies involved in working with women in the Third World in a variety of areas, including education, health, family planning, and development. Some organizations help develop programs and some provide financing for women-owned enterprises. In Chapter 6, books that focus on women in developing countries are annotated; the literature varies from popular accounts to descriptions of primary research and provides a wide perspective on the many issues of importance to women in the Third World. Chapter 7 includes an annotated list of nonprint resources, including films and videocassettes as well as relevant sources of information that can be found on the Internet.

Introduction and Overview

1

The United Nations Fourth World Conference on Women held in 1995 in Beijing focused renewed attention on the status and condition of women throughout the world. In many countries, women find themselves discriminated against, denied basic human rights, and considered second-class citizens. This chapter provides an overview of women in developing countries—their status, the conditions in which they live, and many of the social, political, and economic forces that affect them.

First, we need to define what we mean by the "Third World." This term has come to mean less developed countries, or countries with relatively low per capita incomes, short life expectancies, and high rates of illiteracy. The economies of these countries are generally agriculturally based. "First World" countries are considered to include industrialized, democratic countries, such as the United States, Canada, the European countries, Australia, New Zealand, Japan, and other countries that are not considered communist. "Second World" countries are countries that are part of the communist bloc, and include Poland, Hungary, Romania, Bulgaria, the former Soviet Union, China, and Cuba. "Second World" countries are part of the communist bloc and originally included the Soviet

Union, Poland, Hungary, Romania, Bulgaria, China, and Cuba. Today, many of the countries of the former Soviet Union may be considered "Third World" or developing countries, depending on whether or not they have remained communist.

Third World versus First World Women

Women in the more developed countries often find themselves better off than their counterparts in the developing world. Of course, life for most people, both men and women, in developed countries is better than in developing countries. But women throughout the world may be discriminated against to some degree, and this discrimination is not confined to developing countries.

We also must keep in mind that women in the developed countries are not the only ones who have made great strides. Probably the best-known example is that of women in politics. Women have been elected to lead their countries in India and Pakistan (two Third World countries), as well as in Israel and Britain, while no woman in the United States has held this position. In another example, two women were named to Nicaragua's supreme court in 1982, while the first woman to sit on the United States Supreme Court was named to the Court only one year earlier, in 1981. As we study the conditions of women in the Third World, we must keep in mind that this information should be understood in its proper perspective, that is, in relation to the relative position of women in other, more developed countries and to the condition of men in Third World countries.

Women in the Third World often criticize women in Western democracies for their cultural imperialism, their way of coming into these developing countries and deciding what is wrong with the culture and lives of people there. These Western women (and men) apply Western theories and models to conditions and situations that they find in developing countries, often without a comprehensive understanding of the culture in which these conditions exist. When I talked with young women in India about arranged marriages, I could not understand their acceptance of their situations. One young (21 years old), college-educated woman told me that this is the way it is done in India and she willingly accepts her fate. She did not appear unhappy, even though her husband was many years older than she was, and over time I realized that she would make the best of this situation. Because we had different concepts of marriage, our expectations were different. She was comfortable with her culture's expectations and practices. It is easy to judge a situation based on our own knowledge and experiences; what we must do is put ourselves in these women's shoes and understand their perspective. Scholar Beverly Mack reports on this attitude of acceptance in an article in the *Washington Post:*

> A Hausa woman growing up in her [Nigerian] culture understands the demands made on her and is prepared to deal with them on her own terms. She knows there are certain social expectations to be met: marrying according to parental choice, bearing children and obeying the head of the household. The fulfillment of these obligations gives a devoted woman a sense of security in knowing she has complied with the expectations of both her God and her community. . . . Polygamy . . . offers periodic relief from domestic responsibilities as wives take turns preparing the household's meals, doing laundry and attending to their husband in roughly three-day cycles. Thus co-wives experience a situation in which domestic chores ideally are shared among congenial companions. Of course this is not always the case; in any large household there are complaints about unequal work loads and jealousy among co-wives. (Mack 1984)

Western attempts to study the problems of Third World women also create resentment on the part of those women studied, who complain that Western researchers come in with a grant and a tape recorder, ask questions, and then fly home to write their reports in the relative comfort of their own lives. Often, careers are boosted by these studies but little or nothing is provided to help improve the welfare and lives of the people who are studied. Many researchers ask questions that are meant to elicit intimate details of the lives of these people, but most have no idea of the extent to which this intrusion affects those involved. Outsiders who have little understanding of local culture come in and study polygamy, purdah (the seclusion of women from the public, practiced by Muslims and some Hindus), veiling, dowry (in India, the money and/or goods that a bride's family brings to her husband and his family), brideprice, and child marriages and condemn these practices based on Western beliefs and traditions. Little if any attempt is made to understand these practices within their cultural context before totally condemning them. Many people in the Third World can not understand this type of behavior and resent the implication that their societies are primitive and problematic while Western societies are good and have no problems.

Research conducted today is often more sensitive to the cultures of other people, but we still have a way to go in understanding the many problems that women face within their cultural context. Every society has certain roles that it expects men and women to play; the following section briefly examines the role of gender in society.

Gender Roles and Inequality

Sex roles are behaviors that are determined by the biological differences between women and men, such as pregnancy, lactation, erection, and ejaculation. Gender roles are behaviors that are determined by the social and cultural context in which people live and how they define femininity and masculinity. Gender stratification is defined as "the differential ranking and rewarding of women's and men's roles" (Eitzen and Zinn 1991, 300). All societies use gender as a primary means of determining the division of labor and the provision of rights and responsibilities for citizens. Gender roles are not the same in countries throughout the world. Most countries, however, assign roles in domestic and family areas to women and in political and public areas to men.

Some sociologists believe that male dominance is universal, that is, found in every culture throughout society. They believe that some form of patriarchy is found in all cultures. Others believe that sexual differentiation is found in all societies but that females are not always the ones that are considered of lower status (Rogers 1978; Eitzen and Zinn 1991).

Women's roles vary across cultures. Their status within each society is determined by institutional factors such as family, politics, religion, and economic systems within the culture as well as by the level of power, prestige, and control over property that they have. The power and influence of women may change as they age, with added prestige provided to elderly women in some cultures. Within cultures, women's roles and positions also vary. Women in the upper classes of all societies enjoy many advantages that women in lower classes within the same culture are denied.

Women have both reproductive and productive roles in most societies. Their reproductive role is usually undervalued by most people; it includes biological reproduction (bearing children, rearing children, and maintaining the household) and social reproduction (maintaining the status quo in their society). Productive work includes all activities that generate income or have some sort of exchange value. Most societies do not see reproductive work as productive, that is, having any economic value. As a result, the value of women is considered to be less than that of men because value is usually measured in terms of economic value.

The issue of gender is one of the basic sources of division and definition in a particular society. It determines who is considered a citizen, who is allowed to vote, who is allowed to own land. Gender defines men and women according to the social relationship between them. Approaches to development in terms of gender are concerned with the ways that such relationships are socially constructed.

Patriarchy

Patriarchy is defined as the "principle of male dominance that forms both a structural and ideological system of domination in which men control women" (Chow and Berheide 1994, 14). It is not a static condition or universal in its characteristics. The specific forms that patriarchy may take vary by class, race, and age. Patriarchy is most commonly seen and studied in relation to its role in the family. In the patriarchal family, men have the power to determine the status, privileges, and roles of women and children within the family. This power is also reinforced by traditional gender role belief systems. Hartmann (1976) believes that "patriarchy, as an independent system of domination preceding capitalism, influences the particular forms the sexual division of labor takes in the family as well as in the waged labor economy. Household work, childcare, emotional support, labor, and home-based production are examples of how the family serves as locus of control and how men benefit from women's labor, paid or unpaid, at home" (Chow and Berheide 1994, 15).

Patriarchy can be both public and private. Private patriarchy generally is practiced in the family environment, while public patriarchy is that practiced by the state and within the economy. Patriarchy influences the role of women in the economy in countries around the world. A search of the literature concerning the international division of labor demonstrates a relationship between capitalist accumulation on a world scale and patriarchal family structures and how these factors shape women's place in the global economy's division of labor as well as in the family household (Beneria and Stimpson 1987; Mies 1986; Chow and Berheide 1994). Jiggins sees the influence of patriarchal approaches to politics and international affairs as creating a dangerous and unbalanced world:

> It is a world that counts weapons of destruction as economically productive and women's domestic work as economically valueless. It is a world governed by the public decisions of men who choose to solve problems by force. It is a world in which women and children form the majority of the poor, the displaced, and the hungry. Such a world is not sustainable. (Jiggins 1994, 41)

International relations theory and practice has primarily been developed by men who have based their theories on their own knowledge and experience as men. Women are often left out of this equation, and as a result, their impact on society is not considered or valued. The remainder of this chapter focuses on specific issues of concern to women in Third World countries.

Education

Education is recognized as an inalienable right for every person by the Universal Declaration of Human Rights and the International Covenant on Economic, Social and Cultural Rights. Both have been adopted by the United Nations and its member nations (see Chapter 4 for excerpts of these documents). Most countries recognize the importance of providing education to their citizens. Education enhances citizens' economic, political, social, and cultural development and provides benefits to the community and nation as well. Studies have shown that women who are well educated have more control over their lives, including reproduction, and have fewer children than women with no education (Jejeebhoy 1995).

In developing countries, many citizens do not receive an education that will make them literate, that is, able to read and write and understand the written word. Lack of teachers, school facilities, and transportation to get to school, as well as the cost of schooling, the need to help out at home, and the view that education is not important are some of the many reasons. Researchers have estimated that 95 percent of the world population that is illiterate is living in developing countries (Ballara 1991; UNESCO 1990). Women are more likely to be illiterate in these countries than are men.

Education can provide the impetus to break down stereotypes that exist in a society toward women and their status in society. Throughout the literature concerning women and their status, especially in the Third World, the words *education* and *empowerment* can be found. An education empowers a woman, raises her self-esteem, and offers her options in her life. More than any other factor, education is believed to be the key element in improving the lives of women throughout the world. For young girls who are married and enter a world of restriction, seclusion, or other isolation from family members and friends, the ability to read and write connects them with the outside world. In many situations, an education provides status to a woman in her family and in the community.

Families usually feel a need to educate their sons—that boys need an education to be able to go out into the world, get a good job, and support a family. However, for young daughters in developing countries, the need is not so easily understood—a young girl will eventually get married and have a family and her primary work will be at home taking care of her husband and children—and therefore many families see little need for educating their daughters. They see this as a waste of time and money, for the girls can stay home and help their mothers take care of the housework and care for the other siblings in the family. Young girls also participate in income-generating activities, such as sewing, weaving, and farming activities. Many women agree that an education is not as important for girls as it is for boys. Understanding and changing these attitudes is a difficult task for all advocates of universal education.

For many young girls, especially in developing countries, their informal "education" begins by teaching them that boys have more status and privileges than they do, that boys are better and more important. According to a study of female children in Nepal conducted by the United Nations Children's Emergency

Fund (UNICEF) (1992), researchers found that the process of socializing girls starts early, teaching them that boys are superior to them and that they must accept their situation as natural and normal. The researchers found that "not only are girls and women socially and ideologically unequipped to retaliate against (or even question) the implicit and explicit injustices to which they are subjected, but that, in the absence of alternative models of role and conduct, they actually espouse and propagate the dominant social and cultural values that militate against their gender group" (page 32).

Girls in rural areas of Third World countries are less likely than girls in urban areas to go to school. Families living in rural areas are less likely to have access to a school and may also have a more pressing need to keep children, especially girls, at home to help with child care and subsistence activities. Families living in urban areas are more likely to have access to schools and income to pay for their children's education and are more likely to understand the importance of an education.

Lack of an education affects young girls and women in other ways. For example, many studies have shown a relationship between a lack of an education and teenage pregnancies, unemployment, crime, and health problems (King 1990; King and Hill 1993). For many women's advocates and development workers in developing countries, other problems and needs take precedence over the provision of education. These include food shortages, poor health care, lack of health care facilities, lack of housing or inadequate housing, and lack of employment opportunities.

For married women, as they start families the desire for an education is often lessened by a number of factors, including lack of time, pregnancy, child care, fatigue, agricultural activities, and income-generating activities. Cultural patterns also play a role. In many countries, parents believe that they must educate their sons because they are the ones who will later be required to marry, start a family, and even support their parents in old age. Girls will marry and join their husband's family, thus providing nothing to their birth parents. Religious traditions may encourage girls and women to stay at home, raise a family, and take care of their husbands, thus discouraging the desire for an education. Other factors preventing the education of females are male teachers, classes of mixed gender, distances between home and school, and lack of transportation. Women's learned behaviors, such as submissiveness to male authority, shyness, lack of self-confidence, and isolation from social activities, also contribute to this situation.

More and more researchers are recognizing the important role that women play in economic development activities. The Demographic and Health Survey (1990) conducted in 28 countries in Africa, Latin America and the Caribbean, Asia, and Arab countries in 1990 found a positive relationship between women's education and social and economic development. They also found that family size decreased as the education level of women increased. The use of family planning methods also increased with an increase in women's educational levels.

The relationship between women's educational level and the health of themselves and their families also has been studied. The United Nations Fund for Population Activities (UNFPA) (1989) issued a report on the state of the world population. Studies conducted in 46 countries throughout the world indicated that raising the number of educated women by 1 percent was three times more effective than raising the number of physicians by 1 percent. Ballara (1991) reports on a study conducted by the Research Triangle Institute that examined the enrollment of girls in primary and secondary schools in 80 developing countries. These researchers found that an increase of 70 percent in the enrollment of girls in primary schools as well as in secondary schools could result in lowering infant mortality rates by as much as 40 per 1,000 live births. Caldwell (1979) studied educational levels and child mortality in Nigeria and found that educated women have lower rates of child mortality and tend to be more familiar with doctors and health facilities and use them more frequently. The Demographic and Health Survey (1990) reported a positive relationship between prenatal care and a woman's level of education. Educated women also are more likely to understand the importance of taking their children to see doctors when they are sick.

The relationship between women's educational levels and their participation in the labor force is strong. The Research Triangle Institute study reported on by Ballara (1991) found that a 70 percent increase in the number of girls receiving a primary and secondary education will lead, over time, to an increase in women's participation in the labor force. As women's educational levels increase, the number of self-employed women also increases.

Nongovernmental organizations have instituted programs to encourage literacy among women and girls to improve their lives as well as their position in society. The YWCA of India combines literacy training with classes in health, employment, and social and legal training. Each of the YWCA's programs includes activities in handicrafts, sewing, soap production, and book-binding. The Associated Country Women of the World offers literacy programs in Ecuador, India, Kenya, Pakistan, and Zaire. The United Nations Development Fund for Women (UNIFEM) and United Nations Education, Scientific and Cultural Organization (UNESCO) also have initiated literacy programs for women.

Education is one of the most influential factors in providing advances for women. The more education a woman has, the better off she is. Education provides the knowledge that women need to promote their health, well-being, economic status, family relations, development options, and political rights. The lives of women are enriched by education.

Family Relations

Preference for Males

Even before young women are engaged and married, they understand the place they hold in their families and society. From the time they are born, many girls do not hold an honored place in their families. Many families, especially in developing countries, prefer boys over girls. Girls are biologically stronger than males in their early years, and they are estimated to have a mortality rate lower than males (1 to 1.15) (Royston and Armstrong 1989). However, according to data from the 1983 World Fertility Survey (UNFPA 1989), mortality rates for girls are 1.5 times higher than boys in Sri Lanka and Pakistan, 1.4 times higher in Bangladesh, and 1.3 times higher in Colombia. Many families believe that boys require and deserve more food and better quality food than girls, which may lead to higher mortality rates among girls.

Boys are expected to become wage earners to support their own families as well as to provide support to their parents in old age. In many developing countries, the extended family is still common, with the male usually bringing home his bride to live in their own home or in the home of his parents. The bride helps her husband's mother and father with many of the household chores, especially if she does not have her own job. The preference for males also often extends to access to health care and education. Families are more likely to provide their sons with all available health care and with an education. Girls are seen as providing service to their families, by staying home and helping their mothers with housework, child care, and income-generating activities if available.

Marriage

Most women throughout the world are expected to marry at some time in their lives. In many Third World countries, women are seen as property, having value to their birth families only when they are married off, preferably at an early age, and the family receives money or goods for their "purchase." The wife in many families is expected to care for the husband and to bear children, preferably boys. Throughout the Third World, women bear the burden of taking care of the home; their tasks may include tending the family's garden, caring for live animals that the family may have for future needs, gathering fuel for cooking, gathering water for drinking, cooking, and bathing, caring for the children, and caring for and supporting the husband. In many cases, women are also expected to find paying work to help support the family.

In many Third World countries, arranged marriages are still a common practice. In these cases, parents make all arrangements to find a wife or husband for their child. The prospective bride and groom have no say in the wedding and often do not even have a chance to meet their future spouse until the day of the wedding. Some families are beginning to allow marriages based on love, that is, marriages in which the boy and girl choose each other. As more girls are allowed to go to school, enter college, and find jobs, the opportunities expand for them to find their own mate. However, many families still require the approval of the parents, who are determined to ensure that their sons marry properly.

In some Third World cultures, girls are engaged when they are still very young, even 11 or 12 years old. They will be married when they are older, but they will have no choice in the matter. Some young girls are matched with older men. Especially in Middle Eastern countries, but also in Asia, older men like to marry young virgins.

In India, once a girl marries, she frequently goes to live in her in-laws' home. Her family loyalties are expected to change from her birth family to her new family. Emotionally, economically, and legally, a girl is property that is transferred to another family (Calman 1992). The Indian government passed the Child Marriage Restraint Act in 1929 that set a minimum age of marriage for males at 18 years and for females at 14 years. In 1949, the minimum age for females was changed to 15 years. In 1978, the minimum ages for females was raised to 18 and for males to 21 years. Despite these laws, the 1961 census found that in over one-third of all the districts in India the average age of girls at marriage was below 15 years. The 1971 census revealed that in rural India 14 percent of girls between the ages of 10 and 14 years were married, and in urban areas the figure was 4 percent. The Committee on the Status of Women in India was frustrated that the census did not ask for information on the marriage of girls younger than 10 years because committee members had met many girls younger than 10 years who were already married. In 1986, the health minister of Uttar Pradesh revealed that there were villages in the state in which all girls over the age of 8 years were married, because, as the villagers explained, the dowry expected for an 8-year-old girl was much less than for a girl past puberty (Calman 1992).

In Islamic societies, polygyny, the practice of men having multiple wives, is allowed. The Koran—the holy book of the Islamic faith, which contains the words of God as they were given to the Prophet Mohammed—allows men to take up to four wives in specific circumstances, and many men consider this permission to marry more than one woman whenever they want. In Malaysia, Mohamed Saad Mehmad, Perlis state's Islamic religious department director, claimed at a seminar in 1991 that women should allow "their husbands to take second, third or fourth wives as a way of preventing extramarital affairs and alleviating the problem of unmarried women" ("Malaysia: States Differ on Approach to Polygamy" 1991, 18).

Behavioral Restrictions

In several Islamic countries, women's behavior is severely restricted. The practice of purdah, a Persian word meaning "curtain," is an institutionalized system that requires women to cover their bodies and faces and to remain in seclusion from the rest of society. Purdah has three major parts: women are physically separated with their own living space, they are socially segregated from all but their immediate kinship circle, and they must cover their bodies and their faces whenever they appear in public places. Purdah keeps women secluded and isolated from the rest of society by confining them to the surroundings of their home, family, immediate kinship circle, and neighborhood (Dankelman and Davidson 1988). In other cultures, women are not so $ restricted but still do not have full freedom.

Health Care

All women face a variety of health problems. During pregnancy women can experience vitamin deficiency, high blood pressure, miscarriage, and anemia. Lack of prenatal care endangers the lives of both the mother and the child. Contraceptives may pose their own risks but lack of access to contraceptives may create unwanted pregnancies and result in children that cannot be adequately cared for. Abortion services are not always available. Maternal mortality is higher in developing countries than in developed countries, often because of lack of access to medical care, numerous pregnancies, and overwork. The practice of female genital mutilation in many societies can lead to several health problems, including excessive bleeding, painful menstruation, painful sexual intercourse, and death for some young girls. Sexually transmitted diseases, including AIDS (acquired immunodeficiency syndrome), threatens the health and lives of many women, including those forced into prostitution. During war and internal conflicts, women often are raped by soldiers.

Knowledge of health care issues that affect them as well as access to health care is severely lacking for women in developing countries. Access to health care may be limited for several reasons, including lack of infrastructure, lack of services for referral, poverty, unavailability of midwives, the lack of acceptance of traditional birth attendants by community maternal health programs, lack of information about health care and the need for it, lack of self-esteem, and the position of the woman in the family and her ability to make her own decisions concerning health care.

Medical facilities, hospitals, and clinics, as well as medical staff—physicians, nurses, midwives, and traditional birth attendants—are lacking. If facilities are not located in the same village or town, women need transportation to get to these facilities; many do not have access to cars or bicycles, are not on a bus route, or do not have the money to spend on transportation. Some women do not have the time to go to the doctor or other medical practitioners; they cannot get time off from work or cannot leave their children alone. Some do not have money to pay for medical services. Some women live in rural areas that do not provide easy access to medical facilities. The climate in some countries may affect women's ability to get to health care facilities. Lack of communications, e.g., telephone service, also plays a role in women's ability to gain information concerning their medical conditions or to make appointments.

If midwives or traditional birth attendants (women from the local village who are untrained in modern medicine) are not available, maternal and child mortality levels may increase. For example, in Matlab, Bangladesh, maternal mortality decreased by 68 percent over three years when midwives staffed two health clinic sites (Fauveau 1991). Midwives in Ghana were trained in advanced lifesaving techniques and midwifery skills and, as a result, mortality has been reduced significantly. Midwives have developed good supportive relationships with community and traditional practitioners in Ghana, which has contributed to improved maternal and child health. These cooperative, mutually respectful relationships among all health care workers are critical to the success of health care programs. According to Okafor (1991), traditional birth attendants and midwives have a poor working relationship in many parts of Nigeria, which has led to inadequate services being provided to pregnant women.

The sex of the health care provider also plays a role in whether or not a woman will seek health care. For example, most doctors in Egypt are male; custom dictates that women, once past puberty, should not be seen by any male other than a close relative. Even in an emergency situation, many women must get their husband's permission to seek treatment. A woman's reputation could be ruined if she seeks out a male doctor for treatment of any kind; many will question her purity and accuse her of sexual misconduct (el Saadawi, 1980; Krieger 1991). Islamic married women in Cameroon cannot be touched by a male without the husband's permission. Women interviewed in one study claimed that they would rather die than seek medical care without their husband's approval (Alexandre 1991).

Lack of knowledge concerning the human body and the need for health care in certain circumstances also limits the ability of women to seek help. In some cases, women do not recognize their or their child's need for medical attention. Sometimes women deny, or refuse to acknowledge, their pregnancy in its early stages, when prenatal care may be critical to the health of the mother and of the fetus. Sometimes men do not want to know that their wives are pregnant again, especially if birth control is not available or not encouraged for religious reasons.

Some women do not seek medical care because they have

been taught to believe that suffering is women's lot in life. They accept overwork, back pain, reproductive tract infections, and chronic fatigue as a part of life. Women often deal with life crises by putting the needs of their families first, while putting their own needs last (Moser 1991).

In other cases, traditional beliefs and practices also may preclude a woman from seeking medical attention, especially during pregnancy. Women may believe that it is not necessary to seek help when pregnant, that local midwives will take care of everything during birth, or that certain foods will help, or hinder, a pregnancy.

Nutrition

Because most women put in long hours and have many roles, as wife, mother, and income earner, they are vulnerable to malnutrition. Poverty also influences a woman's nutritional status. Separate studies conducted by Anderson (1991) and Senapati (1991) showed the heavy workload of women in India to be strongly associated with low weight. The nutritional status of women when they are pregnant is especially important. The World Health Organization has estimated that each year 20 million babies are born with low birth weight and 90 percent of this group are born to women living in developing countries (Kramer 1987).

The men and boys in a family often are fed before the girls and the women because boys and men are perceived as more valuable and therefore deserving of as much food as they need to stay healthy and satisfied. According to a report on maternal health by the government of Lesotho (1990), the major factor leading to the poor nutritional status of women is the "tradition of feeding men and boys before women and girls, [where] the nutritious foods are served to male members of the families and females would then have the leftovers" (page 5). A study of rural Bangladesh found that girls were three times more likely to be malnourished than boys (Chen, Huq, and D'Souza 1981). A UNICEF (1986) study determined that in 45 developing countries, mortality rates for girls ages one to four are higher than for boys in 43 of these countries, often as a direct result of malnutrition.

As a result of numerous pregnancies, low food intake, and high work demands, women are not able to meet the nutritional needs of their bodies. They may experience deficiencies of specific vitamins and minerals or a condition of chronic malnutrition may exist. Women tend to suffer from anemia as a result of iron deficiency, or iodine deficiency, or stunted growth as a result of lack of protein and calories. As women age, their health may deteriorate as a direct result of poor nutrition throughout their lives.

According to some researchers, pregnant women may not eat certain foods due to myths and superstitions. Women in some African, Asian, and Middle Eastern countries may be prohibited by local taboos from eating certain foods, including eggs, milk, and occasionally even fruits and vegetables (Acasadi and Johnson-Acasadi 1990). Pregnant women may have a deficiency of iron and become anemic, which may lead to infections and problems with the health of the fetus. Four of the major causes of maternal mortality are related to poor nutrition: hemorrhage, infection, obstructed labor, and eclampsia (Koblinsky, Timyan, and Gay 1993).

Women's occupational health is also at risk in many Third World countries. While few statistics are available to determine the size of the problem, many health hazards do exist. For example, women working in agriculture may be exposed to dangerous pesticides and other chemicals used to enhance crop size. Women working at home may be exposed to eyestrain and more serious vision problems as a result of close production work. Poor lighting may contribute to this problem. Many countries do not have safety laws that protect workers from common dangers in the workplace, including exposed wiring, lack of fire protection equipment such as sprinkler systems, and crowded conditions without adequate exits. Locked doors have proven deadly in several developing countries; fires have started somewhere in the building and women have not been able to get out of the building in time.

Contraceptives

Family planning programs provide individuals and families with the ability to safely regulate and control their fertility. In many countries, government policies and laws determine the availability of contraceptives to the general population. These policies and laws may be based on the need to reduce population growth, since many countries are currently concerned over the growing number of people being born in their countries, which puts heavy pressure on social and economic institutions.

Contraceptives challenge the belief that men have the right to control women's fertility and sexuality. In areas where contraception resources are available, the level of education that a woman has achieved influences her willingness to use contraceptives. The more education a woman has, the more likely she is to use some form of birth control. Educated women are more likely to understand the way contraceptives work and their side effects, and are less likely to be inhibited about discussing their use with their husbands and actually using them (Jejeebhoy 1995).

Even where family planning policies are in effect, some countries prohibit the advertising of services, prevent trained medical personnel from distributing contraceptives, or in some other way prohibit the use of contraceptives. In some countries nurses are not allowed to insert intrauterine devices (IUDs) or distribute oral contraceptives. If women do not have the consent of their husbands or if adolescent girls do not have the permission of their parents (rarely given), contraceptives are not provided. In many developing countries, the decision to use contraceptives is often made by the husband. The prevailing belief in these countries is that a woman's fertility is the property of the husband; the husband is the only one who is allowed to determine whether or not to use birth control and what type to use. For example, a study of men's attitudes and practice regarding family planning in Sudan discovered that men are the ones to decide contraceptive use and were also responsible for procuring the contraceptive (Khalifa 1988).

The cost of contraceptives may be a factor in whether or not a woman uses them. Other problems include the availability of contraceptives, the distance one has to travel to procure them, the poor quality of services provided in procuring them, fear of negative health consequences and side effects, limited choice of method, and the cost of restocking the supply.

One program that is often cited as a highly successful program in supplying contraceptives is the Bangladesh Women's Health Coalition. This program provides a wide variety of contraceptives in an environment supportive of women and their needs. The coalition offers a wide variety of other health care services of interest to women and provided by women paramedics, including gynecological exams, prenatal care, immunizations, early termination of pregnancy, treatment of early childhood diseases, and referrals to hospitals for sterilization. In Ghana, the Ghana National Family Planning Program provides services to rural areas using mobile family planning teams in association with village-based primary health care workers and the Maternal and Child Health

Centers. Services are provided by both women and men, after staff members discovered that in one area almost one-half of the clients were men. Staff members found that men appeared to be more consistent users of contraception and were effective as advocates for family planning (Bouzidi and Korte 1990).

In Nigeria, more than 33,300 family planning service sites exist, but service availability varies widely and there is a limited selection of methods (Kiragu, Chapman, and Lewis 1995). The 1992 Nigeria Family Planning Facility Census found that chemist shops and patent-medicine stores are the most common providers of family planning services (56 percent), while clinics provide 11 percent, and hospitals, health centers, and maternity homes each provide about 7 percent. Fifteen percent of the sites in Lagos and 60 percent of the sites in Benue state report having difficulties in obtaining contraceptive supplies. Counseling services are provided by 41 percent of the sites, while only 4 percent offer informational pamphlets or brochures.

Abortion

Abortion is one of the most controversial topics today throughout the world. Many countries outlaw abortion because it goes against the particular religious beliefs of the country. Other countries allow abortions when the life of the mother is in danger or when the pregnancy is a result of rape or incest. In developed countries as well as in developing countries, discussions and policies concerning abortion are usually controversial.

Induced abortion is probably the oldest and maybe the most widely used form of fertility control (Royston and Armstrong 1989). According to Jacobson (1990), approximately 55 million pregnancies are terminated each year by induced abortions. Approximately one-half of these abortions are illegal and occur in developing countries, while the other half are legal abortions performed in the developed countries, China, and India (Population Crisis Committee 1989). Physical results of unsafe abortions include hemorrhage, uterine perforation, cervical trauma, and even death of the woman. Other costs include psychological trauma, guilt, expense, and the stigma associated with having an abortion.

Unsafe induced abortions are the leading cause of female mortality. These are the most preventable maternal deaths. Abortions by themselves are not responsible for women's deaths; abortions that are unsafely performed are the cause of death. According to Hogberg (1985), deaths per 100,000 legal abortions range from 0.1 in developed countries to 6.0 in developing countries.

According to Dixon-Mueller (1990), approximately one-third of all people in the Third World live in countries in which abortion services are either prohibited or severely limited, usually to cases of rape, incest, or saving a woman's life. In these countries, some women who find themselves pregnant often go to extreme measures to terminate a pregnancy. Abortion policies vary from country to country. Each country's policy is influenced by several factors, including religion, birth rates, and population policies. Countries with large numbers of Muslims or Roman Catholics tend to restrict or prohibit abortion. Countries may watch their birth rates and, as they drop, institute laws restricting abortion. For example, low birth rates in Czechoslovakia led to the government's 1973 decree restricting access to abortion services. On the other hand, as birth rates increase, countries may adopt more liberal abortion policies. Countries such as China and India, with major population increases that have a major impact on society, have liberalized their abortion laws in the wake of unprecedented population growth.

In Bangladesh, under the Penal Code of 1960 induced abortion is allowed only to save the mother's life. This law was waived in 1972 for women who were raped during the War of Liberation. In Nigeria, abortion is a criminal offense for both the woman and the person performing the abortion. The only exceptions made are to save the woman's life (Okabue 1990). However, these laws are rarely enforced and many women crowd Nigerian hospitals suffering from incomplete or problematic abortions or other complications (Ladipo 1989).

In India, abortion was illegal until the Medical Termination of Pregnancy Act of 1971, except in cases in which the life of the mother was in danger. Rapid population growth in India had threatened the country's political stability, economic growth, and social progress. In 1991, its population according to the 1991 Census was 844.3 million people; some estimates push it over the one billion mark by 2001 (Chandrasekhar 1994). Family planning activities have been encouraged throughout India, but were hurt by the coercive methods of Sanjay Gandhi, the son of then Prime Minister Indira Gandhi. As a result of his negative activities, the name of the Ministry of Family Planning was changed to the Ministry of Health and Welfare. Today, over 6,500 medical institutions, including district hospitals, clinics, and private medical centers, provide abortion services. However, many of these institutions are located in urban areas, serving only 25 percent of the total population. Access to abortion services in rural areas is still very limited.

Maternal Mortality

Women's work is often devalued or considered of less value than men's work. This belief often leads to gender discrimination in the distribution of basic resources including food and health care and may lead to early death. Women often die from many of the same causes as men, but one gender-specific cause of maternal mortality is childbirth. Hemorrhage, obstructed labor, infections, hypertension, and complications from induced abortion are the major causes of maternal death during pregnancy, labor, and delivery. Maternal deaths in Third World countries account for a high proportion of all deaths of women in their reproductive years. Maine (1991) found that one of five deaths among women in their childbearing years in Bangladesh, India, Indonesia, and Egypt were related to pregnancy. This compares with one of 200 deaths in the United States.

Female Circumcision

Often referred to as female genital mutilation, the practice of female genital circumcision has seen increased attention in recent years. Even in the United States, many states have attempted to outlaw the practice by families from countries in which it is practiced, considering it a form of child sexual abuse. Physical complications from this "surgery" are often severe, and may include hemorrhage, tetanus, blood poisoning, and shock from the pain of the operation. In a study of the practice in Sierra Leone, Hosken (1988) found that 83 percent of all women who were circumcised were treated at some time in their lives for problems related to the circumcision.

Female circumcision may take several forms. The least damaging form is referred to as mild sunna, which consists of slitting or removing the prepuce of the clitoris. A modified sunna consists of the partial or total removal of the clitoris. A clitoridectomy consists of the removal of part or all of the clitoris and part or all of the labia minora (and is also referred to as sunna in the Sudan). Infibulation or pharaonic circumcision is the most radical form of circumcision and consists of a clitoridectomy, the removal of the labia minora, and the removal of the inner layers of the labia majora. The remaining edges of the labia are sewn together to form a bridge of scar tissue over the opening to the vagina (Lightfoot-Klein 1989).

Young girls in many countries in Africa and a few countries in Asia undergo female genital circumcision. In many rural parts of Africa, traditional midwives often perform the circumcision, although barbers and male priests are also known to perform it. Antiseptics and anesthesia, according to Lightfoot-Klein (1989), are generally not used. In urban areas, doctors, nurses, or midwives perform the procedure and are known to use anesthesia and antiseptics.

According to common belief, circumcision continues today primarily because it has always been done—it is the custom of many cultures. Reasons for continuing the practice include the protection of women from unwanted sexual intercourse; the protection of women from their own sexuality, from an uncontrolled sexual appetite; to keep young girls virgins; to enhance fertility; to enhance femininity; to keep married women faithful; and to keep women from masturbating. Perdita Huston talked with several women in the Sudan about the practice of circumcision and the events of their own circumcision. Huston describes her discussions with these women:

> The views these women expressed seemed somewhat ambivalent. Although they all voiced liberal "theories" on women's rights—and behavior—they nevertheless showed a surprising willingness to perpetuate in practice the very customs they condemned. They said that virginity should not be considered important—even arguing that it would be better to have relations with a man before marriage, in order to know him well. Moreover, although they said they believed the practice of circumcision to be harmful and useless, when I asked if they would circumcise their daughters, they all said, "Yes, I will have to." Clearly these women did not yet dare to act according to their expressed convictions—a reflection of how entrenched the custom of circumcision, particularly, remains in their part of the world. (Huston 1979, 51)

Long-term effects of circumcision include loss of any sexual feeling, chronic urinary tract infections, painful intercourse, pelvic infections, and severe scarring that can result in hemorrhaging during childbirth. Women often must be cut open on their wedding night and when giving birth in order to make sexual relations and childbirth possible.

The movement to prevent female circumcision began in African countries in the 1960s and continues today. Many women's groups are working to eliminate this practice. The Inter-African Committee on Traditional Practices Affecting the Health of Women and Children as well as many professionals, including physicians and nurses, gather information concerning female genital circumcision and advocate for an end to this practice. The African Charter on the Rights and Welfare of the Child calls for an end to harmful social and cultural practices. The Programme of Action of the International Conference on Population and Development as well as the Convention on the Rights of the Child also condemn traditional practices that may negatively impact the health of children.

Sexually Transmitted Diseases

Sexually transmitted diseases, including gonorrhea, syphilis, HIV, and AIDS, affect both men and women throughout the world. In developing countries, these diseases can cause even more problems than in the more developed countries. Many women in developing countries do not seek timely medical attention for many reasons. These reasons include unavailability of doctors or nurses, especially in rural areas; poverty; lack of time; cultural inhibitions; problems in communicating with male doctors; and feelings of shame over their conditions (Koblinsky, Timyan, and Gay 1993).

For some women, the inability to deny sex to their husbands creates an additional vulnerability to sexually transmitted diseases. In many countries, men are allowed, even expected, to seek sex outside of their marriage. If they contract a sexually transmitted disease, they are often unaware of their infection and eventually transmit the infection to their wives. Activities such as prostitution also contribute to women contracting sexually transmitted diseases.

Prostitution

Prostitution has become big business in many countries. In recent years, it has become international in scope. In the past, several southeast Asian countries were known as places in which women could be found for "rest and recreation" activities for foreign military personnel. Today, these countries and several others have expanded these services to include wealthy businessmen and tourists as clients; men traveling alone are creating a new market for prostitutes. Developing countries often encourage these activities, either openly or quietly behind the scenes, because the foreign currency benefits the countries' economies. Some researchers have found that prostitution in the entertainment industry is no longer confined to Asia and South Korea. Kenya, Senegal, and Brazil are now included in the sex tour circuit, countries in which rich businessmen often come for the express purpose of prostitution and other sexual activities (Cincone 1988).

Women involved in prostitution may be participating voluntarily or may have been coerced into this activity. For example, in Thailand, poverty impels rural parents to sell their daughters into prostitution for the survival of the family. In their eyes, economic reality justifies this practice. The government in Thailand has openly encouraged tourism, and Thai officials declared 1980 the Year of the Tourist. Deputy Prime Minister Boonchu Pojanasathian suggested to local governors that they could help the national tourism campaign by "developing scenic spots in your provinces while encouraging certain entertainment activities which some of you may find disgusting and embarrassing because they are related to sexual pleasure" (Holden et al. 1983, as quoted in Turshen and Holcomb 1993, 137).

In South Korea, a coalition of 24 women's organizations called on the government to take action against the growing practice of women being kidnapped and sold into prostitution to meet the needs of the growing entertainment industry. A study conducted in 1989 estimated that over 400,000 businesses in the entertainment field provided prostitutes to their customers, and that between 1.2 and 1.5 million women were participating as prostitutes. This number represents approximately 20 percent of South Korean women between the ages of 15 and 29. Prostitution is big business in South Korea, providing an estimated $5.7 billion to the economy, which is approximately 5 percent of the country's gross national product (Seoul YMCA 1989).

Prostitution places women in danger. The most common danger is from sexually transmitted disease, including gonorrhea, syphilis, and AIDS, but physical violence also endangers women. Male sexual aggression may lead to beatings and other physical harm. In Bangkok, a study sponsored by the United Nations found that two-thirds of women in Bangkok were afraid of being raped or physically assaulted while walking on the city's streets. The researchers found that hospital statistics of rapes and assaults supported this fear (Buendia 1989).

Sterilization

In recent years, attention has been drawn to the issue of sterilization of women. Some countries have been found to sterilize women of childbearing age in order to prevent them from having children. Joselina da Silva, a Brazilian organizer, believes that, in her country, approximately "46 percent of sexually active women between sixteen and fifty-four are now sterilized; the great majority of them are between sixteen and twenty-four years old" (da Silva 1991, 41).

Violence against Women

Throughout the world, women are threatened with violence, including violent acts committed against them by their husbands. In many developing countries, women are expected to obey their husbands and the husbands often have permission to discipline and control their wives in whatever ways they see fit. In Bangladesh, Stewart (1989) found that the murder of wives by their husbands accounted for 50 percent of all murders in the country. Almost 75 percent of all women murdered in Papua New Guinea were killed by their husbands (Bradley 1988).

Many women have died in India as a result of the practice of dowry. The practice of the woman's family providing a dowry to the husband has been prohibited by law since 1961. However, the practice itself, along with bride-burning or dowry deaths has grown in recent years. Many experts believe that providing dowry serves the purpose of elevating the economic status of the husband and his family. When the husband decides that his wife's family has not provided him with enough of a dowry, he may resort to burning his wife alive. Police often have a difficult time proving that the woman was intentionally murdered, primarily because the husbands often make the death look like a cooking accident. Official reports for all of India reported 4,835 dowry deaths throughout the country in 1991, although the Ahmedabad Women's Action Group estimates that over 1,000 women in Gujarat alone may be burned alive each year (Kelkar 1991).

Rape may be one of the most underreported crimes against women throughout the world. The stigma and shame that is often associated with rape appears universal. Estimates in developing countries are believed to be even less accurate than in developed countries because the report rate in developing countries is even lower than in developed countries. Even in developing countries, statistics indicate that most women who have been raped know their assailant. In countries that highly value a woman's virginity, including many Asian, Middle Eastern, and African countries, women who have been raped have lost all value. Fauveau and Blanchet (1989) studied rape in Bangladesh and found that "even when women are victims, a premarital sexual relation is said to spoil something intrinsic in their physical and moral person. . . . Their ruined reputation cannot be amended" (Koblinsky, Timyan, and Gay 1993, 178). Women are driven to suicide, beaten, or murdered as a result of the dishonor that they have brought upon their families.

In some countries, rape is used as a weapon against the women of one's enemies. Within Pakistani society, Ahmed (1992) writes that "feuds are settled through rapes. Men avenge themselves on each other by raping each other's mothers, wives, daughters and sisters. A brave adversary is supposed to break down under the grief and dishonor of the violation of his womenfolk. At times, women are gang raped, then paraded naked in the streets to show to the society that terminal revenge has been taken" (page 36).

In many countries, marital rape is not considered rape. In India, in the early 1980s, many women's groups demanded that forced intercourse by a husband with his wife without her consent should be considered rape. However, the Criminal Law (Amendment) Act of 1983 states that "sexual intercourse by a man with his own wife, the wife not being under fifteen years of age, is not rape" (Calman 1992, 121). Women have a difficult time leaving violent husbands, no matter what country they live in. In many developing countries, it is virtually impossible. For many of these women, returning to their birth families is not an option. The women's parents may have died or may be living with a son or economically dependent on a son and have no room and no economic resources to provide to the woman. In some cases, parents may talk to their son-in-law about his violent behavior and request that he stop. According to Lateef (1992), for many, "marriage is meant to be permanent and women's suffering within marriage is taken for granted" (page 197).

Women and Work

In the formal world of work, women face discrimination and multiple challenges. Access to jobs may be limited within certain cultures that restrict the position of women. The general economic conditions of the area in which they live affect women's standard of living and ability to find work outside the home. Women often earn less than men in many occupations. Women are usually found in lower level jobs than men. Changing economic policies have affected women and their position in the economy of many Third World countries. Women's lack of access to assets such as land and other forms of collateral hurt their ability to get loans to start businesses. However, in many areas, despite the many restrictions faced by women, women are increasing their participation in the workforce and assuming a greater economic responsibility for their families.

Women have traditionally had trouble obtaining credit from banks and other lending institutions. In many Third World countries women have not been allowed to own property; husbands or fathers have had control of property. Therefore, women have been unable to provide any form of collateral to back up a bank loan. However, by the 1980s, some institutions had begun to realize that women are usually excellent credit risks. Nongovernmental organizations and several small business lenders have demonstrated that providing loans to women entrepreneurs is good business. The Grameen Bank in Bangladesh, the Self-Employed Women's Association (SEWA) Cooperative Bank in India, and Banco Solidario in Bolivia have pioneered efforts to provide loans to poor women who have no collateral.

The Grameen Bank provides services to poor landless women in Bangladesh. More than two-thirds of all villages in Bangladesh are covered by this bank, which provides banking and other financial services as well as skills development. Formed by the Self-Employed Women's Association of India, the SEWA Cooperative Bank has one main office, with mobile credit officers. The bank works with rural credit groups and provides individual loans and group lending to rural associations. The Banco Solidario is a commercial bank that offers a variety of services, financial as well as nonfinancial, to clients.

Women's World Banking (WWB) is a global network of over 50 institutions that provides credit, savings, and business services to women. The network offers technical assistance and the local affiliates provide direct financial services to their clients. FINCA International is another affiliate network of nongovernmental organizations in Latin America, the Caribbean, and Africa. Affiliates provide credit through village banks; the main offices provide loan capital and technical assistance. The World Council of Credit Unions, located in Washington, D.C., is a network of 17,000 credit unions in 67 developing countries. Another affiliate network is Friends of WWB/India, an NGO with a national network of grassroots NGOs that provide financial services to poor rural women. The organization offers technical assistance and loan support to NGOs and organizes credit and savings groups.

Agricultural Activities

Women play a major role in the agricultural activities of many Third World countries. Governments are beginning to recognize this role that women play in the local economy. In Kenya, a national agricultural extension system, recently studied by Barbara Herz (1989), specifically targets women in addition to men. Extension agents in Kenya have reported that over half the farmers they meet with are women. This experience has influenced extension efforts in other African counties, including Cameroon, Somalia, Nigeria, and Zimbabwe.

In many Third World countries, women participate in cash crop production more than men. In sub-Saharan Africa, employment is divided generally along gender lines. Women are responsible for providing food; this includes food production and agricultural activities. In the past, men were responsible only for clearing the land for farming. Today, men, for the most part, work in nonagricultural jobs or in agricultural jobs not located on the farms (Joekes 1987). Women in Nicaragua play a large role in coffee and cotton production. Women in Nigeria outnumber men in cocoa, coffee, rice, maize, grain, and cassava production. However, land rights pass down through the male line and current systems of land registration continue this practice. The land is allocated to the men; women are excluded from the legal title (Joekes 1987).

In Asia, many women are involved in rice farming activities, especially at the production and postharvest phases. Their roles vary widely, depending on economic, religious, and social factors within each country. Women can benefit from technological advances in agriculture as long as they have some control over the income received, and this varies from country to country. In Java, women are allowed to own land and control household finances, while women in Bangladesh have little input or control over agriculture-related decisions (Stoler 1977; Abdullah and Zeidenstein 1982).

Industry

Industry is one of the fastest growing sectors in developing countries. Women in many developing countries have found employment in export-oriented industries, including garment and circuit board production. In Bangladesh, the export garment business opened up 500,000 jobs for young women (UBINIG 1991). Even though pay is low, hours are long, health hazards exist, and job security is nonexistent, many women move from rural areas specifically to take these jobs. Many women find that employment frees them from many social and cultural traditions and oppression.

Women have increased their participation in industry in recent years. Their participation often reinforces sexual stratification in the labor market. Unless training and other incentives are provided to women, they will continue to remain in low-paying, dead-end, and often hazardous jobs. The mechanization of tasks may also reduce the number of women employed in this sector, unless other industries move in to provide new jobs. When women participate in wage labor, especially rural women, they are often vulnerable to discrimination, primarily in areas of lower wages. Many employers also find that rural women are usually more docile and less likely to complain about working conditions, low wages, or other problems with their jobs.

In addition to employment in industrial facilities, many industries work from small workshops and women work in their own homes. Wages are usually lower in these cases, women receive fewer fringe benefits, and job security is still nonexistent.

Services

Women participate heavily in several service sectors, including community services, such as health, education, and social welfare;

commerce; and domestic service. Tourism is a major employer of women in many developing countries. Informal activities account for a larger percentage of female employment than employment in the formal sector in most Third World countries. Many reasons for this participation exist. The informal labor market is usually easier to enter, in part because it usually requires fewer skills than the formal market. Informal work can be done at home or at times of the day that enable women to take care of their families and work at the same time. Cultural patterns and expectations about women and work also make it easier for women to enter the informal labor market.

Outwork, or subcontracting work that can be done in the home, is becoming more popular for women, especially in Third World countries. Employers are able to cut costs and avoid paying benefits to many of these workers. Women who work these jobs provide their own tools—for example, sewing machines—and can set their own hours, as long as they meet quotas set by their employer. The drawbacks for women include low wages, little or no benefits, and no formal organization or union to protect rights.

Women in many countries are beginning to see the benefits of organizing among themselves. One of the best-known groups is India's Self-Employed Women's Association, established in 1972 by a group of garment vendors, head-loaders, and vegetable sellers. SEWA has organized over 40,000 women workers in Gujarat and five other states in India, helping them to get licenses, organize industrial and service cooperatives, and obtain legal help. Women members receive assistance in obtaining loans and banking services. The group also advocates for women's rights (Bhatt 1989).

Structural Adjustment Programs

During the late 1970s and early 1980s, the International Monetary Fund instituted "structural adjustment programs" designed to help debtor nations "balance their import and export accounts, cut government spending, and repay their international loans" (Kahne and Giele 1992, 20). In some countries, structural adjustment policies have been harmful influences on women's work and the well-being of children and families. Unemployment has risen, with women losing the most jobs; education, health, and other social programs that were funded by the government have lost funding or have suffered reduced funding; and, in some instances, women's access to land and credit has decreased.

In Africa, structural adjustment programs require reductions in government spending, which often hurt women as well as men. Spending on infrastructure and social programs is frequently cut, and since women and children compose the majority of the poor in any society, they are hurt the most. When governments cut back on spending on infrastructure, such as building and maintaining roads and providing telecommunications services, ease in transporting goods to markets suffers. In Africa, where many women are in agriculture, these policies make it even more difficult for rural areas to succeed in business. Health care services also suffer, as well as education. In a study on structural adjustment programs, Cornia, Jolly, and Stewart (1987) found that reductions in spending on social programs are detrimental to children. These programs also affect women as they attempt to care for their children without any support from the government.

Politics and the State's Role in the Status of Women

Patriarchal policies are often promoted by governments; these policies reinforce gender inequality. Afshar (1987) describes how state policy influences the public and private lives of its citizens and can have a definite impact on women's lives. She specifically explains how, in Iran, the fear of women's sexuality as well as the perception of women as disruptive agents and dangerous to the state led to legislation that secluded women in the home. Afshar believes that, in this way, the state justifies the benefits that men receive as a result of controlling women.

Population Policies

Population policies, or lack of policies, of individual countries provide an opportunity to understand how individual governments treat women, what governments perceive as women's functions in life, and how women are treated and cared for. In recent years, population policies have been adopted or expanded by many countries. These countries recognize the need to examine the effect that family planning programs have on general fertility levels as well as the effect they have on individuals.

Population policies vary from country to country and change over time within countries depending on the focus of the government at the time the policies are adopted. For example, in 1967, the government of Iran adopted its first population control policy. Based on an increasing growth rate, the government legalized induced abortion during the first trimester as long as the husband approved. Contraceptives were provided by the Ministry of Public Health through a network of family planning clinics, and contraceptive use was advocated by the national women's associations and other interested organizations. Efforts were also made to improve women's status within the family structure and in the more public areas of work. When the Shah of Iran fell from power, a conservative Islamic government took over and these family planning activities and programs were dismantled. The government lowered the minimum age for marriage and encouraged early and universal marriage; all family planning activities were opposed by the government. Major problems of overpopulation in Iran eventually led to the adoption of a national birth control policy (Hoodfar 1992).

Several international conferences have focused recently on human rights and population. Participants are searching for ways to define reproductive rights so that these rights are accepted across all cultures. Currently, population policies generally have a broader focus that looks at these policies in their larger social context. The health aspect of reproduction, specifically as it affects women and children, is included. Population policies are seen as only a part of a country's overall development policy. The status and condition of women and their lives are now seen as directly relevant to a country's fertility policies. Reproductive health is a prime focus in these policies.

Female Refugees

Over 20 million people are refugees throughout the world, most from developing countries. They have fled their own countries because of persecution, civil wars, and human rights violations. The United Nations Convention Relating to the Status of Refugees defines a refugee as a person who

> owing to well-founded fear of being persecuted for reasons of race, religion, nationality, membership of a particular social group or political opinion is outside the country of his nationality and is unable or, owing to such fear, is unwilling to avail himself of the protection

of that country; or who, not having a nationality and being outside the country of his former habitual residence as a result of such events, is unable or, owing to such fear, is unwilling to return to it. (quoted in Martin 1991, 1)

The majority of refugees are women and children. Women bear the burden of caring for their children, preparing meals, and dealing with new living arrangements, either in a refugee camp or in a new and strange environment. The role of the woman rarely changes, while her husband's role changes more drastically. The husband may not be able to find productive work or support his family. Women often find themselves responsible for maintaining the traditional culture as well as for supporting the family.

Many organizations are working to help refugee women manage their lives. In a refugee settlement in Zaire, female coordinators are elected by the camp population to help coordinate activities, including distribution of food and other goods, and ensure that women receive adequate care. These coordinators provide basic health education, help pregnant women find prenatal care, and encourage parents to have their children vaccinated. In refugee camps along the border between Thailand and Cambodia, the Khmer Women's Association provides similar services. The association uses social workers to identify needs and problems within the camps and participates in discussions concerning policies and procedures within the camps and the impact of these policies on the women living there. Trainers teach a variety of classes, including basic literacy skills and sewing and weaving. Day care is provided for the children of women enrolled in classes (Martin 1991).

Women refugees need protection from being returned to their country of origin, from armed attacks against them, and from illegal detention; women refugees also must be protected from physical and sexual abuse and exploitation. Women who are separated from their husbands while fleeing often find themselves vulnerable to sexual assault and rape. Once raped, many women are no longer accepted by their families—they are seen as having lost their virginity, their marital dignity, and their value and as an embarrassment to their families.

In order to help rebuild their lives, refugee women often seek income-generating activities, especially when they have been separated from their husbands, they are not married, or their husbands have died. According to Martin (1991), several steps should be taken to help women improve their economic status. These steps include ensuring that these women have equal access to programs designed to improve self-sufficiency; ensuring the full participation of women in designing programs; placing a high priority on integrating refugee women into all development plans; monitoring projects to ensure they provide sufficient income for survival; and providing technical assistance to agencies that are implementing economic development projects.

NGOs have played a large role in helping refugee women find support and protection in their new homes. The NGO Working Group on Refugee Women is a coalition of interested persons from approximately 100 NGOs worldwide. This group keeps its members informed of developments in the field, organizes meetings that coincide with the executive committee meetings at the United Nations High Commissioner for Refugees (UNHCR), and in 1988 convened an international meeting that focused on ways that refugee women's issues could be addressed by the international community.

Women's Rights as Human Rights

Long before the phrase "women's rights are human rights" was prominently used at the Fourth World Conference on Women in Beijing, social reformers, writers, philosophers, and others were writing about human rights and the lack of rights available to most women. In 1792, Mary Wollstonecraft, a British feminist, wrote *Vindication of the Rights of Women,* in which she challenged the prevailing attitudes of the day concerning human rights. Both liberals and conservatives at the time advocated for rights for men but did not think that women needed these same rights. Later, in 1869, John Stuart Mill wrote *The Subjection of Women* in which he advocated equal opportunities for women and suggested ways to eliminate the basic causes of women's oppression. Today, even though many international documents exist to protect women and their rights (see Chapter 4), women in many areas of the world are not aware of their rights or are denied these rights by common practice or by law. In many cases, women are not aware of the fact that they have certain rights or how to gain access to information on how to gain their rights.

In many countries, a woman's status in her social environment is based on the number of children she has. Women's rights too often focus only on issues concerning motherhood and child-rearing, which often diverts attention from other areas in which women face discrimination. This is not to say that motherhood is not important; childbearing and child-rearing are highly valued in most societies. But most women's rights advocates believe that equal rights for women should go beyond motherhood and raising children. According to Tomasevski (1993) "protection of motherhood is compensation to those women who perform a socially valued function, it is not granted them merely because they are women" (page 17).

Issues that relate to motherhood include access to family planning services as well as to abortion services. In all cases, access to family planning should include access to information and services for both men and women. In many cases, family planning services have focused on women, thus perpetuating the view that because women bear children and men do not, women should be the only ones concerned with issues related to family planning. According to most experts in the field, men must be included in this area; their absence only reinforces the often irresponsible behavior of fathers toward their children (Tomasevski 1993; Dixon-Mueller 1993; Sen, Germain, and Chen 1994).

Many international conferences and documents have examined human rights in relation to family planning. The 1968 Teheran Conference on Human Rights declared that parents, not just fathers, have the right to determine the number and spacing of their children. The World Population Plan of Action of 1974, the International Conference on Population held in 1984, the Amsterdam Declaration of 1989, and the Convention on the Elimination of All Forms of Discrimination against Women (Article 16e) all affirmed the rights of both parents to determine the number and spacing of their children.

For women living in Islamic countries, the concept of women's rights is not the same as human rights. According to An-Na'im (1995), "Whereas human rights are, by definition, universal in that they are owed to all human beings by virtue of their humanity without distinction on grounds of gender or religion, the concept of rights under shari'a [the law of God according to the Islamic faith] is fundamentally premised on these distinctions. That is to say, there are different rights for Muslim men, Muslim women, and non-Muslims under shari'a, rather than equal rights for all, regardless of gender or religion" (page 57).

Role of International Conferences and Conventions

Women came from all over the world to attend the 1985 Nairobi Conference during the UN Decade for Women. Stories of the determination of women from rural areas in developing countries inspired all attendees and many women who were not able to attend. In a small town in western Kenya, Elizabeth Wanjara came by bus; her fare was paid for by eight local women who expected her to return and report to them what she found out:

> Elizabeth Wanjara heard about the Decade for Women Conference on a transistor radio at home in the town of Bungoma in western Kenya, 450 miles from [Nairobi]. With eight local women, she saved up by selling honey and knitting sweaters and bought herself a bus ticket. Mrs W. doesn't know exactly how old she is or how many grandchildren she has. She speaks only her tribal Kiswahili dialect and cannot read or write. But she knows exactly why she came to Nairobi. "I have to go back to all the women in my place and tell them how we can be ourselves—no longer just have babies and have babies dying." (Sciolino 1985)

The Convention on the Elimination of All Forms of Discrimination against Women was adopted by the United Nations General Assembly in 1979 and entered into force in 1981 following ratification by the twentieth country (see Chapter 4 for excerpts from this document). By 1989, almost 100 countries had agreed to follow its provisions. By 1993, 120 nations had ratified it. This convention elaborates on the Universal Declaration of Human Rights by affirming women's rights to individual freedoms and to social entitlements as an expression of the equality of men and women. Rights are introduced that specifically concern women, such as right to maternity leave and benefits and the prohibition against dismissal of a woman from her job due to pregnancy. The convention also acknowledges the need for special and temporary affirmative action measures to redress wrongs against women. Finally, the convention focuses on the obligation of states to modify all existing discriminatory social and cultural patterns in order to eliminate practices that treat women as inferior beings.

In order to improve the lives and status of women in Third World countries, more countries must agree to follow the provisions of many of the conventions established by the United Nations and the International Labour Organization. International conferences are enabling more women to know of and understand the rights they have, as women and as human beings. As the number and influence of NGOs throughout the world grows, more and more women will be encouraged to help themselves and help their communities grow and prosper.

Many development NGOs and governmental agencies understand the importance of integrating women into the development process. According to Joekes (1987), "for true economic recovery to occur, women need to be well integrated into the development process. Urban women should be better prepared to work in the modern sector, and rural women should have the opportunity to increase their efficiency as food producers" (page 139). But integrating women into this process changes many aspects of society, including "social and political structures, the distribution of wealth, and cultural mores. It is, in short, revolutionary in its implications" (Franda 1979, 8). According to Fredland (1992), communities thrive when women are included at the decision-making level and in implementing aspects of development activities. She believes that because "life in the villages depends on the work of women in the home and family, in the fields, and at the market, it is important to give attention to the specific needs of women if constructive development is to occur" (page 194).

Many steps are being taken today to improve the lives of women in the Third World. Governments as well as NGOs are realizing the important contributions that women make to society and are acting accordingly. Women's lives have improved in many areas, but work still must be done in other areas, especially for women living in Islamic countries, where their activities are still severely restricted. Many women in Third World countries are currently benefiting from literacy programs, provision of health care facilities, and programs that involve women in economic development. More and more women are becoming involved as activists and advocates in programs that focus on gaining the rights to which women are entitled and on improving their status and lives.

References

Abdullah, Tahrunnesa, and Sondra Zeidenstein. 1982. *Village Women of Bangladesh: Prospects for Change.* Oxford: Pergamon Press.

Acasadi, George, and Gwendolyn Johnson-Acasadi. 1990. "Safe Motherhood in South Asia: Sociocultural and Demographic Aspects of Maternal Health." Background paper prepared for the Safe Motherhood–South Asia Conference. Lahore, Pakistan.

Afshar, Haleh, ed. 1987. *Women, State, and Ideology: Studies from Africa and Asia.* Albany: State University of New York.

Ahmed, Khalil. 1992. "The Sociology of Rape." *Slogan* (February): 36–37.

Alexandre, Marie. 1991. "The Role of Gender: Socio-economic, Cultural, and Religious Pressure on the Health of Women in Cameroon." Paper presented at the 18th Annual NCIH International Health Conference, Arlington, VA.

Anderson, Mary Ann. 1991. "Undernutrition during Pregnancy and Lactation in India: Heavy Work and Eating Down as Determinants." Paper presented at the 18th Annual NCIH International Health Conference, Arlington, VA.

An-Na'im, Abdullahi. 1995. "The Dichotomy between Religious and Secular Discourse in Islamic Societies." In *Faith and Freedom: Women's Human Rights in the Muslim World,* edited by Mahnaz Afkhami. Syracuse: Syracuse University Press.

Ballara, Marcela. 1991. *Women and Literacy.* Atlantic Highlands, NJ: Zed Books.

Beneria, Lourdes, and Catharine R. Stimpson, eds. 1987. *Women, Households, and the Economy.* New Brunswick, NJ: Rutgers University Press.

Bhatt, Ela. 1989. "Toward Empowerment." *World Development* 17: 1059–1065.

Bouzidi, Mohammed, and Rolf Korte. 1990. *Family Planning for Life: Challenges for the 1990s.* London: International Planned Parenthood Federation.

Bradley, Christine. 1988. "The Problem of Domestic Violence in Papua, New Guinea." In *Guidelines for Police Training on Violence against Women and Child Sexual Abuse.* London: Commonwealth Secretariat, Women and Development Programme.

Buendia, Hernando Gomez, ed. 1989. *Urban Crime: Global Trends and Policies.* Tokyo: U.N. University.

Caldwell, J. C. 1979. "Education as a Factor in Mortality Decline: An Examination of Nigerian Data." *Population Studies* 33 (3): 395–413.

Calman, Leslie J. 1992. *Toward Empowerment: Women and Movement Politics in India.* Boulder, CO: Westview Press.

Chandrasekhar, S. 1994. *India's Abortion Experience.* Denton: University of North Texas Press.

Chen, Lincoln, Emdadul Huq, and Stan D'Souza. 1981. "Sex Bias in the Family Allocation of Food and Health Care in Rural Bangladesh." *Population and Development Review* 7 (1): 55–70.

Chow, Esther Ngan-ling, and Catherine White Berheide, eds. 1994. *Women, the Family, and Policy: A Global Perspective.* Albany: State University of New York Press.

Cincone, Lillian. 1988. "The Role of Development in the Exploitation of Southeast Asian Women: Sex Tourism in Thailand." Master's thesis, Department of Social Sciences, San Jose State University, San Jose, California.

Cornia, Giovanni Andrea, Richard Jolly, and Frances Stewart. 1987. *Adjustment with a Human Face,* vol. 1. Oxford: Clarendon Press.

da Silva, Joselina. 1991. "Women Organizing." Presentation to the 18th Annual NCIH International Health Conference, Arlington, VA.

Dankelman, Irene, and Joan Davidson. 1988. *Women and Environment in the Third World: Alliance for the Future.* London: Earthscan Publications.

Demographic and Health Survey Program. 1990. *Women's Education: Findings for Demographic and Health Survey.* Paper presented 5–9 March to World Conference on Education for All. Jomtien, Thailand.

Dixon-Mueller, Ruth. 1993. *Population Policy and Women's Rights: Transforming Reproductive Choice.* Westport, CT: Praeger.

———. 1990. "Abortion Policy and Women's Health in Developing Countries." *International Journal of Health Services* 20: 297–314.

Eitzen, D. Stanley, and Maxie Baca Zinn. 1991. In *Conflict and Order: Understanding Society.* 5th ed. Boston: Allyn and Bacon.

El Saadawi, Nawal. 1980. *The Hidden Face of Eve.* Translated and edited by Sherif Hetata. London: Zed Press.

Fauveau, Vincent. 1991. "Mortality Impact of a Community-Based Maternity Care Program in Rural Bangladesh." Presentation at the 18th Annual NCIH International Health Conference, Arlington, VA.

Fauveau, Vincent, and T. Blanchet. 1989. "Deaths from Injuries and Induced Abortion among Rural Bangladeshi Women." *Social Science and Medicine* 29: 1121–1127.

Franda, Marcus. 1979. *India's Rural Development: An Assessment of Alternatives.* Bloomington: Indiana University Press.

Fredland, Dorane L. 1992. "Empowering Women in Rural India: A Model for Development." In *Women Transforming Politics,* edited by Jill Bystydzienski. Bloomington: Indiana University Press.

Hartmann, Heidi. 1976. "Capitalism, Patriarchy, and Job Segregation by Sex." *Signs: Journal of Women in Culture and Society* 1: 137–169.

Herz, Barbara. 1989. "Women in Development: Kenya's Experience." *Finance and Development* 26 (2): 43–46.

Hogberg, U. 1985. "Maternal Mortality: A Worldwide Problem." *International Journal of Gynecology and Obstetrics* 23: 463–470.

Holden, Peter, et al. 1983. *Tourism Prostitution Development: Documentation.* Bangkok: Ecumenical Coalition on Third World Tourism.

Hoodfar, Homa. 1992. "Population Policy and Gender Equity in Post-Revolutionary Iran." In *Family, Gender, and Population in the Middle East: Policies in Context,* edited by Carla Makhlouf Obermeyer. Cairo, Egypt: American University in Cairo Press, pp. 105–135.

Hosken, Fran. 1988. "International Seminar: Female Circumcision Strategies to Bring About Change." *Women's International Network News* 14 (3): 24–37.

Huston, Perdita. 1979. *Third World Women Speak Out: Interviews in Six Countries on Change, Development, and Basic Needs.* New York: Praeger.

Jacobson, Jodi L. 1990. "Abortion in a New Light." *World Watch* (March/April): 31–38.

Jejeebhoy, Shireen J. 1995. *Women's Education, Autonomy, and Reproductive Behavior: Experience from Developing Countries.* Oxford: Clarendon Press.

Jiggins, Janice. 1994. *Changing the Boundaries: Women-Centered Perspectives on Population and the Environment.* Washington, DC: Island Press.

Joekes, Susan P. 1987. *Women in the World Economy: An INSTRAW Study.* New York: Oxford University Press.

Kahne, Hilda, and Janet Z. Giele, eds. 1992. *Women's Work and Women's Lives: The Continuing Struggle Worldwide.* Boulder, CO: Westview Press.

Kamel, Nahid M. 1983. "Determinants and Patterns of Female Mortality Associated with Women's Reproductive Role." In *Sex Differentials in Mortality,* edited by Alan D. Lopez and Lado T. Ruzicka. Canberra, Australia: Australian National University.

Kelkar, Govind. 1991. "Stopping the Violence against Women: Issues and Perspectives from India." In *Freedom from Violence: Women's Strategies from around the World,* edited by Margaret Schuler. Washington, DC: OEF International.

Khalifa, Mona A. 1988. "Attitudes of Urban Sudanese Men toward Family Planning." *Studies in Family Planning* 19: 236–243.

King, Elizabeth. 1990. *Educating Girls and Women: Investing in Development.* Washington, DC: World Bank.

King, Elizabeth M., and M. Anne Hill, eds. 1993. *Women's Education in Developing Countries: Barriers, Benefits, and Policies.* Baltimore: Johns Hopkins University Press.

Kiragu, K., S. Chapman, and G. L. Lewis. 1995. *The Nigeria Family Planning Facility Census.* IEC Field Report No. 1, Center for Communications Programs, Johns Hopkins School of Public Health, Baltimore, MD.

Koblinsky, Marge, Judith Timyan, and Jill Gay, eds. 1993. *The Health of Women: A Global Perspective.* Boulder, CO: Westview Press.

Kramer, Michael S. 1987. "Determinants of Low Birth Weight: Methodological Assessment and Meta-Analysis." *Bulletin of the World Health Organization* 65 (5): 663–737.

Krieger, Laurie. 1991. "Male Doctor, Female Patient: Access to Health Care in Egypt." Paper presented at the 18th Annual NCIH International Health Conference, Arlington, VA.

Ladipo, Oladipo A. 1989. "Preventing and Managing Complications of Induced Abortions in Third World Countries." *International Journal of Gynecology and Obstetrics,* Supplement 3, 21–28.

Lateef, Shireen. 1992. "Wife Abuse among Indo-Fijians." In *Sanctions and Sanctuary: Cultural Perspectives on the Beating of Wives,* edited by Dorothy Ayers Counts, Judith K. Brown, and Jacquelyn C. Campbell. Boulder, CO: Westview Press.

Lesotho, government of, Health Ministry. 1990. "Lesotho Country Paper." Paper presented at the Conference on Safe Motherhood for the Southern African Development Coordinating Council (SADCC) countries. Harare, Zimbabwe.

Lightfoot-Klein, Hanny. 1989. *Prisoners of Ritual: An Odyssey into Female Genital Circumcision in Africa.* New York: Narrington Park Press.

Mack, Beverly B. "Being Third Wife Beats Having a Career in Moslem Nigeria." *Washington Post,* 4 March 1984.

Maine, Deborah. 1991. *Safe Motherhood Programs: Options and Issues.* New York: Center for Population and Family Health, Columbia University.

"Malaysia: States Differ on Approach to Polygamy." *Far Eastern Economic Review,* 22 August 1991.

Martin, Susan Forbes. 1991. *Refugee Women.* Atlantic Highlands, NJ: Zed Books.

Mies, Maria. 1986. *Patriarchy and Accumulation on a World Scale.* London: Zed Books.

Moser, Caroline. 1991. "Women's Health Is More Than Just a Medical Issue." Presentation at the 18th Annual NCIH International Health Conference, Arlington, VA.

Okabue, Isabella. 1990. "Pregnancy Termination and the Law in Nigeria." *Studies in Family Planning* 21 (4): 197–208.

Okafor, Chinyelu. 1991. "Women Helping Women: Incorporating Women's Perspectives into Community Health Projects." Paper presented at the 18th Annual NCIH International Health Conference, Arlington, VA.

Population Crisis Committee. 1989. *Fact Sheet.* Washington, DC: Population Crisis Committee.

Rogers, Susan Carol. 1978. "Women's Place: A Critical Review of Anthropological Theory." *Comparative Studies in Society and History* 20 (1): 123–162.

Royston, Erica, and Sue Armstrong. 1989. *Preventing Maternal Deaths.* Geneva: World Health Organization.

Sciolino, Elaine. 1985. "Joyous Adventure at Nairobi Forum." *New York Times,* 18 July 1985.

Sen, Gita, Adrienne Germain, and Lincoln C. Chen, eds. 1994. *Population Policies Reconsidered: Health, Empowerment, and Rights.* Boston: Harvard University Press.

Senapati, Shishir K. 1991. "Women's Work Pattern and Its Impact on Their Health and Nutrition." Paper presented at the 18th Annual NCIH International Health Conference, Arlington, VA.

Seoul YMCA. 1989. *The Realities of the Entertainment Culture and Countermeasures.* Report 10, Citizen's Self-Help Movement Series. Seoul: Seoul YMCA.

Stewart, Denise. 1989. The Global Injustice. Ottawa: Canadian Council on Social Development.

Stoler, A. 1977. "Class Structure and Female Autonomy in Rural Java." In Wellesley Editorial Committee, Bunster B. Ximena et al., *Women and National Development: The Complexities of Change.* Chicago: University of Chicago Press.

Tomasevski, Katarina. 1993. *Women and Human Rights.* Atlantic Highlands, NJ: Zed Books.

Turshen, Meredeth, and Briavel Holcomb, eds. 1993. *Women's Lives and Public Policy: The International Experience.* Westport, CT: Greenwood Press.

UBINIG. 1991. *Bangladesh's Textile and Clothing Industry: The Role of Women.* Working Paper prepared for UNIDO (United Nations Industrial Development Organization) and presented at a seminar in Dhaka on 7 October.

UNESCO (United Nations Education, Scientific and Cultural Organization). 1990. *Compendium of Statistics on Illiteracy. 1990 ed.* (Statistical Reports and Studies, No. 31.) Paris: UNESCO.

UNFPA (United Nations Fund for Population Activities). 1989. *State of the World Population Report.* New York: UNFPA.

UNICEF (United Nations International Children's Fund). 1992. *Educating Girls and Women: A Moral Imperative.* New York: UNICEF.

―――. 1986. *Statistical Review of the Situation of Children of the World.* New York: UNICEF.

Chronology 2

The history of the status and rights of women in Third World countries is rich in detail beginning in early history. Because so many events affecting women have occurred throughout history, this chapter focuses on more recent history. Most of the events listed here occurred after 1974, although several items are included from before 1975 to provide a perspective on women's activism and concern for women and their lives in the Third World. References at the end of this chapter provide additional sources of information concerning important dates in women's history.

1919   Women in Egypt participate in street demonstrations to protest the many oppressive policies of the British protectorate, marking the beginning of the fight for their rights as women. Many women believe that religious leaders have more influence than political leaders in preventing women from gaining these rights.

          The Paris Peace Conference is held. The women's delegation to the con-

1919
cont.
ference lobbies for an 8-hour workday, a 44-hour work week, an end to child labor, support for social insurance and pensions, maternity benefits, equal pay, and minimum wages for housework. Most delegates believe that these proposals are too radical, and they are quickly shelved.

The women's delegation to the Paris Peace Conference meets with 14 allied government leaders and urges them to nominate women to positions of influence in the League of Nations, to eliminate traffic in women and children as well as state-supported prostitution, and to recognize universal suffrage. The delegation also wants government leaders to support international education and health bureaus and to control and reduce armaments.

1927
The All India Women's Conference opens with discussions concerning women's education. Participants expand their focus to include the elimination of purdah, child marriage, and other problems that were first tackled by nineteenth-century reformers.

1928
Female delegates to the Conference of American States propose an Inter-American Commission on Women. This group is officially endorsed at the 1933 conference. The commission is the first regional intergovernmental body whose specific purpose is to advance women's rights. Members of the commission are appointed by individual governments. The group will eventually prepare an international treaty on the Nationality of Married Women (1933) and the Declaration of Lima in Favor of Women's Rights (1938). The group encourages "member government to establish women's bureaus, to revise discriminatory civil codes and to take their demands to the LN [League of Nations] in Geneva" (Winslow 1995, 4).

1933
The first women's bank is founded in Indonesia.

1936
Victoria Ocampo leads the effort to form the Argentine Union of Women. The union's main goal is to stop a proposed "reform" of the Argentine civil code that would again consider married women as legal minors, who are

not allowed to control their wages or work without their husband's permission.

1937   In response to requests from several women's organizations, the League of Nations establishes a Committee of Experts on the Legal Status of Women. This committee has the authority to conduct a comprehensive and scientific inquiry into the legal status of women in countries throughout the world. Composed of seven experts and representatives of three international legal institutes, including the Unification of Private Law, Public Law, and the International Bureau for the Unification of Penal Law, the committee will meet in April 1938 to plan the comprehensive study.

1945   Legislation is passed that outlaws infibulation in Sudan. This law will be ignored by many people.

1946   The Sudanese Women's League is formed. This is the first modern women's organization in the Sudan.

        After leaders of 51 governments ratified the United Nations Charter last year, they meet in London for the first time to discuss their role in preventing future wars and in solving the worldwide economic crisis following World War II. Several women serve as delegates to the United Nations General Assembly as representatives or alternates from their countries. The five representatives include Eleanor Roosevelt (United States), Minerva Bernardino (Dominican Republic), Jeane McKenzie (New Zealand), Evdokia I. Uralova (USSR), and Ellen Wilkinson (United Kingdom). The remaining women serve as alternates and come from Czechoslovakia, Denmark, France, Greece, the Netherlands, Norway, the United Kingdom, and the United States.

        The Commission on the Status of Women is established by the United Nations. It is one of the earliest intergovernmental agencies set up to monitor the implementation and status of women's rights throughout the world. Helvi Sipilä, a lawyer from Finland, is its chairperson. It also studies the role of women in social and economic development.

1947   Rani Gaidinliu, an Indian freedom fighter, is released after spending 14 years in jail for her protests against the British occupation and rule of India. At the age of 16, she had led a group of guerrilla fighters and was captured only after the British sent out a large number of troops.

A group of women in Nepal found the Adharsa Mahila Sangh (Model Women's Organization) to fight child marriage. They also fight for the right of widows to remarry.

1950   Planned Parenthood International is founded by Indian family planning advocate Dhanvanthi Rama Rau.

1951   The marriage of girls under 12 is allowed in Sri Lanka as long as the marriage is approved by a religious court.

1952   The United Nations General Assembly adopts the Convention on the Political Rights of Women (see Chapter 4 for excerpts) prepared by the Commission on the Status of Women for the Economic and Social Council.

1953   The United Nations General Assembly elects Indian diplomat Vijaya Pandit as its first female president.

The Federation of Ghana Women, a trade and business association, is founded by Dr. Evelyn Amartiefio.

1954   Divorce is legalized in Argentina; women have worked for decades for this legal reform. The law will be repealed, however, the next year.

Women in Nepal stage a protest over the lack of women in the King's Advisory Assembly. As a result, the government forms a second assembly, and includes 4 female members out of 113 total members. These women include Punya Prava Dhungana, Mangla Devi, Maya Devi Shah, and Prativa Jha.

The National Federation of Indian Women, a broad-based, moderate feminist group, is founded in India.

1955   In India, legislation outlaws polygyny for Hindus, but Muslim men are still allowed to marry up to four women. Both women and men may sue for divorce on the grounds of adultery, desertion, physical or mental cruelty, religious conversion, insanity, leprosy, sexually transmitted disease, disappearance for seven years, or persistent and long-term refusal of conjugal rights. Women are also allowed to sue for a divorce from a husband who is found guilty of rape, sodomy, or bestiality. Women who marry before 15 have until the age of 18 to divorce their husbands, as long as the marriage is not consummated.

Women band together in India to found Bharatiya Grammen Mahila Sangh. This organization offers family planning services, maternity and child care, and vocational training for women.

1956   In India, legislation is passed that outlaws sati, reaffirms the father's right to custody of his children, allows equal inheritance rights to both Hindu sons and daughters, allows women to adopt children, and provides equal rights to adopted sons and daughters. (Sati, also known as suttee, is the practice of Bengali widows (in India) throwing themselves on the funeral pyres of their husbands. They were believed to have failed in using their traditional female powers to ensure the long life of their husbands.)

Recognizing the need for an organized approach to family planning, the government of Egypt establishes the Supreme Council of Family Planning.

Believing that girls should be able to go to school, Saudi Arabian queen 'Iffat, the wife of King Faisal, establishes a government school for girls.

1957   Lee Tai Young, Korea's first woman lawyer, establishes the Korean Legal Aid Center for Family Relations. She helps women who have a variety of legal problems, especially women needing help getting divorces from their husbands.

The United Nations General Assembly approves the Convention on the Nationality of Married Women. This

1957
cont.

document "protects the nationality of the wife. It pro-vides that neither the celebration nor dissolution of marriage between a national and an alien, nor the change of nationality by the husband during marriage, automatically affects the wife's nationality" (Winslow 1995, 19).

1958

Afghanistan's prime minister calls for women to reject the veil.

Recognizing the need for family planning programs, the Nepal Family Planning Association is founded.

Nigeria opens its first birth control clinic.

The Economic and Social Council of the United Nations and the Commission on the Status of Women call on the World Health Organization (WHO) to study the persistent customs of female genital circumcision and the steps that governments plan to take to end the practice. The following year, the WHO rejects this request because circumcision is based on local social and cultural practices and therefore is outside the realm of WHO's interest.

1960

The Commission on the Status of Women urges governments to affirm women's access to all levels of education. The Convention on Eliminating Discrimination in Education is adopted by the United Nations.

Sirimavo Bandaranaike becomes the prime minister of Ceylon following the assassination of her husband, Solomon Bandaranaike. She is the first female prime minister.

1961

The Dowry Prohibition Act is passed in India. This legislation makes the act of asking for a dowry illegal, but the law has little effect on actual practices throughout the country. "Presents" can still be legally offered to the groom's family by the bride's family. If a groom's family believes that these "presents" are not sufficient, the groom's family may still harass the bride, and sometimes kill her. This practice, known as dowry murder, continues despite protests from India's many women's groups.

The Mount Carmel International Center for Community Training is formed at a meeting in Haifa, Israel. The meeting is attended by women from 23 African and Asian countries who are inspired by Golda Meir's desire to help rural women in Third World countries. The center offers agricultural and business training for women.

1962   Feminists in Brazil win a change in the law that considers women legal minors. Women are now considered as adults.

Thailand outlaws prostitution, primarily as a result of the efforts of Pierra Hoon Veijjabu, Thailand's first female physician.

1967   The Declaration on the Elimination of All Forms of Discrimination against Women is written by the Commission on the Status of Women. It is the first comprehensive measure concerning women's rights.

1968   Iranian politician Farrokhrou Parsa, who had become one of the first six women in the Iranian Parliament in 1964, becomes her country's first female cabinet minister. She is named minister of education.

The idea that family planning is a human right is first recognized at the United Nations International Conference on Human Rights in Teheran, Iran.

1969   The government of Ecuador institutes a "malaria control" program throughout the country. In reality, this program is an excuse to sterilize peasant women.

Several women are elected or appointed to office in this year. These women include Jordan's first female ambassador, Laurice Hlass; Ecuador's first female senator, Isabel Robalino; Venezuela's first female cabinet minister, Minister of Development Aura Celina Casanova; South Africa's first female judge, Leonora Neethling; and Puerto Rico's first female cabinet member, Secretary of Labor Julia Rivera de Vincenti.

1969   The first feminist group in Venezuela, the Movimiento de
cont.   Liberacion de la Mujer (Women's Liberation Movement),
          is founded.

1970   In Libya, women who are employed receive a pay bonus
          when they get married. A new law now mandates that
          women receive equal pay for equal work, but restrictions
          are placed on women working under certain conditions.
          These restrictions are that women cannot hold jobs that
          are dangerous, cannot work at night in most cases, and
          cannot work more than 48 hours per week.

1971   Women in India win the right to have an abortion (one
          and one-half years before *Roe v. Wade* legalizes abortion
          in the United States).

          Women's rights forces continue to lose ground in the Is-
          lamic countries. President Numairi of the Sudan is
          openly hostile to the radical Sudanese Women's Union
          and forces the dismantling of the group.

1972   Aida Gindy of the Social Development Division of the
          United Nations recognizes the need for more under-
          standing on the role of women in economic develop-
          ment. She calls for and plans an Expert Group Meeting to
          discuss these issues. Sir Arthur Lewis, president of the
          Caribbean Development Bank, presides over the meet-
          ing; he is joined by Inga Thorssen (Sweden), Aziza Hus-
          sein (Egypt), Annie Jiagge (Ghana), Vida Tomsic
          (Yugoslavia), Mina Ben Zvi (Israel), Laticia Shahani
          (Philippines), and Elizabeth Koontz (United States).
          Margaret Snyder is the Economic Commission of Africa
          (ECA) Observer. Members discuss common strategies to
          effectively integrate women into the development
          process.

          The Economic Commission of Africa establishes its own
          Women's Programme, explaining that women are ne-
          glected as resources and that their contributions to so-
          ciety are rarely seen or measured. Women's social and
          economic activities and contributions within their fam-
          ilies, communities, and nations are not acknowledged
          or supported, which leads to missed opportunities for

development and negative effects on productivity. The ECA Women's Programme is designed to help communities and nations recognize women's contributions.

1973   The Institute of Women's Studies in the Arab World is created as part of Beirut University College. Its goals are focused on academics and include creating and maintaining contacts with people throughout the world interested in women's issues, increasing awareness of the advances made by Arab women, and advocating for the integration of women into development activities. The institute compiles bibliographies of resources concerning women written in Arabic, French, and English.

1975   The first regional conference on Gulf women is organized by the Kuwaiti Women's Social and Cultural Society, an NGO that works closely with government officials to encourage the participation of women in the development process.

International Women's Year is proclaimed by the United Nations. The Conference of International Women's Year is held in June in Mexico City and is the first world conference of governments focusing on women. It creates the World Plan of Action, the first international public policy to improve women's status. The conference is the largest consciousness-raising event held on this subject and advances women's claim to full citizenship. The conference is significant because it marks the beginning of the bringing together of two distinct agendas: the women's agenda, defined and developed by the Commission on the Status of Women (CSW), and the larger political agenda of the United Nations. Delegations from 133 nations and representatives from 8 UN agencies, 12 UN programs, and 192 NGOs in consultative status attend the Conference on International Women's Year. Over 6,000 participants come to an unofficial parallel conference at the opposite end of Mexico City.

In October, the World Congress for International Women's Year is held in Berlin. Almost 2,000 delegates, observers, and guests from throughout the world gather to unite diverse social forces to encourage the women of

1975
cont.

the world to maintain peace and to fight for democracy and the fulfillment of their legitimate rights. Delegates come from 29 European countries, 33 Asian countries, 44 African countries, and 33 countries in North, Central, and South America, Australia, and New Zealand. Over 700 journalists from 48 countries also attend. Nine commissions meet for three days to focus on specific areas of concern to women; these areas include equality of women in society; women and work in industry and agriculture; women and development; the family and society; the education of women; women and the struggle for peace, detente, and international security; women and the struggle for national independence and international solidarity; the effect of mass media, literature, and art on the attitude of public opinion toward women; and cooperation and joint action of women of the world and of governmental and nongovernmental organizations and the United Nations for the realization of the aims of International Women's Year.

The Committee on the Status of Women in India publishes their findings in a report, *Towards Equality.* This government report examines the ways in which the status of women affects the lives of women. For example, the report notes that from 1901 on the ratio of females to males in the population has declined. In 1901, there were 972 females for every 1,000 males; by 1971 the number of females had declined to 930 per 1,000 males. The strong preference for sons, the effect of childbearing on women, and the general neglect of women all have an impact on these statistics, according to the report. Other customs examined include patrilocality, the practice of a young woman moving to the home of her husband once she is married. This practice forces a woman to change her loyalty from her own birth family to the family of her husband; the implication of the practice is that a woman is considered property and her feelings and her connections to her own birth family are not considered important.

1976

The International Tribunal on Crimes against Women convenes in Brussels to discuss the violence against women that occurs throughout the world. Over one thousand women from around the world discuss the extent and prevention of violence, including rape, battering, genital mutilation, and imprisonment.

The United Nations develops its World Plan of Action, which suggests ways to integrate both men and women into the development process. Among its recommendations are the development of women's bureaus, advisory committees, commissions, ministries, and government offices at all levels to monitor and promote the causes of women.

Egypt becomes the first Arab nation to reverse the gains that women have made throughout the region. The government amends article 2 of the constitution to make the shari'a, or Islamic law, the principal law of the country.

At the National Conference of the Mozambican Women's Organization, members define the problems that face them in Mozambique—illiteracy, unemployment, tribalism, racism, prostitution, and forced marriage.

1977   The World Bank creates the post of adviser on women. The president of the World Bank pledges to monitor the impact of bank activities on women and to ensure that attention will be paid to the role of women in development activities.

In the summer, a ten-day Pan-African Conference on the Role of Trade Women is held in Nairobi. It is sponsored by the African-American Labor Center, AFL-CIO. Issues debated include why more women do not actively participate in their unions and what can be done to increase women's participation.

General Zia al-Haq seizes power in Pakistan. He removes all the advantages that women had under the first president of Pakistan, Mohammad Ali Jinnah (who founded Pakistan in 1947). Jinnah believed that women should not be confined and that Islamic law did not require their subjugation and confinement. Zia issues a

1977
cont.
series of directives that remove all freedoms that Pakistani women once had; he requires that they wear Islamic dress, including the chador.

In Buenos Aires, Argentina, the Mothers and Grandmothers of the Plaza de Mayo publicly protest against military rule and begin their search for missing relatives. The military government has a network of more than 340 secret concentration camps to hold those they perceive as enemies of the state. Over 30,000 people, including approximately 10,000 women, are kidnapped from homes, schools, or places of employment. Families are not notified of the kidnapping or location of their relatives. The women who protest in the Plaza de Mayo bring world attention to the abuses of power of the military government.

1979
In February, the World Health Organization holds a conference in Khartoum, the capital of Sudan, on traditional practices affecting the health of women. As a result of this conference, the practice of female circumcision is examined, and many participants begin to question the reasons for this type of genital mutilation (according to some). Many estimate that as many as 30 million girls have been circumcised to some extent. Most participants are health officials of countries in which female circumcision is practiced. The conference participants unanimously condemn circumcision as a practice that is disastrous to the health of women in these countries that cannot be defended on either medical or humane grounds.

Egyptian feminist Nawal El Saadawi publishes *The Hidden Face of Eve: Women in the Arab World*, in which she discusses female genital mutilation, rape, the Arab emphasis on female virginity before marriage, family honor, and women in Arab history.

On March 8, 6,000 women march in Tehran, Iran, to protest the oppressive policies of Iran's new leader, Ayatollah Ruhollah Khomeini. They chant, "In the dawn of freedom, there is no freedom." On March 10, Iran's Palace of Justice is seized by 15,000 women, protesting the loss of their rights. On March 13, two women attack Khomeini's spokesman. They do not win any reforms of the repressive policies.

The market in Accra, Ghana, is destroyed by the government, which believes that the market women are responsible for food shortages throughout the area. The women become scapegoats and are persecuted because many people believe that the women are wealthy and powerful. The women have no real power and no way to fight back.

The first widely publicized demonstrations take place against dowry murder in India. Women march through neighborhoods in New Delhi to the home where one dowry murder has recently occurred; other demonstrators march to the homes where suspected dowry murders have also occurred.

The first global feminist meeting is held in Bangkok, Thailand.

In Medellín, Colombia, a National Women's Congress is held. Representatives from 19 women's groups meet to discuss abortion and the abuse of sterilization procedures.

The Hudood Ordinances are passed in Pakistan. These four laws govern adultery, fornication, rape, and prostitution. The testimony of women is banned in certain types of serious criminal trials, including trials for murder, theft, adultery, and rape. A woman must have four adult male witnesses who are Muslim to prove that they have been raped. However, if the accused rapist is found not guilty, the woman can be sentenced to 80 lashes for "false testimony."

In Iran, Farrokhrou Parsa, Iran's first female cabinet member, is executed by firing squad as a result of her feminist views. She believes that schoolgirls should not have to wear the veil. She also advocates that schools use nonsexist teaching materials.

1980   The King of Saudi Arabia decrees that brides and grooms must be permitted to meet each other before the wedding. Most Saudi Arabian women are married by the time they are 16 years old and are bought by the groom with a bride price.

The United Nations Children's Emergency Fund (UNICEF) pledges to assist community groups and organizations willing to work toward the prevention of female genital circumcision. As a result, several women's organizations are formed, including the Somali Democratic Women's Organization, Women's Group against Sexual Mutilation (in France), Le Mouvement Femmes et Société (Senegal), and the Babiker Bedri Foundation for Women's Studies and Research (Sudan).

In Namibia, Ida Jimmy makes a speech at the South West African People's Organization (SWAPO) and is sentenced to seven years in prison. Gertrude Kandanga, deputy secretary of SWAPO's Women's Council, also is arrested and held in jail for one year without being charged with a crime or given a trial.

A workshop on national liberation and development is held at the Hague, the Netherlands. Women from all over the world converge to discuss the liberation struggles they have been involved in (for example, in South Africa, Angola, Namibia, Mozambique, and Zimbabwe). They examine their participation and the gains, if any, they have made in their own liberation struggles, once national liberation has succeeded. Most often, they discover, women return to their old (subservient) status following the national struggle.

The mid-decade Conference for the International Women's Decade is held in Copenhagen. It has two goals: to measure progress in the first half of the Decade for Women and to develop strategies and programs for the remaining five years. Politics appears to enter into every major item of discussion—the Iran delegation withdraws; Jihan el-Sadat, the wife of President Anwar Sadat of Egypt, discusses Middle East issues and prompts a walkout by Palestinian representatives; and the concept of sexism (discrimination based on sex) is not included in the draft of the Programme of Action because many women insist that it does not exist in their countries. At the conclusion, four delegations—from the United States, Canada, Australia, and Israel—vote against the Programme of Action, while the remainder of the Western delegations abstain. U.S. representatives believe that the conference is a diplomatic defeat and many others believe that the women's movement has been damaged beyond repair.

Following the murders of two women by their husbands, Brazilian feminists establish the Center for the Defense of the Rights of Women.

1981   The government arrests Egyptian feminist Nawal el Saadawi because she has published articles that criticize President Sadat's policies. Many other feminists also are arrested because of their activities protesting government actions and policies. El Saadawi is held in prison for 80 days and released after Sadat is assassinated.

The first All Latin American Women's Conference is held in Colombia. The conference is attended by 250 delegates from 25 countries and focuses on the status of women in Latin America.

The first battered women's shelter is opened in Thailand by activist Kanitha Wichiencharoen.

Peruvian feminists protest pornography and violence against women.

In Geneva a conference on Women and Health is convened. Over 250 women from 35 countries gather to discuss health issues of importance to women.

Several NGOs appear before the UN Working Group on Slavery to to argue that female circumcision and other traditional practices are a human rights problem. The Working Group recommends that a study be conducted to examine the extent of this problem.

1981
cont.

The International Labor Conference adopts a new convention, the Workers with Family Responsibilities Convention (No. 156) and a new Workers with Family Responsibilities Recommendation (No. 165). This is the first time at the international level that child care is considered to be the concern of men as well as women. Convention 156 requires that member states of the International Labor Organization develop national policy that will "enable persons with family responsibilities who are engaged or wish to engage in employment to exercise their right to do so without being subject to discrimination and, to the extent possible, without conflict between their employment and family responsibilities" (Article 3). Recommendation 165 elaborates on the steps that can be taken to implement the convention. These include reduced working hours and overtime, flexible work schedules, parental leave of absence following maternity leave, and protection for part-time workers.

1982

Two women in Nicaragua become justices on the Supreme Court (Sandra Day O'Connor becomes the first woman on the U.S. Supreme Court in 1981).

An Expert Meeting on Multidisciplinary Research on Women in the Arab World is held in Tunis. The meeting is sponsored by the United Nations Educational, Scientific and Cultural Organization (UNESCO). As a result of this meeting, the Association for the Development of Research on Women in the Arab World is formed.

In Chile, the Movement of Women Slum Dwellers (MOMUPO) is founded with the purpose of uniting and coordinating the activities of grassroots women's groups. There are over 50,000 people in the Santiago area who belong to 500 organizations to fight poverty.

The Islamic Ideology Council of Pakistan proposes passage of a Law of Evidence, which values a woman's testimony in court as worth half as much as a man's testimony. It also recommends that the lives of murder victims who are women should be valued at half as much as murder victims who are male.

A pro-contraceptive campaign is begun in India to curb the large population increases. Women are paid $22 to be sterilized, and men are paid $15.

Kenya outlaws traditional genital mutilation of women.

1983   UNESCO begins to implement strategies with member states and NGOs to encourage literacy programs among women in developing countries. It launches Equal Opportunities in Education for Women and Girls, a special program whose aim is to reduce gender inequities in all areas, but especially in education.

The second Latin American and Caribbean Feminist Meeting is held in Lima, Peru. The focus is decidedly feminist; topics include patriarchy and the church, feminist research, domestic work, women in exile, health, literature, development programs, sexuality, power, violence and sexual slavery, paid work, family, peasant women, psychotherapy, feminism, and general problems in daily life.

Thirteen women's organizations send a memorandum requesting government action to the lieutenant governor of Delhi (India) claiming that the number of young women who have died as a result of burns in New Delhi grew from 311 in 1977 to 610 in 1982 (*Indian Express,* 3 December 1983).

Several women's organizations publicly protest the Pinochet regime in Chile. The Manifesto of the Feminist Movement is written, with the slogan "Democracy in the Country and in the Home." Several organizations coordinate their activities in opposition to military rule.

In Brazil, women are outraged when a woman who killed her husband is sentenced to 14 years in prison, while a man who murdered his wife is given a two-year suspended sentence. The court's position is that the man was defending his honor and therefore had a right to murder his wife.

1984   In Egypt, the Committee on the Conditions of Women is created by the Arab Lawyers Federation. This committee provides women with their own committee to examine the status of women and encourage interest in human rights in general and women's rights in particular.

In Kuwait, the Women's Cultural and Social Society of Kuwait works to mobilize women and to encourage them to work with and lobby key government officials to extend voting rights to women. Members are primarily upper- and middle-class women.

The first Regional Meeting on Women and Health in Latin America is held in Colombia and includes 70 participants from 10 countries. This is one of many conferences in which women's health concerns are being made known and protests are registered against the male-dominated health policy decisions being made.

The Inter-African Committee on Traditional Practices is formed. The committee's two major tasks are to support the creation of national organizations to address the issue of female circumcision and other traditional practices and to encourage research into those practices that are harmful to women. The committee also proposes strategies for eliminating female circumcision.

The Dowry Prohibition (Amendment) Act of 1984 is passed in India. The purpose of this act is to strengthen the Dowry Prohibition Act of 1961, which was ignored by most Indians. But this new act is denounced by several women's organizations because too many loopholes exist and prosecution of those who murder young brides will be difficult if not impossible. Punishment is difficult to enforce, and there are no provisions for enforcing the act.

In Argentina, the world's first Housewives' Trade Union is created to provide support and advocacy for housewives. The union demands wages and pensions for housework. The group is formed by women in politics, trade unions, housewives, and human rights organizations and demands equal pay for women and pensions for housewives and also a state department for women.

In Amsterdam, the International Tribunal and Meeting on Reproductive Rights is held.

1985   The Tunisian Human Rights Organization creates a women's committee to defend the rights of women. The committee circulates a petition that supports women's equal access to work, education, civil and political rights, divorce, guardianship of children following the death of the husband, and improvement in the inheritance rights of single female children. A series of debates is organized on these issues and many of them are discussed on television and radio programs. The campaign concludes with a large demonstration to show popular support for the fight for women's rights.

The lack of progress in improving women's health is a major concern at the annual meeting of the World Health Assembly, which consists of representatives of all members of the World Health Organization. The group also notes that women's rights should be protected and recognizes the link between equal rights and women's participation in health activities.

Nairobi, Kenya, hosts the final conference of the United Nations Decade for Women, 1975–1985, and the parallel nongovernmental organization Forum '85. Approximately 1,900 official delegates and more than 14,000 NGO representatives arrive in Nairobi for these meetings. The main purpose of the meeting is to review and appraise the achievements of the Decade for Women and to adopt the major conference document, the *Nairobi Forward-Looking Strategies for the Advancement of Women.*

The National Conference on Perspectives for Women's Liberation is held in Bombay, India. Almost 400 delegates from over 100 women's organizations throughout India attend the conference.

Over 5,000 landless peasants from the Paraguayan Peasants' Movement (MCP) organize a mass public demonstration for their rights. Over 1,000 peasant women participate in a demonstration to celebrate the formation of the Women's Commission of the MCP.

1986 The International AIDS Conference recognizes the impact of HIV and AIDS on women for the first time and begins to focus attention on the neglect of women in AIDS prevention activities.

    The United Nations Economic and Social Council recognizes that family violence violates the rights of women.

1987 Eight international agencies and organizations launch the Safe Motherhood Initiative, which focuses on attempts to reduce the number of maternal deaths throughout the world by half by the year 2000. Organizers place high priority on improving the socioeconomic status of girls and women, providing family planning services to all women, offering high quality prenatal and delivery care for all women, and providing skilled obstetric care for emergency and high-risk cases.

    In Uruguay, the Women's Institute is established within the Ministry of Education and Culture to promote policies that help women improve their status and lives.

    Women from Latin America and the Caribbean meet in Taxco, Mexico, to discuss major issues of concern to them. The 1,500 participants include women from government ministries, nongovernmental organizations, and Catholic feminist organizations. Lively discussions lead to little agreement on many issues. Women represent different classes, ages, and regions, and agreement on local issues is difficult. Many participants want to focus on major gender issues and leave local issues out of the discussions.

    In Costa Rica, the fifth International Women and Health Conference is held.

1988 The Korean Women's Association United, a coalition of 24 women's organizations in South Korea, holds a news conference to announce the launching of a crusade against trafficking in women and to focus attention on the increasing number of women who are being kidnapped off the streets and sold into prostitution. The coalition calls for the government to take action against this practice and to slow down the rapidly growing entertainment industry, thought by many to be the cause of the increase in prostitution.

The NGO Working Group on Refugee Women holds a meeting of 150 representatives from refugee women's groups, NGOs, intergovernmental groups, and governments to discuss refugee women's issues and to determine how these issues can be more effectively addressed. Five major themes are the focus at the meetings—protection, health, education, cultural adjustment, and employment. The group produces a report entitled "Working with Refugee Women: A Practical Guide," which includes a discussion of the five major themes and recommendations for action.

May 28 is set aside by women's groups and organizations throughout the world as an international day of action for women's health. Protests and demonstrations, lobbying activities, and publicity events are held to focus attention on the need to provide women with accessible, humanized, and competent health services and to lower maternal mortality. This becomes an annual event.

1989   The International Conference on the Implications of AIDS for Mothers and Children is held in Paris, France. Two conclusions are reached at this conference concerning women and children with AIDS. First, AIDS prevention programs for women and children do not exist in most countries. Second, in countries that have prevention programs for women, the programs often focus on reaching female sex workers, that is, prostitutes and others involved in promiscuous sexual activities, rather than on women in the general population who are at risk of contracting AIDS.

1990   Recognizing the importance of education, especially in developing countries, the United Nations declares International Literacy Year. International, national, and regional activities are encouraged to promote literacy throughout the world. UNESCO begins an awareness campaign to promote the idea of achieving total literacy for all by the year 2000. Many programs focus on providing women with literacy activities and providing

1990
cont.

them with an understanding of the need for educating their children.

The South Asian Association for Regional Co-operation declares the Year of the Girl Child, recognizing the detrimental attitudes of many parents toward their daughters. The association claims that the common and widely held preference for male children encourages the neglect and exploitation of female children, robbing these children of their self-esteem. Males receive the majority of resources as they are growing up, including food, parental attention, health care, and education, while females are treated as second-class citizens both as children and later as adults. The association believes that this attitude must change to eliminate gender discrimination from all aspects of society.

The Permanent Working Group on the Situation of Women in the United Nations High Commissioner on Refugees (UNHCR) suggests that more women professionals should be hired at UNHCR. Because the majority of refugees are women and children, the Working Group believes that more women on staff at local sites will encourage more refugee women to participate in activities designed to help them and their children.

UNICEF and WHO convene a top-level panel of policymakers in Italy to examine breast-feeding and to determine ways to encourage mothers throughout the world to breast-feed their babies. This panel develops the Innocenti Declaration on the Protection, Promotion and Support of Breast-feeding, which states that breast-feeding is both a mother's and a child's right; ambitious goals are set to expand the number of women who breast-feed their children.

Women from Latin America and the Caribbean meet in San Bernardo, Argentina, to discuss relevant women's issues. Almost 3,000 participants come from a variety of fields and levels of activism and include ecologists, pacifists, union organizers, squatters, parliamentarians, political party militants, Christians, lesbians, indigenous women, and black women. The women form new women's networks and coordinate regional campaigns on issues such as abortion and how women are perceived in the media.

In Riyadh, Saudi Arabia, 47 women drive their cars to protest the law against women driving. They are briefly imprisoned, with religious leaders believing that they have tried to corrupt society by their behavior. They are fired from their jobs, some are threatened, and many of their families are also threatened. The government reinforces the ban on driving by women.

In Algeria, Islamic fundamentalists increase their efforts to suppress women's rights and force women to follow strict Islamic practices.

In Chile, the government creates the National Women's Service (SERNAM) to develop and promote programs that focus on women.

1991   The International Association of Women Judges is formed. Members come from 53 countries, including Brazil, Chile, Nigeria, and the Philippines.

The Inter-American Development Bank (IDB) develops an action plan for changing its approach to women in development (WID) activities. This plan changes the ways that the IDB participates in various country programs, project development, and project analysis. The plan calls on the IDB to treat women's participation as an integral part of all IDB activities and mandates that WID issues will be addressed at the beginning of projects or during the planning process.

In Kenya, over 300 schoolboys attack a girls' dormitory following the girls' refusal to join a protest against the headmaster. The boys kill 19 girls and rape 71. When questioned about the boys' behavior, a deputy principal claims that the "boys never meant any harm against the girls. They just wanted to rape."

The Pakistani government adopts Islamic law. Women's rights as witnesses, judges, and lawyers are limited.

1991   According to a report by the United Nations, the number
cont.   of rural women in developing countries who are living
        in poverty has increased by 50 percent in the past 20
        years. The number of rural men living in poverty is
        found to be much lower.

1992   An Expert Group Meeting on Population and Women is
        held in Botswana. Participants develop several recom-
        mendations concerning the promotion of responsible fa-
        therhood. Recommendations encourage the participation
        of both parents in the provision of material and emo-
        tional support to their children. Governments are en-
        couraged to support responsible parenthood and to
        develop measures to facilitate this practice through edu-
        cational activities, information services, employment leg-
        islation, and institutional support. Family responsibilities
        should be equitably shared by both parents.

        At the annual meeting of the World Health Assembly,
        which consists of representatives of all members of the
        World Health Organization, a call is made to implement
        international policies that focus on improving women's
        health. The group recognizes that although recommen-
        dations have been made throughout the years to im-
        prove the health of women throughout the world, little
        progress has actually been made.

        The United Nations Conference on Environment and De-
        velopment is held in Rio de Janeiro. Participants focus at-
        tention on women as managers of natural resources and
        as the moving force for sustainable development and on
        the need for planners to recognize women's role in de-
        velopment when creating development projects. Experts
        at this meeting blame the growing population in
        Rwanda on husbands who refuse to let their wives use
        birth control pills because of the belief that pills weaken
        women, making them unable to work in the fields.

        In Kenya, 50 women, some over 70 years old, demon-
        strate for the release of political prisoners and are at-
        tacked by police with batons and tear gas. Four of them,
        including environmental activist Wangari Maathai, are
        knocked unconscious.

Religious leaders in Nigeria blame a severe drought in the country on "indecent" women. Women who are wearing nontraditional dress are attacked and many women protest these attacks. The offices of the Association des Femmes Nigeriennes are burned.

1993   In June, at the United Nations World Conference on Human Rights in Vienna, Austria, the women's caucus demands that violations of female human rights be examined when UN Treaty Committees meet to monitor and enforce the provisions of their treaties. Women's rights are finally seen as an important component of international human rights. But at the meeting, many Muslim governments who had supported the Universal Declaration of Human Rights in 1948 withdraw their support, believing that universal human rights is a Western concept, that Muslim societies should not be judged by these Western concepts, and that Islam can provide the basic elements of a fair society, including women's basic rights.

The Canadian government grants refugee status to a female Saudi national on the basis of gender-related persecution. The woman's advocates argue that her basic human rights to life, liberty, and security of the person are threatened because she does not accept the restrictions imposed on her by Saudi society. Her freedom to work, study, or dress as she wants is restricted, along with her freedom of movement in and out of the country. In addition, government policy, as well as public attitudes, led to her persecution, since she was subjected to violence whenever she walked down the street without covering her face.

The United Nations General Assembly unanimously adopts the Declaration on the Elimination of Violence against Women. The Declaration defines violence against women as "any act of gender-based violence that results in, or is likely to result in, physical, sexual or psychological harm or suffering to women, including threats of such acts, coercion or arbitrary deprivation of liberty, whether occurring in public or in private life." The declaration states that acts of violence against women include

1993
cont.

battering, sexual abuse of female children, dowry-related violence, marital rape, female genital mutilation, non-spousal violence, rape, sexual abuse, sexual harassment, intimidation at work and in schools, trafficking in women, and forced prostitution.

The World Health Organization condemns the genital mutilation of women following lengthy and intense lobbying on the part of Ghanaian-British feminist Efua Dorkenoo.

In Tehran, Iran, almost 800 women are arrested for violating Islamic dress codes requiring that women cover everything but their hands and face when they are out in public. Some of the women arrested are sentenced to be flogged.

Over 1,300 women in Latin America meet for their biannual *encuentro* (encounter) in Costa del Sol, El Salvador. They discuss human rights violations, women's rights, electoral quotas, and problems of discrimination they face within the women's movement. The organizers of the meeting receive death threats and consider moving the gathering to another country.

1994

The International Conference on Population and Development is held in Cairo, Egypt. Participants agree that population and development policies should focus on women's equality, empowerment, reproductive rights, and sexual health. Attendees state that women must be empowered and their status improved in order for them to realize their full potential in the areas of economic, political, and social development. Empowering women is also an important goal in and of itself. As women achieve status, opportunities, and social, economic, and legal rights equal to men, human health and well-being will be enhanced. At the conference the Muslim governments join forces with representatives from the Vatican to oppose human rights for women.

The Inter-American Development Bank forms a Task Force on Women in response to requests by the bank's Professional Women's Network. The task force analyzes gender differences in hiring practices, pay, assignments, advancement opportunities, work quality, and other areas of concern. Recommendations are made to improve the situation of women employees.

The United Nations declares 1994 the International Year of the Family to promote policies that foster equality between women and men within the family and to bring about a fuller sharing of domestic responsibilities and employment opportunities.

Women's World Banking (see Chapter 5) convenes the United Nations Expert Group on Women and Finance in preparation for the Fourth World Conference on Women to be held in Beijing. The group focuses on transforming financial systems to open access to low-income women entrepreneurs and producers. Delegates to the meeting include world leaders in banking with the poor and from NGOs, financial institutions, research organizations, and funding sources.

The United Nations Secretariat for the Fourth World Conference on Women convenes an Expert Group Meeting on Women and Economic Decision-Making. Women leaders from government organizations, the private sector, NGOs, and research organizations participate in this meeting.

1995   The Geneva-based Women's World Summit Foundation awards the 1995 Prize for Women's Creativity in Rural Life to ten rural women and women's groups from eight countries. The award honors the women's courage and creativity and their innovative projects that enhance their quality of life and contribute to sustainable development. The women, who win cash awards, come from Africa, Asia, and Latin America and include Domitila Barrios of Bolivia, an internationally known grassroots leader; Lia Junqiao of China, who has built a village skills-training school; Lai Xiao, a Mongol herdswoman who has developed a scientific strategy for breeding and raising sheep; Gawaher Saad El Sherbini Fadi of Egypt, a leader of land reclamation cooperatives; Joan Abgo of Ghana, who coordinates activities of rural women in

1995
cont.

farming and trading; Samuben Ujabhai Thakore and Ranbai Jemalji Rauma of India, who shared one prize for leading a union of 14,000 rural women to secure employment programs from the government; Samake Nekani and Sangare Aminata of Mali, who shared a prize for being effective group leaders; Huda Abdel-El-hameid of Sudan, who expanded her fishing abilities into a successful business; and the Coordinating Bureau for Women's Groups in Togo, led by Segou Tida, which trains women in poverty-stricken areas to earn and manage money and provides health care, food, housing, and clothing.

President Alberto Fujimori of Peru, in his second-term inaugural speech, announces an aggressive government campaign to provide family planning services to low-income Peruvians. The Peruvian bishops conference protests the campaign, arguing that contraception is not morally acceptable. Although Peru is 90 percent Roman Catholic, a poll suggests that many people support the president's position on family planning.

The World Summit for Social Development is held in Copenhagen. In addition to having women's issues on the agenda, at this meeting women also help set the agenda. Women's empowerment is a major issue; this is also accepted as a necessary element in all strategies that seek to solve social, economic, and environmental problems. Participants recognize the importance of empowering women politically, socially, and economically in order to eliminate poverty, unemployment, and other social problems.

The Fourth World Conference of Women is held in Beijing, China, in September. The key points established in the Platform for Action involve the importance of seeing women's rights as human rights, superseding cultural restrictions on women's rights, ensuring reproductive and sexual rights, a call for review of laws that call for punishment of women who have an abortion, recognition of adolescent rights, and the right of women to control their sexuality. Prior to this meeting, five regional conferences are held in Indonesia, Argentina, Austria,

Senegal, and Jordan to focus on specific regional priorities. These meetings help each region offer concrete suggestions for the meetings in Beijing.

Over 30,000 participants attend the NGO Forum on Women '95 in Huairou, China. It is the largest international gathering on women.

The First International Conference on Dowry and Bride-Burning convenes at Harvard Law School. The conference organizers focus attention on the practice of dowry-related violence toward women in India. The National Crimes Bureau of India reports that there were 5,817 dowry deaths in 1993 and 5,199 deaths in 1994, although the Supreme Court of India estimates that up to 15,000 women die each year from dowry disputes. All of these deaths occur despite the fact that the Indian government, in 1961, enacted the Dowry Prohibition Act, prohibiting the practice of dowry. The conference suggests practical ways that dowry and bride-burning can be eliminated, such as providing residential training centers and apartment complexes for abused women.

An International Symposium on Women and the Media—Access to Expression and Decision-Making is organized by UNESCO and held in Toronto. As one of UNESCO's contributions to the Fourth World Conference on Women, the symposium brings together 200 media experts, journalists, researchers, and representatives from international organizations and NGOs. Participants examine success stories of women, women's access to expression and decision making in and through the media, and ways to encourage more female representation in the media.

1996   The city of Khartoum in the Sudan issues a public law that orders the separation of the sexes in public in order to conform to strict fundamentalist Muslim law. The law requires that barriers must be erected between men and women at social events, weddings, parties, picnics, and all other social gatherings. Buses must display a verse from the Koran that reminds people that they are prohibited from looking at members of the opposite sex.

1996 Male students are to be separated from female students.
cont.

Forty Kuwaiti women—lawyers, scientists, and teachers—protest outside the Kuwaiti legislature to demand the vote and the right to run for parliament. Many of the women were members of the civilian resistance during Iraq's occupation from 1990 to 1991; during the occupation Sheik Jaber al-Ahmad al-Sabah said that he would consider giving women the vote because of their bravery during the resistance to Iraqi rule. In Kuwait, women occupy top positions in the civil service, oil industry, and education; they are allowed to drive and to wear Western-style clothes. However, they do not have political rights and equality with men on social issues.

References

Franck, Irene, and David Brownstone. 1995. *Women's World: A Timeline of Women in History.* New York: HarperPerennial.

Greenspan, Karen. 1994. *The Timetables of Women's History: A Chronology of the Most Important People and Events in Women's History.* New York: Simon and Schuster.

Hafkin, Nancy J., and Edna G. Bay, eds. 1976. *Women in Africa: Studies in Social and Economic Change.* Stanford: Stanford University Press.

Hahner, June, ed. 1980. *Women in Latin American History: Their Lives and Views.* Los Angeles: University of California at Los Angeles.

India, government of. Department of Social Welfare, Ministry of Education and Social Welfare. 1974. *Towards Equality: Report of the Committee on the Status of Women in India.* New Delhi: Ministry of Education and Social Welfare.

Miles, Rosalind. 1989. *The Women's History of the World.* Topsfield, MA: Salem House.

Miller, Francesca. 1991. *Latin American Women and the Search for Social Justice.* Hanover, NH: University Press of New England.

Olsen, Kirstin. 1994. *Chronology of Women's History.* Westport, CT: Greenwood Press.

Read, Phyllis J., and Bernard L. Witlieb. 1992. *The Book of Women's Firsts.* New York: Random House.

Reeves, Minou. 1989. *Female Warriors of Allah: Women and the Islamic Revolution.* New York: E. P. Dutton.

Trager, James. 1994. *The Women's Chronology: A Year-by-Year Record, from Prehistory to Present.* New York: Henry Holt.

Winslow, Anne, ed. 1995. *Women, Politics, and the United Nations.* Westport, CT: Greenwood Press.

Biographical Sketches 3

Throughout history women have played major roles in politics, social activism, health care, education, and other areas that contribute to their local communities, nations, and at an international level. Thousands of women have participated in major United Nations conferences and have contributed to the movement to improve women's status and the fight for equal rights throughout the world. This chapter provides short biographical sketches of individuals who play or have played a key role in one or more of the above-mentioned areas. But the women included here are only a few of the many women actively involved in working to improve women's lives. At the end of the chapter, a list of resources is provided to direct the reader to sources of information on the many thousands of women advocates, educators, and politicians.

Aminah Al-Said (b. 1914)

Born in Cairo, Egypt, Aminah Al-Said is a writer and advocate for women's rights. Her father, a doctor, believed that daughters should be educated along with sons. Karimah Al-Said, her sister, was a teacher who in 1965 became the first female minister of education in the Egyptian government. In

1935, Aminah was among the first small group of women to attend and graduate from Cairo University.

She became the editor of *Hawa*, a weekly women's magazine that has the largest foreign circulation of all Arabic papers. The first woman elected to the Egyptian Press Syndicate Executive Board, Al-Said is a member of the Supreme Board of Journalism, president of Dar al Hilal Publishing House, and a popular participant in international conferences. She delivers many lectures on the status and lives of Arab women and helps audiences throughout the world understand the differences between Arab women and Western women.

Aduke Alakija (b. 1921)

A well-known Nigerian lawyer, Aduke Alakija attended primary and secondary school in Lagos, Nigeria, and continued her secondary education in the United Kingdom. After studying medicine at Glasgow University, she changed her major to social science and attended the London School of Economics. While attending Cambridge, she started the West African Students' Union. She returned to Nigeria to work as a welfare officer, but when she realized she needed to be better prepared to fight for women's rights, she returned to England to study law. She joined the Nigerian delegation to the United Nations in 1961 and spent five years as a delegate. She has been a trustee of the Federal Nigeria Society for the Blind and the International Women's Society; she was an adviser to the International Academy of Trial Lawyers, the first black African female director of Mobil Oil, and a president of the International Federation of Women Lawyers. She received an honorary Doctor of Laws degree from Columbia University in 1964.

Corazon Aquino (b. 1933)

Corazon Aquino was president of the Philippines from 1986 until 1992. She was born in Luzon to one of the important landowning families of her country. Her family was active politically—her father was a congressman, and both of her grandfathers were senators. Growing up in a Catholic family, Aquino was educated at Catholic schools in Manila and the United States. She received her B.A. from Mount St. Vincent College in New York City and then returned to the Philippines to attend law school at Far Eastern University.

In 1954, she left law school after one year to marry Benigno 'Ninoy' Aquino, Jr., a successful young journalist. Soon after they were married, Benigno left journalism for politics. When Ferdinand Marcos came to power in the Philippines in 1965 and declared martial law in 1972, many politicians and activists were arrested by the Marcos regime, including Benigno Aquino. During the seven years that her husband spent in prison, Corazon became an activist, changing from a shy wife raising their five children to her husband's major link to the outside world.

In 1979, Benigno was released from prison and traveled to the United States for medical treatment; in 1980 he settled with his family in Newton, Massachusetts. In 1983, Marcos decided to allow elections the following year and Benigno flew home to the Philippines. Moments after his plane touched down, he was assassinated. Corazon flew home, buried her husband, and began her political career. She worked for anti-Marcos candidates and, in 1985, when many of these politicians won election to the National Assembly, people realized that Corazon was an effective leader—her ability to mobilize people was clear evidence of this ability. People started calling on her to run for president; the movement for her to run for president gained momentum, and she was elected president in 1986.

Aquino believed she should continue her husband's fight for democracy. She called for a new constitution that would set additional limits on presidential power. The military made many attempts to gain control; seven of these attempts led to the deaths of over 150 people. Aquino continued to fight for what she believed would most benefit her country's citizens—freedom and democracy. She initiated military reform, appointed many women to high government positions, and appointed three women to the Philippine Supreme Court. She also focused attention on helping nongovernmental organizations (NGOs) and cooperatives organize. She continues to work with NGOs and other organizations since leaving office in 1992.

Aung San Suu Kyi (b. 1945)

Aung San Suu Kyi is known throughout the world for her work in human rights and her fight for democracy in Burma (now referred to as Myanmar by its military leaders). Her father, Bogyoke Aung San, was a legendary Burmese hero. Her education focused on politics, philosophy, and economics at St. Hugh's College, Oxford University. In 1967, she received a B.A. in English from Oxford. She became a researcher for the United Nations in 1968 and worked in the New York office.

In 1972, she married Michael Aris, a scholar of Tibetan civilization, and they moved to Bhutan. She worked in the foreign ministry as a researcher on United Nations affairs. In 1973, she and Michael returned to England and she gave birth to their first son, Alexander. Their second son, Kim, was born in 1977. She cared for the children while her husband taught at Oxford University and became increasingly interested in learning more about her father, whom she never really knew because he was assassinated in 1947. Aung San went to Japan as Visiting Scholar at the Centre for Southeast Asian Studies at the University of Kyoto and continued her research on her father while there. She moved again in 1986, to Simla, India, where she joined her husband and became a researcher for the Indian Institute of Advanced Study.

Returning to Burma in 1988, she became involved in pro-democracy demonstrations and decided to enter politics, quickly becoming the symbol of the fight for democracy. The opposition hurriedly moved to silence her by disqualifying her candidacy, claiming that she could not run because she had married a foreigner. The authorities placed her under house arrest in 1989. During this eleven-month period, Aung San traveled throughout the country, urging her people to be courageous and to support democratic reform. Despite her name's absence on the ballot, her party, the National League for Democracy, won in a landslide victory, but the ruling army council refused to honor the election results.

In 1991, she won the Nobel Peace Prize for her work in human rights and the European Parliament's Andrei Sakharov Human Rights Prize. The Nobel Prize committee recognized her as "the leader of a democratic opposition that employs nonviolent means to resist a regime characterized by brutality" (Schlessinger and Schlessinger 1996, 173). She was released from house arrest in 1995 but continues to be harassed by government forces. Many of her supporters are frequently arrested by the current military government. She currently serves as the secretary-general of the National League for Democracy in Burma and continues to fight for human rights and for democracy in her country. In September 1996 the authorities accused her of working with the United States to foment unrest.

Sirimavo Bandaranaike (b. 1916)

As president of the Sri Lanka Freedom Party since 1960 and prime minister of Sri Lanka, Sirimavo Bandaranaike has participated in politics for many years. She was prime minister and minister of defense and external affairs from 1965 through 1970; a member of the Senate until 1965; leader of the opposition party from 1965 through 1970; and prime minister, minister of defense, and minister of foreign affairs, planning, economic affairs and plan implementation from 1970 to 1977. Her husband was prime minister of Ceylon from 1956 through 1959.

She was born into a wealthy family that was actively involved in politics. Sent to a Catholic school in Colombo, she married Solomon Bandaranaike, an Oxford-educated lawyer and politician, after her graduation. He was elected to the House of Representatives, served as minister of health and local government, and became prime minister in 1956. Following much unrest in the country as a result of proposals to replace English with Sinhalese as the national language and to make Buddhism the national religion, he was assassinated in 1959. When the Sri Lanka Freedom Party asked Sirimavo to campaign on their behalf, the party won 75 out of 151 seats in the House of Representatives and, as party leader, she was appointed prime minister. During her second term, Ceylon became the Socialist Republic of Sri Lanka and cut off all political ties to Great Britain. She ran for president in 1986 but did not win. In 1989, she won a seat in the National Assembly at the age of 73. In 1994, her daughter, Chandrika Bandaranaike Kumaratunga (see separate entry), became the new prime minister of the country.

Ela Bhatt (b. 1936)

Ela Bhatt is a well-known politician and women's organization executive in India who is a founding member and chairperson of the executive committee and board of directors of Women's World Banking (see Chapter 5). She is also the founder of the Self-Employed Women's Association (SEWA), which is one of the most successful organizations for economic empowerment of self-employed women in India. In 1989, she became the first woman appointed to the Planning Commission in India. Prior to this, Bhatt was a member of the Indian Parliament, a member of the Union Planning Committee, chairwoman of the Global Video Network, a member of the National Committee on Self-Employed Women and the advisory committee of the All-India Weavers' Foundation. Mrs. Bhatt's many awards include the Right Livelihood Award and the Ramon Magsaysay Award for Community Leadership. Her publications include *Profiles of Self-Employed Women*, published in 1975.

She understands the importance of helping women organize. She sees increasing levels of self-esteem among women who have organized to improve their lives and how these women learn to work together despite their differences (Snyder 1995). SEWA has helped women in many ways. Individual cooperatives have been organized, including groups of artisans, dairy workers, traders, and vendors. A wide variety of support services such as the SEWA Bank, health care, legal aid, housing assistance, child care, and affiliations with international labor groups are provided.

Benazir Bhutto (b. 1953)

Born at Pinto Hospital in Karachi, Pakistan, to her father's second wife, Benazir Bhutto was born into politics. Raised as a Sunni Muslim, Benazir's parents were progressive thinkers and allowed her to do more than most girls in Pakistan were allowed to do. She graduated from Radcliffe College in 1973 and completed a second B.A. in philosophy, politics, and economics at Oxford University. Staying on one more year to study international law and diplomacy, she was elected president of the Oxford Union in 1976, becoming the first Asian woman to serve as president. Following her graduation in 1977, she returned to Pakistan to work in the office of her father, Zulfikar Ali Bhutto, the prime minister of Pakistan.

Her father was overthrown in a coup in July 1977 by General Zia and kept under house arrest for several weeks. Later charged with conspiracy to murder at least one of his political opponents, her father was found guilty along with four codefendants and sentenced to death by hanging. He and his codefendants were hanged in 1979. Earlier, in 1978, Benazir's father had encouraged her to travel through the Northwest Frontier Province and the Punjab to encourage support for the Pakistan People's Party. She traveled throughout the country and was arrested, along with her mother, several times while her father was in prison.

Moving to London to escape the wrath of General Zia, Benazir continued to lead the Pakistan People's Party in opposition to Zia and his policies. Over the next several years, Benazir traveled back to Pakistan and, along with other party members, was arrested, confined to her home, and generally harassed by the Zia government. When General Zia was killed in a plane crash in August 1988, Pakistani president Ishaw Khan asked Benazir to become prime minister and form a new government. She became the first woman to lead a modern Muslim nation as well as the youngest head of state in the world.

She promised to deal with the serious drug problem throughout the country as well as growing ethnic violence, poverty, other social problems, and problems between India and Pakistan. She established women-only police stations in response to widespread rape and torture of women prisoners. Many people note her failure to take on the repressive Hudood Ordinance although she promised to eliminate it during her campaign. This ordinance specifies punishment for adultery, rape, fornication, and prostitution; rape may be considered as adultery or fornication if there are not four male witnesses to testify that the woman was raped. Women are not allowed to testify, and these crimes are punishable by death. She was not able to overturn this ordinance. In elections held in early 1977, Bhutto was turned out of office.

Ester Boserup (b. 1910)

Ester Boserup is a noted Danish rural economist. She received her Ph.D. in economics from the University of Copenhagen. In 1970, she wrote what is now considered a classic text, *Women and Economic Development,* which caused most experts in the field of economic development to rethink their ideas concerning development, especially the roles that women play in development activities. For this book, Boserup gathered and analyzed data from official statistics and research. She provided clear and concise evidence that women played a crucial role in economic development, although their contributions usually were uncounted when measuring national economic productivity. She was one of the first experts in the field of development to believe that women had not been included in capitalist development activities and programs and that their exclusion widened an already wide gap between women's and men's economic power.

Boserup has been a member of the United Nations Expert Committee of Development Planning, the Scandinavian Institute of Asian Studies, and the International Research and Training Institute for the Advancement of Women (INSTRAW). In 1972

Boserup prepared the working document for and attended the Meeting of Experts on the Integration of Women in Development, which was co-sponsored by the Commission on the Status of Women and the Commission on Social Development of the United Nations. This historic meeting provided advice to the United Nations and its member states concerning policy measures that should be followed in regard to women's role in economic and social development.

Elise Boulding (b. 1920)

Born in Oslo, Norway, Elise Boulding is a sociologist with a global view of the world and the role that women play in it. She received a B.A. in English from Douglass College, an M.S. in sociology from Iowa State University, and her Ph.D. in sociology from the University of Michigan. She has conducted numerous transnational and comparative crossnational studies on conflict and peace, development, and women in society. She has committed herself to working for peace throughout the world and has worked internationally on problems of peace and world order as an activist as well as a scholar. She served as a member of the governing board of the United Nations University from 1980 to 1985, as a member of the International Jury of the United Nations Educational, Scientific and Cultural Organization (UNESCO) Prize for Peace Education, and as a member of the U.S. Commission for UNESCO from 1981 to 1987.

Boulding taught in the Department of Sociology and Institute of Behavioral Science at the University of Colorado at Boulder from 1967 through 1977. She was a professor and chair of the department of sociology at Dartmouth College from 1978 to 1985. From 1988 to 1991 she was secretary general of the International Peace Research Association.

She was a member of the Commission on Proposals for a National Academy of Peace and Conflict Resolution which recommended that Congress establish a U.S. Institute of Peace. She served as editor of the International Peace Research Newsletter from 1963 to 1968 and from 1983 to 1987. Her many books focus on women, their role in history, and their status as women and include *Handbook of International Data on Women* (with Carson, Greenstein, and Nuss) published in 1977 by Halsted Press; *Women in the Twentieth Century World*, published in 1977 by Halsted Press; *Women and Social Costs of Development: Two Case Studies* (with Moen, Lilleydahl, and Palm); and the *Underside of*

History: A View of Women Through Time (2 volumes). She has been actively involved in the peace movement, and has written several books on this topic.

Angie Brooks-Randolph (b. 1928)

Angie Brooks-Randolph is a well-known Liberian lawyer and diplomat. She worked her way through high school as a typist, working as a stenographer in the justice department of the Liberian government. When she became the first woman to become a legal apprentice in Liberia, people laughed at her during her first court appearance. Brooks-Randolph later received a grant to attend school in North Carolina and received her degree from the University of Wisconsin. She traveled to London to study at the University College and then returned to Liberia to practice law. Becoming assistant attorney-general in 1953, Brooks-Randolph also taught law. From 1958 until 1978 she was assistant secretary of state, and for three years (1964–1967) she was president of the International Federation of Women Lawyers.

She became the second woman to preside over a session of the United Nations General Assembly, serving from 1969 through 1970. She represented Liberia at the United Nations Plenary Session from 1970 to 1973 and was also the Liberian ambassador to Cuba. She has been a strong advocate for women's rights—especially for professional opportunities and better educational opportunities. During her life, she has provided care for 47 foster children. She has participated in many international conferences and committees, has served on advisory panels, has been awarded many honors, and has received 18 honorary degrees from several universities in the United States.

Charlotte Bunch (b. 1944)

As a well-known feminist author, teacher, organizer, and activist, Charlotte Bunch has played a leading role in the women's movement for more than 20 years. She received a B.A. in history and political science from Duke University. She was the first woman resident fellow at the Institute for Policy Studies in Washington, D.C., and founded DC Women's Liberation and *Quest: A Feminist Quarterly*, which she edited during the 1970s. She has edited seven anthologies, including *Learning Our Way: Essays in Feminist Education*, *Women Remembered: Biographies of Women in History*, and *International Feminism: Networking against Female Sexual Slavery.* Her most recent book is a collection of her essays from 1968 to 1986 entitled *Passionate Politics: Feminist Theory in Action.* In 1979 she participated in an international workshop, "Feminist Ideology and Structures in the First Half of the Decade for Women," which was sponsored by the United Nations Asian and Pacific Centre for Women and Development in Bangkok, Thailand. Bunch helped organize a worldwide conference on the topic of traffic in women and female sexual slavery, held in Rotterdam, Netherlands, in 1983. Currently she is the director of the Center for Global Issues and Women's Leadership at Rutgers University.

Violeta Barrios de Chamorro (b. 1929)

Born in Rivas, Nicaragua, Violeta Chamorro was educated in a Catholic high school in San Antonio, Texas, and, for one year, at Blackstone College in Virginia. She married Pedro Chamorro Cardenal in 1950, the publisher of the newspaper, *La Prensa,* which openly criticized the government of General Somoza. Throughout the 1950s, Pedro was repeatedly arrested and jailed for his opposition to the government. He was banished in 1957 and he and his family escaped to Costa Rica and stayed there for several years. Pedro and the family returned during a period of amnesty in 1960 and he continued his vocal opposition to the regime of Somoza's sons, Luis Somoza Debayle and Anastasio Somoza Debayle. He was assassinated in 1978; most people believed his murder was ordered by the government. His murder ignited the final rebellion against the Somoza regime.

Violeta Chamorro took over the task of publishing *La Prensa* after her husband's death. She oversaw the attacks against the Somoza regime and endured bomb threats at the newspaper. She contributed money to the Sandinista National Liberation Front that focused on overthrowing the corrupt Somoza regime. Following the downfall of General Somoza in 1979, she became a member of the civilian junta that held the executive powers of the Government of National Reconstruction. She resigned her membership in 1980 after she became disillusioned with the new Sandinista government and its Marxist leanings and excessive militarism.

She often wrote articles denouncing the Sandinista government and the paper was frequently closed down by the government, in 1986 indefinitely; this shutdown lasted for 15 months. Chamorro became a target of the leftist regime, and harassment continued even after the paper reopened. She became leader of the opposition party, the Union Nacional Opositora (UNO) in September 1989 and was elected president of Nicaragua in February 1990. Voters looked to her to bring peace and outside aid to the country's battered economy. During her presidency, she ended the draft and greatly reduced the size of the Sandinista army.

Eugenia Charles (b. 1919)

Eugenia Charles is the current president of the Commonwealth of Dominica. She attended Catholic schools on Dominica and Grenada and received a bachelor's degree in law from the University College of the University of Toronto in 1946. She was called to the English bar in 1947 and enrolled at the London School of Economics for additional study. When she returned to Dominica, she became the only woman practicing law on the island.

As a co-founder and the first leader of the Dominica Freedom Party, she has been a member of Parliament since 1975 and prime minister and minister of foreign affairs, finance, and development since 1980. Dominica achieved independence from Great Britain in 1978 amid concerns that the country was not ready economically or socially for independence. Charles is strongly anticommunist and has received millions of dollars from the United States during the 1980s to strengthen the country's weak infrastructure.

Gaositwe Keagakwa Tibe Chiepe (b. 1926)

Born in Serowe, Botswana, Gaositwe Keagakwa Tibe Chiepe attended Fort Hare University in South Africa from 1944 to 1947 and Bristol University from 1955 to 1957. Returning to Botswana, she worked as an education officer and became director of education in 1968. By 1970, she was appointed high commissioner to the United Kingdom and to Nigeria and held ambassadorial positions in Europe and Scandinavia. She became minister of commerce in 1974, minister of mineral resources and water affairs in 1977, and minister of external affairs in 1984.

Jeanne Martin Cissé (b. 1926)

Jeanne Martin Cissé started her career as a teacher in 1945 and became a well-known Guinean diplomat. She was director of a school until she decided to move into politics in 1958. She became a member of the Democratic Party in 1959 and worked in the federal office of the Kinda Region, focusing on activities to improve the lives and status of women. She served on the National and Regional Women's Committees of the National Assembly and eventually became secretary-general of the Conference of African Women in 1962. She remained in this role for ten years and at the same time was a member of the United Nations Committee on the Status of Women. As her country's permanent representative to the United Nations from 1972 to 1976, she was the first woman appointed as a delegate and the first to preside over the United Nations Security Council. She was awarded the Lenin Peace Prize in 1975. In 1976, she returned to Guinea to become minister of social affairs until her retirement in 1984.

Nawal El Saadawi (b. 1930)

A well-known Egyptian doctor, novelist, and militant writer, Nawal El Saadawi was born in a small village on the banks of the Nile and graduated from Cairo University in 1955. She refused to accept the role that Egyptian society offered women: She studied medicine at Columbia University in New York and returned to Egypt and joined the staff of Cairo University Hospital as a doctor practicing in rural areas. She later became a psychiatrist, and her book, *Women and Sex* (1972), caused a great deal of controversy because it openly discusses chastity and the taboos that women face in Arab society. She called for radical changes in the position of women within the family and as wage earners. She had been Egypt's director of public health but lost this position following the publication of her radical views; highly placed political and religious authorities called for her dismissal. She has written seven novels and five nonfiction books, including *The Hidden Face of Eve: Women in the Arab World* (1979), which describes her horrifying personal experience with female genital circumcision and examines the price that Arab women pay for being seen as second-class citizens and the property of their husbands. In 1981, she was imprisoned at the notorious Qanatir prison with several other women on the order of President Anwar Sadat because she was publishing a feminist magazine (*Confrontation*) and stirring up protest among women. She was released in 1982 and started the Pan-Arab Women's Organization.

Ana Figuero (1908–1970)

Chilean feminist Ana Figuero was born in Santiago and gradu-ated from the University of Chile. She taught school until the start of World War II when she traveled to the United States to study at Columbia University and Colorado State College. An ac-tive advocate for women, she was president of the committee to gain the vote in Chile. She directed the national secondary school system from 1947 to 1949 and then became the head of the Women's Bureau in the Ministry of Foreign Affairs in the Chilean government. In 1951 she was her country's special envoy to the United Nations. As chair of the Social, Humanitarian, and Cul-tural Committee, Figuero was the first woman to head a United Nations committee of the General Assembly. She became the first woman on the Security Committee in 1952 and became the first female assistant director general of the International Labour Or-ganization (ILO). In 1967, she retired from the ILO.

Indira Gandhi (1917–1984)

Indira Gandhi was the daughter of Jawaharlal Nehru, the first prime minister of India following independence from Great Britain, and the granddaughter of Motilal Nehru, who played a prominent role in India's struggle against British colonial rule. She grew up an only child and was frequently without the pres-ence of her father and grandfather, who were often arrested for their freedom activities. She attended school in Switzerland and England and married journalist Feroze Gandhi in 1942. Upon their return to India in 1942, Gandhi and her husband were im-prisoned for 13 months because they supported the indepen-dence movement.

When India gained independence in 1947, Gandhi and her two sons moved home to help her father during his years as prime minister. Her marriage to Feroze ended—although they were never divorced—about the time she moved into her father's home. She became his hostess and confidant, meeting many world leaders and traveling with her father to many foreign countries. During this time, she also served as chairperson of the Central Social Welfare Board and as president of the All India Youth Congress and was a member of the Congress Working Committee and the Central Election Committee. Following her father's death in 1964, she was elected to fill his seat in Parlia-ment. The same year she was appointed minister of information and broadcasting by Lal Shastri, who succeeded her father as prime minister. After Shastri's death in 1966, Gandhi was elected leader of the Congress Party and became prime minister of India.

Her years as prime minister were often stormy. Congress Party members split the party over opposition to her policies and Gandhi called for a general election in 1971. She traveled throughout the country campaigning for public support and won an overwhelming majority of votes. The country experienced economic difficulties in 1974 and she declared an emergency rule, following demonstrations throughout India. She imprisoned political adversaries and censored the press, outraging many Indians because of these actions. Although she released many prisoners from jail and lifted the press censorship before elections were held in 1977, voters removed her from office. By October 1977, she was charged with official corruption and jailed briefly.

In 1978, she ran for office in a rural district in South India after forming her own party, Congress-I Party (I—for Indira) and was elected to Parliament. During national elections in 1980, she was swept back into power, with her party gaining two-thirds of the seats in Parliament. Many Indians forgave Gandhi for her excesses while in office, believing that she was the best the country had to offer. She became a forceful speaker and advocate for Third World countries, while trouble again mounted at home. During 1983 and 1984, she sent government troops to stop disturbances in the Punjab, and these troops destroyed the large Sikh temple. Two of her Sikh bodyguards assassinated her in New Delhi in June 1984 in retaliation for the destruction of the temple. Her son Rajiv followed in her footsteps and was sworn in as prime minister of India.

Lydia Gueiler Tejada (b. 1921)

A well-known accountant, politician, and diplomat from Bolivia, Lydia Gueiler Tejada played an active role in the Bolivian revolution of 1952. She received a B.A. in accounting from the Institute Americano in Cochabamba, Bolivia. She was the Bolivian ambassador to Colombia from 1983 to 1986 and she spent some time in charge of Bolivian business affairs in Germany. She was political director and secretary general of Partido Revolucionario de Izquierda. After serving as president of the National Congress from August through November 1979, Gueiler Tejada became president of Bolivia on 17 November 1979. However, she was overthrown in a coup on 17 July 1980 and was exiled to Paris.

Before being exiled, Gueiler Tejada was undersecretary of farmers' affairs in the Bolivian government, served six years as a national deputy, and represented Bolivian women at the Comision Interamerica de Mujeres. She authored several laws to help Bolivian women gain their rights. The author of *La Mujer y la Revolucion* (Women and Revolution) in 1959, she received Bolivia's highest decoration, Condor de los Andes Gran Cruz, in 1979. At the United Nations in 1979, along with Margaret Thatcher and Indira Gandhi, Gueiler Tejada received the United Nations Woman of the Year award.

Asma Jahangir

As a well-known Pakistani lawyer, Asma Jahangir has fought legal inequities and human rights violations and continues to fight to end discrimination against women. Her father was a well-known liberal politician and she was active in student politics while in college. After graduation, she married a very successful businessman. She moved in with her husband's family, had children, and acted appropriately for her position as a woman. Finally disgusted with herself, she asked her family to allow her to study law. She studied at home, attending college only when she was required to take exams. After graduation, her husband would not allow her to work in a "man's law office"; therefore, in 1980, she and three other women started their own law firm, the first woman's legal practice in Pakistan. Today, about 70 percent of their cases are pro bono, or handled without charge. In 1983, she was beaten, tear-gassed, and arrested by police after protesting the Proposed Law of Evidence, in which a woman's testimony in court is valued at half that of a man's testimony.

Visakha Kumari Jayawardena (b. 1931)

Visakha Kumari Jayawardena is a well-known Sri Lankan political scientist, historian, and feminist. She received her Ph.D. in 1964 at the London School of Economics and Political Science. She studied at the Ecole de Sciences Politiques in France and received a diploma in 1956. She has been a senior lecturer in economics at the University of Sri Lanka (formerly the University of Ceylon) since 1969 and director of the Workers Education Programme. She has written *Rise of the Labour Movement in Ceylon* in

1972 and *Feminism and Nationalism in the Third World* in 1986. She has also been the director of the World Institute for Development Economics Research (WIDER).

Annie Ruth Baeta Jiagge (b. 1918)

Annie Ruth Baeta Jiagge, a prominent jurist in Ghana, received a teacher's certificate from Achimota College in 1937 and her LL.B. from the London School of Economics and Political Science in 1949. She has been a teacher and headmistress and operated her own legal practice from 1951 to 1956. Jiagge has had broad experience in the legal profession, as a senior magistrate, a circuit court judge, a high court judge, a judge in the Court of Appeal, and as president of the Court of Appeal. She was chairperson of the Commission on Investigation of Assets of Senior Public Servants and Named Political Leaders. She was the author of the draft of the 1968 United Nations Declaration on Elimination of Discrimination against Women and has written many articles in various journals. She has been president of the World Council of Churches (1975–1983), moderator of the WCC Programme to Combat Racism (1984–1991), on the UN Commission on the Status of Women (1962–1974) and president in 1968, and chairperson of the Ghana National Council on Women and Development (1975–1982). In other nongovernmental organizations, she has been vice president of the YWCA at the international level, Ghana YWCA president, and chairperson of the Committee of the Churches Participation in Development, Christian Council of Ghana.

Fatima Jinnah (1893–1967)

Born in Karachi, Pakistan, Fatima Jinnah went to live with her brother in Bombay when she was eight years old, following the death of her father. She attended a mission school and later studied dentistry. She and her brother attended a Round Table Conference in London in 1929 and then remained in England for four years. Returning to Pakistan in 1934, she joined the Muslim League, which opposed the conservative orthodox attitudes of Pakistani society toward women; this was the start of her active participation in the fight for the emancipation of women. She led the All-India Muslim Women's Committee in 1938. She traveled throughout India, founding branches of the committee and student federations and inspired the establishment of industrial schools, collectives, and other associations. She also founded the Fatima Jinnah Women's Medical College in Lahore.

When her brother, Ali Jinnah, became the first governor-general of Pakistan in 1947, she lived with him and served as his hostess; he died in 1948 and Fatima Jinnah retired from all public activity. In 1954 she re-entered the public eye, campaigning for the Muslim League and becoming an outspoken critic of the totalitarian government in East Pakistan. Persuaded to run against Ayub Khan in presidential elections as the representative of the combined opposition parties, she gained many staunch supporters. Although she lost the election, she continued to maintain a strong base of support. Known as the "mother of the country," she was a popular public figure; riots broke out during her funeral in Karachi in 1967, as her supporters mourned her death.

Begum Liaquat Ali Khan (b. 1905)

Born to an aristocratic Muslim family in India, Begum Liaquat Ali Khan received her education at the universities of Lucknow and Calcutta. At the age of 26 she moved to New Delhi, where she taught economics at Indraprastha College for Women. In 1941, she submitted as her master's thesis a carefully thought-out plan to develop a women's association. Eighteen years later, she finally founded such an organization, the All Pakistan Women's Association, which consisted of over two million women who were nurses, teachers, and administrators. Her husband, Liaquat Ali Khan, became prime minister of Pakistan in 1947; he was assassinated four years later in Rawalpindi.

In 1952 the All Pakistan Women's Association became a major force in the women's movement, encouraging women to become involved in politics and social causes. The organization founded schools, hospitals, and craft industries. Continuing her involvement in politics, she became the first Muslim woman ambassador from Pakistan; she served as ambassador to Belgium and the Netherlands in 1954 and later as ambassador to Italy and Tunisia. She has participated on committees of the United Nations and in studies for the International Labour Organization. She became the first woman to become governor of a province in Pakistan (Sind). She has also been the chancellor of the University of Karachi. In 1978 she was awarded the Human Rights Award from the United Nations.

Gwendoline Konie (b. 1938)

Gwendoline Konie was born in Lusaka, Zambia, and received her early education from local schools, the University College in Cardiff, Wales, and the American University in Washington, D.C. Following her return to Zambia, she found a job in the ministry of local government and social welfare. In 1963, Konie became a member of the Legislative Council and then joined the ministry of foreign affairs the following year.

In 1972 she joined the staff of the presidential office and was the Zambian ambassador to Sweden, Norway, Denmark, and Finland from 1974 to 1877. In 1977, she represented Zambia at the United Nations, leading the UN Council for Namibia. Since 1979, she has been a permanent secretary in the Zambian Civil Service, acted as an adviser and consultant to many organizations, and is a member of executive boards of several organizations that focus on adult education and family planning.

Chandrika Bandaranaike Kumaratunga (b. 1946)

Following in her mother's footsteps, Chandrika Bandaranaike Kumaratunga has been president of Sri Lanka since 1994. Kumaratunga's father, Solomon Bandaranaike, served as prime minister until his assassination in 1959. Her mother, Sirimavo Bandaranaike, served two terms, from 1960 to 1965 and from 1970 to 1977.

She received a degree in political science from the Sorbonne in Paris in 1985. Although she has held teaching positions in England and India, she has focused primarily on political activities. During her mother's second term, she headed the land reform office. With her husband, a politician and film star, she formed the People's Alliance, a coalition to the right of her mother's Freedom Party and to the left of the United National Party. Following her husband's assassination in 1988, Kumaratunga assumed leadership of the alliance. She was named prime minister in 1994 following her party's narrow win in Parliament.

While in office, she pledged to end the 12-year-old civil war between the government and the Liberation Tigers of Tamil Eelam. Women, especially in rural areas, have been vulnerable to rape, kidnapping, and torture, according to human rights groups. Kumaratunga has fought to protect these women. She has advocated and won progressive revisions in the country's rape laws to increase penalties for this crime.

Bertha Lutz (1899–1976)

Bertha Lutz was a well-known Brazilian feminist who founded the Brazil Federation for the Advancement of Women in 1922 and was the federation's president until her death in 1976. At the same time, she was a permanent delegate to the Inter-American Commission of Women from Brazil. She studied biology at the Sorbonne in Paris and returned to Rio de Janeiro to become the first woman to enter government service at the National Museum. She organized and led the fight for women's suffrage, which was won in 1931. In 1936 she developed a government department to deal with the specific problems that women face in society, and she has represented her country at many international conferences. She participated in the campaign to organize the United Nations Commission on the Status of Women. She has also taught zoology at the University of Rio de Janeiro.

Wangari Maathai (b. 1940)

Known around the world for her environmental and human rights activities, Wangari Maathai was born in Nyeri, Kenya, and raised in a farming community. Her parents were subsistence farmers from the Kikuyu tribe. After winning one of the many scholarships awarded to Kenyans by the Kennedy administration, Maathai attended Mount St. Scholastica College in Kansas, where she received a B.A. in biology in 1964. She earned her M.S. from the University of Pittsburgh, the first woman in all of eastern and central Africa to earn an advanced degree. In 1971, she earned a Ph.D. in biology from the University of Nairobi. She later became the first woman to hold an associate professorship at the University of Nairobi and was the first woman invited to chair a department there.

During her husband's campaign for a seat in Parliament, she realized the problems that people in the lower economic class face in finding a job and supporting their families. Following her husband's election, she started an employment agency to help people find work either cleaning the homes of wealthy people or planting trees and shrubs. She believed that planting trees would help stop desertification and soil erosion and support beautification.

Even though her agency was not successful, she continually was committed to finding ways to involve Kenyans in preserving the environment.

In 1977 Maathai succeeded in persuading the National Council of Women of Kenya to support her cause. First known as the Save the Land Harambee, the group soon became known as the Green Belt Movement (GBM). On World Environment Day in 1977, her group planted seven trees in a small Nairobi park, gained the public's attention, and eventually grew to a large, influential organization. The group has the support of the United Nations, several European governments, and hundreds of individual donors throughout the world. She has written several books about the movement, including *The Green Belt Movement* (1985) and *The Green Belt Movement: Sharing the Approach and the Experience* (1988).

During her early involvement in the Green Belt Movement, her husband filed for divorce, in large part, because he had never gotten used to the fact that she held a Ph.D.—African women are supposed to be dependent and submissive, not better than their husbands. During the divorce hearing, her husband accused her of adultery, the judges believed him, and she stated that the judges were "either incompetent or corrupt" for believing him. She was found in contempt of court and sentenced to six months in jail but served only three days after making an apology to the judges. She then decided to run for Parliament but was not allowed to run because of a technicality. In the meantime, she had resigned her position in the university in order to run for Parliament and the university refused to allow her to resume her duties.

In 1989, the Kenyan government wanted to construct a large, 62-story building in Nairobi's Uhuru Park that would include hotels, theaters, the newspaper, and a television station. This project, projected to cost $200 million, would have forced the country to take on more debt, not an economically sound idea, according to Maathai. She proposed a public debate on the construction and many people supported her efforts. These supporters, despite harassment, were successful in their efforts to stop the project.

She has continued to play an active role in politics. She is a member of the Forum for the Restoration of Democracy, and she established the Tribal Clashes Resettlement Volunteer Service to encourage the government to stop inciting tribal violence. She has won many awards, including the Woman of the Year Award in 1983, the Right Livelihood Award in 1984, the Better World Society Award for the Protection of the Global Environment in 1986, the Windstar Award for the Environment in 1988, the Woman of the World Award in 1989, and the Africa Prize for Leadership for the Sustainable End to Hunger in 1991. She continues to fight for the environment and for human rights.

Rigoberta Menchú Tum (b. 1959)

Rigoberta Menchú is an internationally known civil rights activist who works for the rights of the Mayan and Aztec people of Guatemala. Born in Chimel, Guatemala, she witnessed the brutality of government forces toward her people, the Quiché Mayan Indians. She has tirelessly traveled throughout the world to bring attention to the plight of Guatemala's indigenous people who have been persecuted by the landowning class and the military. Human rights organizations estimate that the number of indigenous people killed during the 33-year civil war has exceeded 15,000 people. Menchú traveled the country with her father, activist Vincente Menchú, who was a founding member of the Peasant Unity Committee (CUC), until he was tortured and killed by the Guatemalan security forces. Her mother and younger brother were also tortured and killed. In 1981, she escaped to Mexico.

Menchú won the Nobel Peace Prize in 1992 for her work in human rights. The Nobel Prize Committee cited Menchú as a "vivid symbol of peace and reconciliation across ethnic, cultural, and social dividing lines." The committee noted that "by maintaining a disarming humanity in a brutal world, Rigoberta Menchú appeals to the best in us. She stands as a uniquely potent symbol of a just struggle" (Schlessinger and Schlessinger 1996, 174). She is the youngest person and the first indigenous person to win the Nobel Peace Prize. In a book about her life, *I, Rigoberta Menchú: An Indian Women in Guatemala,* she describes many of her civil and human rights activities. She currently lives in Mexico and continues her human rights activities on behalf of native peoples.

With her prize money, she set up the Vincente Menchú Foundation, with headquarters in Mexico City and branch offices in Guatemala City and Berkeley, California, in honor of her father. The foundation advocates for human rights and education for indigenous people. It helps Indian street children and the widows of murdered political prisoners. She is a member of the United

Nations International Indian Treaty Council. She served as the goodwill ambassador to the United Nations in 1993 for the Year of the Indigenous Peoples.

Fatima Mernissi

Fatima Mernissi is a well-known Moroccan sociologist and feminist and the author of several publications; she is best known for her classic *Beyond the Veil: Male-Female Dynamic in Modern Muslim Society* (1975, 1987, revised edition). This book vividly describes the status and lives of women and their interaction with men in Muslim society. She has reinterpreted classical Islamic texts from a feminist perspective and supervised publication of a series of books on the legal status of women in Morocco, Algeria, and Tunisia. In 1992, she wrote *Islam and Democracy: Fear of the Modern World* in which she argues that the Islamic faith has been used and compromised by Arab leaders to control their countries and prevent democratic reforms. These rulers have distorted Islamic beliefs to fit their needs and have abused human rights by suppressing democratic reforms. In 1994, she wrote *Dreams of Trespass: Tales of a Harem Girlhood* (published in England as *The Harem Within: Tales of a Moroccan Girlhood*), which recounts her childhood growing up in a harem. Life was repressive and boring, and she and the other women and girls in the harem were restricted in what they could do and where they could go. Her latest publication is *Dreams of Trespass* (1994), a collection of interviews she conducted during the mid-1970s. This collection provides incredible insight into the lives of Moroccan women. Mernissi is currently a professor of sociology at Mohammed V University in Rabat, Morocco.

Swasti Mitter (b. 1939)

Born in West Bengal, India, Swasti Mitter was educated at Calcutta University, the London School of Economics, and Cambridge University. She is the deputy director of the United Nations University Institute for New Technologies located in Maastricht, the Netherlands. In this position, she is responsible for coordinating the research program focusing on gender, technology, and development. She is currently the coordinator of a collaborative research project involving 28 women workers' organizations from eight Asian countries. Mitter also holds the chair of gender and technology studies at Brighton University, United Kingdom. As a consultant on a wide variety of assignments for international agencies, including the European Commission, the International Labour Organization, the United Nations Development Programme, and the United Nations Development Fund for Women (UNIFEM), Mitter has focused on the areas of women and industrialization. Her books include *Common Fate, Common Bond: Women in the Global Economy* and, with Sheila Rowbotham, *Dignity and Daily Bread: New Forms of Economic Organization among Poor Women in the Third World and the First.*

Shushila Nayar (b. 1914)

Born in Gujarat, Pakistan, Dr. Shushila Nayar received her education at Lahore College for women, Lady Hardinge Medical College in Delhi, and at Johns Hopkins University in Baltimore, Maryland. As medical attendant to Mahatma Gandhi, she supported the Indian struggle for independence and was arrested and imprisoned from 1942 to 1944. Following India's independence from Britain, she worked as senior medical officer. She became minister of health, rehabilitation, and transport in Delhi State, and was Speaker of the Delhi Legislative Assembly from 1952 to 1956. She was elected to the Lok Sabha (lower house of Parliament) in 1957. Appointed minister of health from 1962 through 1967, Nayar lost her seat in Parliament in 1971 but remained a highly influential figure. In 1969, she was named director of the Mahatma Gandhi Institute of Medical Sciences, where she was professor of preventive and social medicine. During this time, she was also secretary of the Leprosy Board of the Mahatma Gandhi Memorial Trust.

Naomi Nhiwatiwa (b. 1940)

Naomi Nhiwatiwa is one of three women in the government of Robert Mugabe in Zimbabwe. She serves as deputy minister for posts and telegraphs. She was actively involved in the struggle for the creation of Zimbabwe. With a degree in psychology, Nhiwatiwa is actively involved in the fight for women's rights, often campaigning for the abolition of the practice of *lobola,* or arranged marriages for a bride-price.

Joice Nhongo (b. 1955)

Born to peasant parents, Joice Nhongo ran away from her family and village to join the boys who were fighting in the bush for the creation of Zimbabwe. By the time she was 18 years old, she was a member of the Zimbabwe African National Liberation Army's (ZANLA) general staff and was 21 years old when she was named camp commander of Chimoio, which was the largest guerrilla and refugee camp in Mozambique. She met and married Rex Nhongo, who was deputy head of the ZANLA forces. During her time fighting with the guerrilla forces, she became one of the most famous guerrillas in Robert Mugabe's forces. She was hunted by the Rhodesian security forces but never captured. Following the creation of Zimbabwe, Nhongo was named the minister of youth, sport, and recreation in 1980 and became minister of community development and women's affairs in 1981.

Isabel Peron (b. 1931)

Not as well known as Eva Perón, Juan Perón's second wife, Isabel Perón was the third wife of Juan Perón, president of Argentina and the first woman to serve as president of a nation. She gave up a career as a dancer to become Perón's secretary and then his wife. In 1955, they were exiled from Argentina during his second term as president because of his suppression of free speech and the faltering economy. Following many years of political ups and downs, Juan and Isabel Perón were allowed back into the country in 1973. Encouraged to run for the presidency, Juan Perón chose his wife to be his running mate. They won in a landslide victory in September 1973. Isabel, as vice president, championed the cause of women's rights. With her husband's health failing, Isabel assumed the duties of head of state. She presided over the cabinet, traveled to Paraguay, traveled to Geneva to address the International Labour Organization, and went on to Madrid and Rome, where she met with Pope Paul VI. The day following her return to Argentina, Juan turned over full presidential power to her; he died on 1 July 1974. She had a troublesome presidency, with many factions fighting for power, and was ousted in a coup in March 1976 by the military junta. She was held under house arrest in a remote government resort, then arrested and charged with corruption. In 1981, she was released and went into exile to Spain until 1983 when she returned to Argentina to quietly live out the remainder of her life.

Fumilayo Ransome-Kuti (b. 1900)

An active feminist from Nigeria, Fumilayo Ransome-Kuti received her education from Anglican primary and secondary schools and then studied domestic science at Wincham Hall College in England. She returned to Nigeria and took a job teaching; she also became involved in advocating for women's rights, women's suffrage, and for abolishing heavy taxation of market women in Egbaland. She was honored with an honorary degree in law and she also holds a chieftancy title.

Aisha Ráteb (b. 1928)

Aisha Ráteb received her law degree from the Faculty of Law in Cairo and rose to become the first professor of international law at Cairo University. She became the minister of social affairs in the Egyptian government in 1971, the first woman to hold a ministerial position. Remaining in this position until 1977, she went on to become the minister of insurance. Ráteb became chair of the Legislative Affairs Committee in 1973 and the Egyptian minister of foreign affairs in 1978. She became ambassador from Egypt to Denmark in 1979 and to Germany in 1981.

Dhanvanthi Rama Rau (1893–1987)

Dhanvanthi Rama Rau was a well-known social worker from India who was born into an aristocratic family and educated at the University of Madras in southern India. She was one of the first Indian women to attend college. She was a lecturer in English at Queen Mary's College in Madras from 1917 to 1921 and met and married Sir Bengal Rama Rau, a leading Indian diplomat. Following her marriage, she began to work for social reform. She became the secretary of the All-India Child Marriage Abolition League in 1927, a member of the International Alliance for Suffrage and Equal Citizenship in 1932, and president of the All-India Women's Conference in 1946. She became interested in family planning, and from 1949 to 1963 she worked for the Family Planning Association of India. In 1963 she became the president of the International Planned Parenthood Association; she held this position until 1971. She published her memoirs in 1977.

Nibuya Sabalsajaray (1951–1974)

Nibuya Sabalsajaray, the daughter of a poor family, was an active unionist from Uruguay. She studied in local schools and qualified as a teacher. Becoming a union organizer and leader, in 1974 she participated in a major demonstration against the Uruguayan dictatorship. She was arrested, tortured, and died two days after her arrest, at the young age of 23 years. She is now revered and admired as one of the martyrs of the country's repressive policy toward the unions during the 1970s.

Gita Sen (b. 1948)

Gita Sen is a leading researcher on women-in-development issues, conducting policy research on women, development, health and population, and the environment. She is professor of Economics at the Indian Institute of Management in Bangalore, India, and an adjunct professor of Development Economics at the Harvard Center for Population and Development Studies. A founding member of DAWN (Development Alternatives with Women for a New Era), Sen received her M.A. from the Delhi School of Economics and her Ph.D. in economics from Stanford University. She has taught at the New School for Social Research in New York, Radcliffe College, Vassar College, and at the Center for Population and Development Studies at Harvard University. She is currently on the staff at the Centre for Development Studies in Trivandrum, in Kerala state in India, and teaches at Harvard. Her publications include *Women and the New World Economy: Feminist Perspectives on Alternative Economic Frameworks; Development, Crises, and Alternative Visions: Third World Women's Perspectives* (with Caren Grown); *Population Policies Reconsidered: Health, Empowerment, and Rights* (with Adrienne Germain and Lincoln Chen); and *Power and Decision: The Social Control of Reproduction* (with Rachel Snow).

Leticia Ramos Shahani (b. 1929)

Leticia Shahani has been involved in a variety of political and advocacy activities. Born in Lingayen, Pangasinan, the Philippines, she received a B.A. in English literature in 1951 from Wellesley College, an M.A. in comparative literature in 1954 from Columbia University, and a Ph.D. in comparative literature and sociology in 1961 from the University of Paris (France). She has been on the faculty at the University of the Philippines, the New School for Social Research in New York, and the International Study and Research Institute in New York. Other positions include dean of the graduate school, Lyceum of the Philippines, and president of the national YMCA of the Philippines.

She is a senator in the Congress of the Philippines and has had a varied and active career in politics. At the international level, she has participated in many United Nations activities, such as representative to the United Nations Commission on the Status of Women (1970–1974), member of the Philippine delegation to the United Nations General Assembly (1974–1979), member of the Philippine delegation to the United Nations World Conference on International Women's Year (1975), Philippine representative to the Preparatory Committee for the United Nations Conference on the Mid-Decade for Women (1978–1980), chairwoman of the Philippine delegation to the World Conference on the UN Mid-Decade for Women (1980), UN assistant secretary general for Social Development and Humanitarian Affairs (1981–1986), and secretary general of the World Conference to Review and Appraise the Achievements of the UN Decade for Women (1985).

Her awards include being named one of the Outstanding Women in the Nation's Service in 1974, being named to the Order of Teodor Vladimirescu by the government of Romania in 1978, and receiving an honorary Doctor of Laws degree from the Centro Escolar University in 1976. Among her publications is *The Philippines: The Land and People.*

Huda Shaarawi (1882–1947)

A well-known Egyptian women's rights advocate, Huda Shaarawi was born into a wealthy family in Minia and educated in Turkish and French, the language of the wealthy. She taught herself Arabic. She started a school for girls in 1910, with general educational classes instead of courses such as midwifery that women were usually taught in vocational classes.

Shaarawi organized hundreds of women to participate in the demonstrations against the British during the nationalist movement. She helped organize and became head of the first women's association in Egypt in 1920. Three years later she traveled to Rome as the Egyptian representative to the International Conference of Women. In 1924 she organized the Women's Feminist

Union. She and Saiza Nabarawi started the open feminist movement in Egypt by taking off their veils at the Cairo train station as they returned from an international feminist conference. Shaarawi and the union advocated for women's rights and the integration of urban women into public life. They wanted changes in the personal status laws, equal access to secondary and university education, expanded professional opportunities in business, and support systems for working mothers to provide child care; they advocated for the end to legalized prostitution. Union members lobbied the government for these and other changes.

She also founded *Egyptian Women,* a journal published in both Arabic and French that described the goals of the Women's Union to its readers. In 1935 and 1939, Shaarawi attended the international women's conferences. In 1944 she helped organize the All Arab Federation of Women. In 1945 she advocated for the abolition of all atomic weapons.

Helvi Sipilä (b. 1915)

After receiving her education at the University of Helsinki, Helvi Sipilä became an acting judge in the rural district courts in Finland. Between 1941 and 1951 she held various legal posts on the Supreme Court and the Supreme Administrative Court. She has been a member of various Finnish government committees on matrimonial legislation, protection of children, social benefits for children, citizenship education, and international development. She has been a member of the Council of the Human Rights Institute in Strasbourg, France, since 1969.

As an attorney, she founded and operated her own law office in Finland from 1943 to 1972; at the same time she was actively involved in United Nations activities. Sipilä retired from her post of assistant secretary general of the UN's Centre for Social Development and Humanitarian Affairs (CSDHA) in 1980. She played a major role in planning the 1975 International Women's Year (IWY) Conference in Mexico City. CSDHA administered the IWY Trust Fund and its Branch for the Advancement of Women acted as the secretariat for the Commission on the Status of Women. Before taking the post at CSDHA, Sipilä served as international president of Zonta International, a professional women's organization.

During International Women's Year, she appealed to governments to set aside prejudices of race, sex, language, or religion in order to confront problems affecting everyone. She traveled extensively to government capitals around the world to build understanding and interest in International Women's Year. In 1981, she founded the Finnish National Committee on UNIFEM, which consisted of 400 individual and 30 organizational members.

Margaret Snyder (b. 1929)

Margaret Snyder has been involved in women's development activities for many years and is the founding director of the United Nations Development Fund for Women. She received her Ph.D. from the University of Dar es Salaam and was honored at Makerere University in 1993 for her valuable contributions to the advancement of women in agriculture and education. She has recently been a Visiting Fellow in International Studies at Princeton University.

Snyder has long been involved in development policies and women's issues in Africa. As a regional adviser for the United Nations Economic Commission for Africa, she initiated their Women's Programme, led the Voluntary Agencies Bureau, and cofounded the African Training and Research Centre for Women. She is also a cofounder of Women's World Banking, an organization that provides loans and other business services to women through a network of affiliate organizations (see Chapter 5). Her publications include *Farmers and Merchants: Some Observations on Women and the State in Africa; Politics, Poverty and Participation: A History of Women's Leadership in Development;* and *Women: The Key to Ending Hunger.* In writing *Transforming Development: Women, Poverty and Politics,* Snyder traveled to 15 countries to examine the projects that UNIFEM has assisted; she interviewed women and men who were helped by projects supported by UNIFEM. She was the founder and first director of UNIFEM (see Chapter 5).

Mary Tadesse (b. 1932)

As a former vice minister for education and culture as well as an assistant minister of education in Addis Ababa, Ethiopia, Mary Tadesse has worked extensively with policy development and programs concerning women and development. These activities include developing and advancing policies and strategies for the advancement of women in developing countries on a regional as well as global level. She has worked with organizations such as the Council of African Advisers to the World Bank, the Board of

Trustees of the International Research and Training Institute for the Advancement of Women (INSTRAW), the Federation of African Women Entrepreneurs, and the Africa Regional Coordinating Committee for the Integration of Women in Development. She has participated in many academic and governmental conferences. With Margaret Snyder, Tadesse wrote *African Women and Development: A History* in 1995.

Mother Teresa (b. 1910)

Born Agnes Gonxha Bejaxhia in Skopje, Macedonia, Mother Teresa entered the Roman Catholic order of the Sisters of Our Lady of Loretta in Ireland at the age of 18 years. After training in Ireland and India, she took her vows. As Sister Teresa, she joined the Loretta nuns in Calcutta in 1929 and taught high school for 20 years. Moved by the incredible suffering she saw on the streets of Calcutta, she received what she saw as a sign from God telling her to leave the Sisters of Loretta and devote her life to working and living with the poor people living on the streets.

The pope allowed her to leave the convent, and in 1948 Mother Teresa started her lifelong ministry among the poor. She and those working with her became the new order of the Missionaries of Charity in 1950. Other women who joined Mother Teresa took four vows—of poverty, chastity, obedience, and service to the poor. Mother Teresa believes that by serving the poor she and her sisters are serving Christ. Since founding her order, the work has spread to 50 Indian cities and more than 25 countries. In 1952, Mother Teresa founded the Nirmal Hriday (Pure Heart) Home for Dying Destitutes in Calcutta. She has written a book about her life, *Gift from God,* published in 1975.

She won the Nobel Peace Prize in 1979 for her work in helping the poor. In choosing her, the Nobel Prize Committee said that "this year, the world has turned its attention to the plight of children and refugees, and these are precisely the categories for whom Mother Teresa has for many years worked so selflessly (Schlessinger and Schlessinger 1996, 174). In 1985 she received the Presidential Medal of Freedom from the United States.

While many people marvel at the work she has done and her dedication to her cause, some critics do not understand her firm opposition to abortion and to all types of artificial birth control. Many feminists have been alienated by her views of the role of women, especially in India. She has urged women to build stable and strong families and to allow "men to do what they are better suited to do" (Wasson 1987, 1048).

Begum Khaleda Zia (b. 1945)

Begum Khaleda Zia is the prime minister of Bangladesh. She also serves as the minister for establishment, information, and mineral resources and is leader of the Bangladesh Nationalist Party. She attended primary and secondary school and then married Zia-ur Rahman when she was 16 years old. He was a captain in the Pakistani army at the time of their marriage. He would later serve as the country's president from 1977 until 1981 when he was assassinated while in office. H. M. Ershad came to power, martial law was declared, and political parties were abolished. The Bangladesh Nationalist Party continued to exist, and Khaleda Zia led her party as chairwoman in 1984. Khaleda Zia was at the center of the fight to end martial law and restore free elections, participating in strikes, street protests, and mass demonstrations. During this time, she was placed under house arrest several times. Ershad resigned his position in 1990, elections were held in 1991, and Khaleda Zia became prime minister. She has focused her attention on population control, mass literacy, compulsory primary education, fighting poverty, and extending electricity to rural areas.

She has been criticized by many women for her silence on women's issues, especially the conditions of women working in the garment industry. Over two million women work in appalling conditions in sweatshops. She has also been criticized for her unwillingness to fight the growing Islamic fundamentalist movement in her country. Also, her country has not ratified the United Nations Conventions that guarantee equal political, marriage, and pay rights to women.

References

Corke, Bettina, ed. 1993. *Who's Who in Latin America: Government, Politics, Banking and Industry.* 3d ed. New York: Norman Ross Publishing.

International Who's Who of Women. London: Europa Publications, 1992.

Kay, Ernest, ed. 1996. *The World's Who's Who of Women.* 13th ed. Cambridge, England: Melrose Press.

Liswood, Laura A. 1995. *Women World Leaders: Fifteen Great Politicians Tell Their Stories.* London: HarperCollins.

Schlessinger, Bernard S., and June S. Schlessinger, eds. 1996. *The Who's Who of Nobel Prize Winners, 1901–1995*. 3d ed. Phoenix: Oryx Press.

Snyder, Margaret. 1995. *Transforming Development: Women, Poverty, and Politics*. London: Intermediate Technology Publications.

Uglow, Jennifer S., ed. 1989. *The Continuum Dictionary of Women's Biography*. New York: Continuum Publishing.

Wasson, Tyler, ed. 1987. *Nobel Prize Winners*. New York: H. W. Wilson Company.

Who's Who of Women in World Politics. 1991. London: Bowker-Saur.

Facts and Statistics 4

This chapter presents basic facts and statistics of interest concerning women and their lives and status in the Third World—statistics describing major aspects of women's lives such as education, family, health, violence toward women, work, politics, migration, and female refugees. The chapter includes excerpts from major international agreements and United Nations documents that protect or extend certain rights to women and young girls.

The Status of Women in the Third World

The lives and status of women are improving in many areas of the world. However, in many areas and in many individual situations, women are still discriminated against and refused basic human rights and still find their lives difficult and often dangerous. Women throughout the world, not just in Third World countries, find themselves denied an education, denied a job, and discriminated against in a number of ways. In Third World countries, as in many other countries, women in upper socioeconomic classes are better off than women in lower classes. Statistics provide a general indication of what women in developing countries face in their daily lives, although the reader must keep in mind that these statistics do not describe all women in all situations. Also, the range of opportunities open to women must be examined within each individual country. For example, in some western Asian countries, while higher education for women is the norm, few women in these countries participate in politics or in the labor force (except for unpaid family labor). With these caveats in mind, this section offers statistics to provide a better picture of what life is like for women in developing countries.

Education

The United Nations Educational, Scientific and Cultural Organization (UNESCO) defines a person as literate if he or she can read and write a short description of his or her daily life and understand this description. According to this definition, many people in developing countries are illiterate, in contrast with developed nations, where literacy rates are over 90 percent for both men and women. Further, in all developing countries, as in most developed countries, literacy rates for men are higher than for women.

Over the past few decades, basic literacy rates for women, as well as for men, have increased in many parts of the world. Many countries have passed legislation that requires equal access to education for both boys and girls, schools are being built in many rural areas, and traditional attitudes that girls should not be educated are slowly changing. In the developing world, most countries in Latin America, the Caribbean, and in eastern and southeastern Asia have increasing literacy rates for women. However, some countries in Africa, Asia, and the Middle East have seen declines in literacy rates.

In 1990, literacy rates for women between the ages of 15 and 24 in Third World countries ranged from a low of 7 percent in Burkina Faso to a high of over 98 percent in Chile, Uruguay, Brunei, and Thailand. For women over the age of 25, literacy rates ranged from less than 10 percent in Benin, Burkina Faso, Guinea-Bissau, Mali, Mozambique, Niger, Senegal, Togo, Nepal, Yemen, and Papua New Guinea to over 90 percent in Argentina, Chile, Uruguay, and the Philippines (United Nations 1995).

Literacy rates for men are at least 25 percent higher than for women in many countries, primarily in sub-Saharan Africa. These countries include Benin, Central African Republic, Guinea-Bissau,

Mozambique, Togo, Tanzania, and Morocco, as well as India, Nepal, Syria, and Yemen (United Nations 1995). In many developing countries, women are not expected to receive an education, and many people do not believe that girls should be educated. Countries in which the literacy rate is 25 percent or less for women include Benin, Burkina Faso, Guinea-Bissau, Mali, Mozambique, Niger, Nepal, Pakistan, and Yemen (United Nations 1995).

Literacy rates for older women and women living in rural areas are generally lower than for women living in urban areas, because widespread education for girls has only recently been encouraged in most developing countries and is found more often in cities than in rural areas. For example, in 1990 in Honduras, the literacy rate for women was over 90 percent in urban areas and 70 percent in rural areas; in Mali, the rate is over 40 percent in urban areas and only 10 percent in rural areas; and in Iraq the rate is over 90 percent in urban areas and in rural areas closer to 65 percent (United Nations 1995).

Sex ratios of girls to boys in secondary school enrollment vary from region to region and country to country. In eastern and southeastern Asia secondary school enrollments are almost identical for girls and boys. In western Asia and northern Africa slightly more boys than girls are enrolled in secondary schools. However, boys greatly outnumber girls in secondary schools in sub-Saharan Africa (68 girls per 100 boys) and southern Asia (60 girls per 100 boys). A positive sign is that in the past 20 years girls have been gaining ground in most developing countries. For example, in 1970 in southeastern Asia the ratio was approximately 65 girls per 100 boys; by 1990 the ratio was approximately 92 girls for every 100 boys (United Nations 1995).

Many researchers have found a strong relationship between education and fertility rates; higher literacy rates among women are strongly related to lower fertility rates (Jejeebhoy 1995). Literacy rates for women were under 50 percent in Africa and southern Asia in 1990 and fertility rates were over five births per woman. Women in Latin America and southeastern Asia have literacy rates over 80 percent with overall fertility rates of less than four births per women.

In higher education, women outnumber men in the social science and health fields but are outnumbered by men in science, engineering, and law. This applies to women in developing countries as well as women in the more developed regions. For example, in 1990 in Latin America the ratio was 254 women per 100 men in liberal arts, and only 74 women per 100 men in science and engineering and 80 per 100 men in law. In eastern and southeastern Asia in 1990 there were 164 women per 100 men in liberal arts, 274 women per 100 men in medical and health fields, but only 73 women per 100 men in science and engineering (United Nations 1995).

Population and Family

Although there are more men in the world than women, the ratio of elderly women to elderly men is increasing, as is the proportion of elderly women in the general population. Women live longer than men in almost every country.

In general, if no deliberate measures are taken to reduce the number of births, especially female births, the sex ratio is biologically stable. There are between 93 and 96 female births for every 100 male births. In some countries in Asia, the sex ratio varies from this norm; in India in 1988/1989 there were 91 girls born per 100 boys; in the Republic of Korea there were 88 girls born per 100 boys; and in Pakistan 92 girls were born per 100 boys (United Nations 1992b). In Pakistan, the ratio in 1982 was 98 girls per 100 boys and 92 per 100 boys in 1988/1989; for some reason the ratio is dropping. Boys may outnumber girls for several reasons: from parents who see no need to report the birth of a daughter, since girls aren't important in many societies, to the more serious desire for sons, which may lead to female infanticide or the use of new technology to determine the sex of the fetus with resulting sex selective abortion if the fetus is female.

Household size decreased significantly between 1970 and 1990 in many developed regions, in Latin America, and in eastern and southeastern Asia. The average household size dropped to 3.7 in eastern Asia, 4.9 in southeastern Asia, and 4.7 in Latin America. Other areas have seen increases in household size— from 5.4 to 5.7 in northern Africa. Higher household size indicates higher fertility rates and/or the prevalence of extended families living together (United Nations 1992d).

Throughout the world, women marry at an earlier age than men, but the age at which both women and men marry varies among regions. Between 10 and 12 percent of women between the ages of 15 and 19 are married in northern Africa, South America, central and southeastern Asia; this compares with between 1 and 3 percent of men the same ages. Between 16 and 17 percent of women between the ages of 15 and 19 are married in western

Asia and Central America; 29 percent of this group is married in sub-Saharan Africa; and in southern Asia 41 percent of women between 15 and 19 are married. The highest rate for men in the same age group is 9 percent in southern Asia. Individual countries and smaller regions may have higher rates; for example, over 50 percent of women between the ages of 15 and 19 are married in west Africa (United Nations 1995).

Differences also exist between urban and rural areas. Rural women generally marry at a younger age than urban women. The Demographic and Health Surveys (DHS), a project sponsored by the United States Agency for International Development, has conducted national sample surveys on fertility, family planning, and maternal and child health. Results from these studies indicate that women in rural areas consistently marry at a younger age than women in urban areas (United Nations 1985). For example, the researchers found that 25 percent more women in rural areas were married at a younger age than urban women in sub-Saharan Africa, 34 percent more in Latin America, 42 percent more in northern Africa, and 45 percent more in Asia (United Nations 1995).

A relationship also appears to exist between lack of education and early age at marriage for women. The DHS study found that in over 67 percent of the countries studied, women with no education were twice as likely to marry before the age of 20 as those with a primary school education. The study found that statistics for women in Egypt were the most extreme: 77 percent of women with no education were married by the age of 20, while only 13 percent of those women with at least a primary school education were married by the age of 20 (United Nations 1992a).

In many countries women find themselves living at some point in their lives without a partner and father for their children. Many reasons for this pattern exist—polygynous unions in which the husband has more than one wife and spends times with each wife; visiting unions in which the male partner visits from time to time; or male partners who may need to migrate to other areas within the country or to other countries in order to obtain work.

The majority of women in most countries become mothers at some point in their lives. In some regions, many women start giving birth to children while they are still teenagers themselves, while in other regions the majority of women give birth to children when they are 21 years or older. Generally, women start having children when they are still teenagers most often in countries in which women are seen primarily as wives and bearers of children. Traditions in these countries support the idea that a woman's only role is as a wife and mother and that women do not generally need to receive an education or enter the job market. Women tend to marry at a later age and also tend to have smaller families in countries in which women are seen as more than wives and mothers, in which they receive an education, and in which they are encouraged to enter (or at least not discouraged from entering) the job market.

In developed countries, the use of contraceptives was fairly widespread by 1980 and did not grow significantly over the following ten years. However, in developing countries, the use of contraceptives was not widespread by 1980. Following the growth of organizations encouraging the use of contraception, growing numbers of women in developing countries began to use contraceptive devices. For example, in eastern Asia 79 percent of the population used some type of contraceptive by 1990, 58 percent in Latin America, 42 percent in the rest of Asia, but only 18 percent in Africa. This compares with 72 percent in developed areas of the world (United Nations 1994b).

Sterilization is the most widely used method of contraception for women in developing countries. One-third of the women and one-tenth of the men in Asia choose this method, while 21 percent of the women and only 1 percent of the men in Latin America choose sterilization. The intrauterine device (IUD) is the most popular method in eastern Asia and is used by 31 percent of women (United Nations 1995). Statistics on the prevalence of abortion as a method of birth control are difficult to find, primarily because abortion is illegal in many countries.

Over the past 25 years, the number of births per woman has declined throughout most of the world. In the developed countries, it currently averages 1.9 births per woman. Women in eastern Asia also have a low number of births per women—2.3 births; women in countries in sub-Saharan Africa average 6.1 births per woman, although the rate is lower in Botswana, Kenya, Lesotho, Mauritius, South Africa, Swaziland, and Zimbabwe (United Nations 1995). The current number of births per woman in Latin America is 3.2, in eastern Asian countries, 2.3, and in southern Asia, 5.3 (United Nations 1995).

Fertility rates are lower among women living in urban areas and among educated women. Women living in urban areas are more likely to have access to information concerning contraceptives, have contraceptives available to them, and not have a need for more children to help work on the farm and in the home. Women living in cities also have more opportunities to find work and thus to postpone having children.

Adolescent fertility has also declined recently in many countries. Countries in northern Africa have seen a small decline, as have countries in Latin America and eastern and western Asia, and rates have generally fallen in southeastern and southern Asia, although rates for adolescents in India and Pakistan have increased (United Nations 1995).

Health

Women generally have a longer life expectancy then men—in the developed nations often six to eight years longer. In the Third World, the differences are not as great. For example, women can be expected to outlive men by only three years in Africa and four to five years in the rest of the developing countries, except for southern Asia, where the life expectancy for women and men is about the same (about 58 years). However, in Bangladesh and Nepal men outlive women by one year (United Nations 1992e).

In most countries life expectancy is increasing, although it has dropped significantly for both men and women in two sub-Saharan countries because of AIDS. In Uganda life expectancy has dropped for women from 48 to 43 years and for men from 46 to 43 years. According to a report from the Population Division of the United Nations Secretariat, these two countries will continue to see decreases in life expectancy. Other sub-Saharan countries will also begin to see either a decrease or no increase in life expectancy; these countries include the Central African Republic, the Congo, Ivory Coast, Malawi, Rwanda, Tanzania, Zaire, and Zimbabwe (United Nations 1994a).

In many developing countries, statistics on infant and child mortality are scarce and unreliable. In countries in which there is a strong preference for sons over daughters, reliable data may not be available. In developed nations, the ratio of female to male infant deaths is 0.8, or 8 female deaths for every 10 male deaths. Where statistics are available in developing countries, girls enjoy a similar advantage. However, one study on child mortality in developing countries reports that 17 out of 38 developing countries showed higher rates of infant mortality for girls than for boys. Highest rates were for Egypt, with a ratio of 1.4, or 14 female deaths for every 10 male deaths, and Pakistan, with a ratio of 1.6 (United Nations 1995).

For adolescent girls, the greatest risks to reproductive health include sexually transmitted diseases, early motherhood, unwanted pregnancy, and unsafe abortion. Many girls, especially in developing countries, do not have access to information related to reproductive health and do not have access to health services. According to the World Health Organization (WHO), adolescent girls have a 20 to 200 percent higher risk of dying from pregnancy-related causes than older women. The younger the girl is when she becomes pregnant, the higher the risk of complications or maternal death (World Health Organization 1989).

Abortion, especially unsafe abortion, also has higher risks for adolescent girls. Studies have been conducted in the Congo, Kenya, Liberia, Mali, Nigeria, and Zaire that examine hospital records of women seeking treatment as a result of complications for abortion. These studies have found that between 38 and 68 percent of all women seeking care for these complications were under the age of 20 years (United Nations 1995).

Adolescent girls in several developing countries are also at risk for developing complications from female genital circumcision (or female genital mutilation, as many people refer to this procedure). In a survey of 300 women living around Mogadishu, Somalia, researchers found that almost all women undergo the severest form of circumcision, infibulation. The researchers found that approximately 40 percent of the women experience severe and significant immediate complications from this procedure and another 40 percent experience long-term complications (United Nations 1995).

According to the WHO, more than 16 million adults and 1 million children have been infected with HIV. Women represented 40 percent of the estimated cases of HIV infection in 1994. By the year 2000, the number of women infected with HIV will equal the number of men, according to WHO estimates. Between 10 and 15 million new infections are expected by 2000, primarily in developing countries (World Health Organization 1994). Women, especially in developing countries, are becoming infected in greater numbers than men. Over one-half of people infected in Africa are believed to be women, while between one-third and one-fourth of those infected in Asia are expected to be women. Female sex workers are at particularly high risk of infection, especially in parts of India, urban areas of Burma, and in Thailand. By the year 2000, over 8 million people in Asia may be infected with HIV (United Nations 1995).

In recent years, heterosexual activity has increasingly caused the spread of HIV. Women are becoming infected in growing numbers. Young women are most susceptible. According to a

United Nations Development Program review of studies concerning HIV in two Asian and three African countries, young women between the ages of 15 and 25 account for 70 percent of the women who contract and later die from HIV. Women between the ages of 15 and 25 are twice as likely as men to contract HIV. Approximately 25 percent of young women who become pregnant in Rwanda before they reach the age of 17 years will contract HIV (Reid and Bailey 1993).

Pregnancy and childbirth increase risks to women's health. Each year over 150 million women become pregnant. Prenatal care is critical to protecting the health of both mother and child. Availability of prenatal care varies widely throughout the world, including Third World countries. For example, prenatal care is widely available in southern Africa, eastern Asia, and Latin America, with 70 percent or more of women covered. Prenatal care is available to 54 percent of the women in western Asia. However, in other areas of the world coverage is available to less than half the women who become pregnant. Only 49 percent of the women in northern Africa and 35 percent of the women in southern Asia and in southern Asia have access to prenatal care (World Health Organization 1993).

Women who have access to trained medical personnel while they are pregnant and while giving birth have a higher survival rate than women who do not. More women die during pregnancy and during childbirth in regions of the world that have few trained maternity care personnel than in areas where trained medical personnel are available. In developed regions most women (99 percent) give birth attended by some type of trained medical person. Women in developing countries are much less likely to give birth with any trained medical staff in attendance; only 55 percent of births in developing countries occur with a trained attendant, and only 37 percent take place in hospitals or clinics. In sub-Saharan Africa, only 40 percent of births occur with a trained attendant and only 31 percent do in Southern Asia. Women in Latin America are more likely to have a trained attendant while giving birth; in Central America, 74 percent, and in South America 76 percent of births occur with a trained attendant (World Health Organization 1993).

Maternal mortality rates also vary from one area of the world to another. In developed regions, in 1988, there were 26 maternal deaths per 100,000 live births. In developing regions, the rate varied from 120 per 100,000 live births in eastern Asia to almost 700 deaths per 100,000 live births in sub-Saharan Africa (World Health Organization 1991).

According to the WHO, 20 million unsafe abortions are performed throughout the world each year and over 70,000 women die each year as a result of these unsafe procedures. Women in South America have the highest incidence of unsafe abortion—approximately 41 per 1,000 women between the ages of 15 and 49 undergo unsafe abortions. For women in eastern and western Africa, the rate is also high, with 30 unsafe abortions per 1,000 women. Asia has the lowest rate among developing regions, with 12 unsafe abortions per 1,000 women (United Nations 1995).

Violence toward Women

The most common form of violence against women is domestic violence, in which either a husband or intimate partner abuses a woman. According to studies conducted in 10 countries, between 17 and 38 percent of women have been physically assaulted by an intimate partner (United Nations 1995). Most studies concerning domestic violence in developing countries in Africa, Latin America, and Asia have reported rates of up to 60 percent or more of women being assaulted by an intimate partner. Other studies report that women can also be the aggressors—but these attacks are usually less frequent and less serious (United Nations 1989).

Rape and sexual assault are more difficult to measure, especially in developing countries, although experts believe that sexual assaults occur in greater numbers than statistics would suggest. Studies concerning rates of sexual assault in select urban areas in 14 developing countries found rates of 10 percent or more over five years in six countries. Highest rates reported were 22 percent in Kampala, Uganda; 17 percent in Dar es Salaam, Tanzania; 15 percent in Buenos Aires, Argentina; 14 percent each in Indonesia and Papua New Guinea; and 10 percent in Rio de Janeiro, Brazil (Del Frate, Zvekic, and van Dijk 1993). In a study of 133 postgraduate, middle- and upper-class students in India, researchers found that 26 percent reported that they had been sexually abused by the time they were 12 years old. Researchers in Kingston, Jamaica, found that among 450 schoolgirls between the ages of 13 and 14, 13 percent had experienced an attempted rape; half of these occurred before the girls reached the age of 12 years (United Nations 1995).

In 1949 the United Nations General Assembly adopted the Convention for the Suppression of the Traffic in Persons and of the Exploitation of the Prostitution of Others. But despite the convention's efforts, this practice continues in many areas throughout the world. An estimated two million women are involved in prostitution in India; one-fifth of them are under 18 years of age, according to the Commission on Human Rights Working Group on Contemporary Forms of Slavery (United Nations 1995). The commission also believes that between 5,000 and 7,000 young girls come from Nepal and are sold into brothels each year. According to Asia Watch and the Women's Rights Group, at least 20,000 women and young girls work in brothels in Thailand (Human Rights Watch 1993). In a report to the International Organization for Migration, the government of the Philippines (1994) estimates that the number of Filipina women, often between the ages of 16 and 23 years of age, migrate to other countries as entertainers. The authors of the report believe that most of these women have been tricked into working as prostitutes or in some other sex-related business.

As the demand for cheap domestic labor grows throughout the world, women will continue to migrate from poorer to richer countries in search of work. According to the Asia and Pacific Development Centre, between 1 and 1.7 million foreign women are currently estimated to be working as domestic workers in Asian countries. Often these women are illegal, undocumented immigrants lured to foreign countries with the promise of work as domestic servants or in the entertainment field. Many of these women end up being forced into prostitution. Others are abused in other ways. Employers may take away their passports, withhold their salaries with the claim that the women owe them money, or physically or sexually abuse them.

The plight of Asian women working as maids and cooks in Kuwait has received attention recently. According to a report by Middle East Watch (1992), these women endure abuse, confinement, and debt bondage. For a period of 12 months, beginning in May 1991, the report estimates that 1,400 Filipina domestic servants as well as hundreds of maids from India, Bangladesh, and Sri Lanka sought safety in their countries' embassies in Kuwait. The report claims that other women were arrested by police while attempting to run away from their employers; in many cases these women were returned to their employers by the police. Investigation by Human Rights Watch/Middle East (formerly Middle East Watch) in 1993 and 1994, as well as later updates, determined that while most domestic workers in Kuwait are not abused by their employers, a significant number are abused in some way, including rape, physical assault, mistreatment, debt bondage, and illegal confinement. Kuwaiti labor law excludes domestic workers from the law's protection, so these women have little recourse, except to escape from their employers and find some way to return home (Human Rights Watch 1995).

Another form of violence against women is the rape of women during war. Estimating the numbers of women raped during war is difficult. For example, the number of women raped in the former Yugoslavia has never been known or accurately measured. According to an investigation conducted by the European Community (n.d.), 20,000 women were raped. According to the United Nations Commission of Experts (United Nations 1992c), 800 victims were identified. A team of physicians estimated that 11,900 rapes occurred, based on the number of pregnancies as a result of rape and on a formula predicting the chances of becoming pregnant (Swiss and Giller 1993).

Work and Economic Activity

Women work in both paid and unpaid work. Most women, especially in Third World countries, work at home, taking care of the household and the children. In addition to these duties, women may be involved in other labor. In poor agricultural regions, women are the primary growers and preparers of food, gatherers of fuel for cooking, and collectors of water, among other tasks. With all this work, women are still responsible for caring for the family. In other regions, women may find paid employment, either working for someone else or working at home in some entrepreneurial activity. In most of these cases, they are still responsible for household and family care.

Research has shown that when women have access to and engage in paid work activities, they gain a measure of self-reliance and self-esteem. They also contribute to the economic well-being of their families. Unfortunately, when women work in unpaid labor activities, their contribution to society is largely uncounted—hardly even acknowledged. Most countries gather statistics on those economic activities that add value to the society, usually without considering that care of the family and the home contributes economically to society.

In studies of housework and other activities in India, Nepal, and Bangladesh, researchers found that women and girls spend between 3 to 5 more hours per week than men in unpaid subsistence activities, including gathering fuel, carrying water, and growing and processing agricultural products for their families' use. These 3 to 5 hours are in addition to the 20 to 30 hours more per week that women spend in unpaid housework activities. Studies found that women spend between 31 and 42 hours each week in maintaining the household, while men spend only between 5 and 15 hours (United Nations 1995).

Many women throughout the world find that they must find paid employment in order to help support their families. In the developing world, only 30 percent of the women in western Asia engage in paid economic activity; women in countries in central Asia had the highest participation rate of paid activity (58 percent).

For women, participation in paid economic activity is higher in rural areas in sub-Saharan Africa and most of Asia than in urban areas. In rural areas of sub-Saharan Africa, 50 percent of the women participate in economic activity, compared with 35 percent in urban areas. In southern Asia 27 percent of the women participate in economic activity and in western Asia 15 percent participate. Women in Latin America find better opportunities in the cities than in rural areas, with 34 percent working in urban areas and 21 percent in rural areas. In northern Africa, 19 percent of the women work in urban areas while 12 percent find work in rural areas (United Nations 1995).

When examined by industry type, more men work in industry than women, although women are well represented in agriculture and services. However, the majority of women participating in economic activity in Latin America work in the service sector (75 percent), while the majority of working women (75 percent) in sub-Saharan Africa work in the agricultural sector. In Asia, women are represented throughout the agriculture and services sectors, with the fewest in industry. For example, in southern Asia 55 percent of the working women are involved in agricultural activities; 20 percent are in the service sector. In western Asia 23 percent are in agriculture, only 14 percent in industry, and 61 percent in services (United Nations 1995).

When jobs in formal wage employment are difficult to find, people look to the informal sector to find work. In most African countries, more than one-third of women who are economically active outside of agriculture work in the informal sector, ranging as high as 62 percent in Gambia and 72 percent in Zambia. In Asian countries, women's participation in the informal sector varies widely from country to country. Economically active women in western Asian countries participate at the rate of 10 percent while 65 percent of the women in Indonesia participate.

Women in Latin America participate less actively in the informal sector, with less than one-third of all economically active women participating (United Nations 1995).

In all countries in the developing world, but also those in developed regions, women earn less than men for doing the same job. For example, in 1990, in the area of manufacturing in the countries studied, women earned only 50 percent of what men earned in the Republic of Korea, 54 percent of what men earned in Swaziland, up to 88 percent in Sri Lanka, 94 percent in El Salvador, and 97 percent in Burma. In many cases, women in developed nations do not fare much better. For example, in Japan women earned only 41 percent of what men earned, 68 percent in the United Kingdom, 77 percent in New Zealand, and 89 percent in Norway (United Nations 1992e). These differences exist despite the fact that many countries have enacted equal pay laws. Many countries have also endorsed several United Nations Covenants that deal, at least in part, with equal pay for equal work, such as the International Covenant on Economic, Social and Cultural Rights, the Convention Concerning Equal Remuneration for Men and Women Workers for Work of Equal Value, and the Convention on the Elimination of All Forms of Discrimination against Women.

Along with the right to work and the right to equal pay, many women also are concerned with maternity benefits. These benefits are provided for women in many countries—women are allowed a certain amount of time off work before and after they give birth and a certain percentage of their pay while on leave. Most countries in Africa, except Swaziland, provide maternity leave, ranging from 30 days in Tunisia to 15 weeks in the Congo. Women in these countries receive between 50 and 100 percent of their current salary. In Latin America maternity leave ranges from ten weeks in Honduras to four months in Costa Rica, with pay usually at 100 percent of the salary. Women in Asia generally receive between 25 and 100 percent of their salary and receive 10 weeks of maternity leave (United Nations 1995).

However, for many women, the place of work does not provide maternity benefits, primarily because they work at unpaid labor in the home, in agriculture, or in the informal sector. In many countries, women have little access to child care, so when they give birth, they may have trouble going back to work because there is no one to care for their children. Many women are forced to quit working to care for their children unless an older child stays home to care for the infant, other family members live in the home or nearby and can provide child care, or extended family members are available.

Power and Politics

One measure of the power that women have (or do not have) is the number of women who hold positions of power in their own governments. Few women have held ministerial or senior level positions; only 24 women have been elected as heads of state or government, and half of these have been elected since 1990. By 1994, ten women were leading their governments. Women serving as presidents include
- Vigdis Finnbogadottir in Iceland
- Mary Robinson in Ireland
- Violeta Chamorro in Nicaragua
- Chandrika Bandaranaike Kumaratunga in Sri Lanka

Women prime ministers include
- Khaleda Zia in Bangladesh
- Eugenia Charles in Dominica
- Gro Harlem Brundtland in Norway
- Sirimovo Bandaranaike in Sri Lanka
- Tansu Ciller in Turkey
- Benazir Bhutto in Pakistan

Other women presidents have included
- Isabel Martinez de Perón in Argentina (1974–1976)
- Lidia Gueiler Tejada in Bolivia (1979–1980)
- Ertha Pascal-Trouillot in Haiti (1991)
- Corazon Aquino in the Philippines (1986–1992)
- Milka Planinc in Yugoslavia (1982–1986)

Other women prime ministers have included
- Sylvia Kinigi of Burundi (1993)
- Kim Campbell of Canada (1993)
- Edith Cresson of France (1991–1992)
- Indira Gandhi of India (1966–1977)
- Golda Meir of Israel (1969–1974)
- Hanna Suchocka of Poland (1992–1993)
- Maria de Lourdes Pintasilga of Portugal (1981–1985)
- Agathe Uwilingiyimana of Rwanda (1993–1994)
- Margaret Thatcher of the United Kingdom (1979–1990) (United Nations 1995)

Over half of the countries that these women have led or are leading are developing nations. (See Chapter 3 for short biographies of many of these women.)

Women have made some progress in reaching top government positions. For example, between 1987 and 1994, the number of countries in which women held no top positions dropped from 93 to 59. Only 3.3 percent of the world's cabinet-level ministers were women in 1987, but this number grew to 5.7 percent in 1994. At the subcabinet level, the number of countries in which women served here grew from 15 countries in 1987 to 23 in 1995. As one United Nations document noted, "Women's higher representation at ministerial and subministerial levels is usually tenuous, however. Most countries with women in top ministerial positions do not have comparable representation at the subministerial level" (United Nations 1995, 151).

Countries in the Third World in which more than 15 percent of ministers or subministers are women in 1994 include Bhutan, the Central African Republic, Guinea-Bissau, Lesotho, Niger, São Tomé and Principe, Seychelles, Zimbabwe, Antigua, Bahamas, Barbados, Dominica, Guatemala, Guyana, Honduras, Jamaica, and Trinidad and Tobago.

Areas of government throughout the world in which women are most often found are the ministries of social welfare and law and justice. In developing nations, the highest percentage of women in social ministries occurs in sub-Saharan Africa (13 percent), South America (12 percent), eastern Asia (4 percent), southeastern Asia (5 percent), central Asia (9 percent), and western Asia (4 percent). The field of law and justice is the field with the highest percentage of women in northern Africa (17 percent). In Central America, women are split evenly between the social and the law and justice fields (15 percent each) (United Nations 1995).

Even though the Charter of the United Nations expressly refers to equal rights of women and men by saying that the "United Nations shall place no restrictions on the eligibility of men and women to participate in any capacity and under conditions of equality in its principal and subsidiary organs," few women have participated at this level. Only 2 of the 49 people elected to preside over the General Assembly have been women: Vijaya Lakshmi Pandit of India in 1953 and Angie Brooks of Liberia in 1969. At the fourth session in 1949, only 4 percent of the delegates to the General Assembly were women. By 1994, that number had increased to 20 percent. Regions with the highest participation were from the Caribbean (29 percent) and Latin

America and the developed regions (22–24 percent). The delegations with the fewest numbers of women were from eastern Europe (5 percent) and southern and eastern Asia and Oceania (8–9 percent) (United Nations 1995).

Migration

Urban areas in many countries are rapidly expanding, with more and more people moving to the cities to find work and improve their lives. When women move away from their traditional rural communities to cities, they usually gain greater freedom to participate in many activities, including educational activities and work. These opportunities frequently alter gender and family relations. In many cases, however, women are more restricted than men in their ability to move from one area to another. In Latin America more women than men live in urban areas, but in Africa and Asia, because women are more restricted in their movements, men outnumber women in urban areas (United Nations 1995).

Statistics are difficult to find concerning women who migrate from one country to another country. Because many men migrate to other countries in search of work, the women who travel with them are counted only as dependents. The United Nations conducted a study on the international migration of women and found that "so pervasive is the idea that most international migrants are men that the sex of migrants is often unrecorded or, if recorded, the information is not used to prepare tabulations for publication" (United Nations 1996, 1).

Many women who migrate to another country find work in their new country. Residents in some countries actively seek foreign women to work as maids, housekeepers, and nannies for their children. In some cases, these women are taken advantage of by their employers—they are paid less than minimum or fair wages, they may be threatened with being sent home if they don't comply with their employer's wishes, or employers may ask or demand sexual favors of them.

Women as Refugees

The experiences of refugee women are of particular concern to many persons working in this field. Women are particularly vulnerable to physical and sexual abuse, including rape. According to statistics gathered in 1993, men outnumber women among refugees in most areas of the world, except in Africa where women outnumber men (102 women per 100 men). For all refugees, there are 91 women per 100 men. Regionally, there are 89 women per 100 men in Latin America and 75 per 100 in Asia and the Pacific (United Nations High Commissioner for Refugees 1994). Some sources estimate the total number of refugees throughout the world at 20 million (Martin 1991).

International Agreements

The Charter of the United Nations and the International Bill of Rights are two documents that provide a forceful statement on women's rights in the international arena. The International Bill of Rights includes the Universal Declaration of Human Rights, the International Covenant on Civil and Political Rights, and the International Covenant on Economic, Social and Cultural Rights. The UN Charter is the first international document to specifically mention equal rights of women (and men). Relevant passages of the Charter of the United Nations, the Universal Declaration of Human Rights, the International Covenant on Civil and Political Rights, and the International Covenant on Economic, Social and Cultural Rights are provided below.

Several other international agreements are also excerpted in this section. The Convention Concerning Maternity Protection extends protection to agricultural and nonindustrial workers and to those women earning wages while working at home. The Convention Concerning the Employment of Women on Underground Work in Mines of All Kinds protects women from being forced to work in positions requiring them to work underground. The Convention Concerning Equal Remuneration for Men and Women Workers for Work of Equal Value obligates those countries ratifying it to work to eliminate wage discrimination based on sex. The Convention Concerning Night Work of Women Employed in Industry sets standards by which women can work at night. The Discrimination (Employment and Occupation) Convention works to eliminate all discrimination in employment. The Convention against Discrimination in Education prohibits educational discrimination, including all phases and aspects of education.

Concerning women and marriage, the Convention on Consent to Marriage, Minimum Age for Marriage, and Registration of Marriages ensures the free consent of all parties to a marriage, requires states to legislate a minimum age for marriage, and sets up a system of official registration for marriages. The Convention on the Nationality of Married Women addresses the many problems that women face when they marry men whose nationalities are different from their own. States ratifying the Convention on the Political Rights of Women are required to allow women to vote, stand for election, and hold public office.

The Convention for the Suppression of the Traffic in Persons and of the Exploitation of the Prostitution of Others as well as the International Convention for the Suppression of the Traffic in Women of Full Age focus attention on curbing the forced prostitution of women and girls. Finally, the Convention on the Elimination of All Forms of Discrimination against Women is the most comprehensive international treaty. It brings the female half of the world into the focus of human rights concerns—the legal status of women and their reproductive rights—and is an attempt to increase understanding of the influence of culture and tradition on restricting women's enjoyment of their fundamental rights.

The Charter of the United Nations

Preamble

We the peoples of the United Nations, determined to . . . reaffirm faith in fundamental human rights, in the dignity and worth of the human person, in the equal rights of men and women and of all nations large and small . . .

Article 1 (3)

To achieve international cooperation in solving international problems of an economic social, cultural, or humanitarian character, and in promoting and encouraging respect for human rights and fundamental freedoms for all without distinction as to race, sex, language or religion . . .

Article 8

The United Nations shall place no restrictions on the eligibility of men and women to participate in any capacity and under conditions of equality in its principal and subsidiary organs.

Article 55 (c)

With a view to the creation of conditions of stability and well-being which are necessary for peaceful and friendly relations among nations based on respect for the principle of equal rights and self-determination of peoples, the United Nations shall promote: universal respect for, and observance of, human rights and fundamental freedoms for all without distinction as to race, sex, language or religion.

The Universal Declaration of Human Rights (adopted in 1948)

Preamble

Whereas recognition of the inherent dignity and of the equal and inalienable rights of all members of the human family is the foundation of freedom, justice and peace in the world,

Whereas disregard and contempt for human rights have resulted in barbarous acts which have outraged the conscience of mankind, and the advent of a world in which human beings shall enjoy freedom of speech and belief and freedom from fear and want has been proclaimed as the highest aspiration of the common people,

Whereas it is essential, if man is not to be compelled to have recourse, as a last resort, to rebellion against tyranny and oppression, that human rights should be protected by the rule of law,

Whereas it is essential to promote the development of friendly relations between nations,

Whereas the peoples of the United Nations have in the Charter reaffirmed their faith in fundamental human rights, in the dignity and worth of the human person and in the equal rights of men and women and have determined to promote social progress and better standards of life in larger freedom,

Whereas Member States have pledged themselves to achieve, in cooperation with the United Nations, the promotion of universal respect for and observance of human rights and fundamental freedoms,

Whereas a common understanding of these rights and freedoms is of the greatest importance for the full realization of this pledge,

Now, therefore, the General Assembly proclaims this universal declaration of human rights as a common standard of achievement for all peoples and all nations, to the end that every individual and every organ of society, keeping this Declaration constantly in mind, shall strive by teaching and education to promote respect for these rights and freedoms and by progressive measures, national and international, to secure their universal and effective recognition and observance, both among the peoples of Member States themselves and among the peoples of territories under their jurisdiction.

Article 1

All human beings are born free and equal in dignity and rights. They are endowed with reason and conscience and should act towards one another in a spirit of brotherhood.

Article 2

Everyone is entitled to all the rights and freedoms set forth in this Declaration, without distinction of any kind, such as race, colour, sex, language, religion, political or other opinion, national or social origin, property, birth or other status.

Article 16

1. Men and women of full age, without any limitation due to race, nationality or religion, have the right to marry and to found a family. They are entitled to equal rights as to marriage, during marriage and at its dissolution.
2. Marriage shall be entered into only with the free and full consent of the intending spouses.
3. The family is the natural and fundamental group unit of society and is entitled to protection by society and the State.

Article 25

1. Everyone has the right to a standard of living adequate for the health and well-being of himself and his family, including food, clothing, housing and medical care and necessary social services, and the right to security in the event of unemployment, sickness, disability, widowhood, old age or other lack of livelihood in circumstances beyond his control.
2. Motherhood and childhood are entitled to special care and assistance. All children, whether born in or out of wedlock, shall enjoy special protection.

The International Covenant on Civil and Political Rights (1966)

Preamble

The State Parties to the Present Covenant,

Considering that, in accordance with the principles proclaimed in the Charter of the United Nations, recognition of the inherent dignity and of the equal and inalienable rights of all members of the human family is the foundation of freedom, justice and peace in the world,

Recognizing that these rights derive from the inherent dignity of the human person,

Recognizing that, in accordance with the Universal Declaration of Human Rights, the ideal of free human beings enjoying civil and political freedom and freedom from fear and want can only be achieved if conditions are created whereby everyone may enjoy his civil and political rights, as well as his economic, social and cultural rights,

Considering the obligation of States under the Charter of the United Nations to promote universal respect for, and observance of, human rights and freedoms,

Realizing that the individual, having duties to other individuals and to the community to which he belongs, is under a responsibility to strive for the promotion and observance of the rights recognized in the present Covenant,

Agree upon the following articles:

Article 2(1)

Each State Party to the present Covenant undertakes to respect and to ensure to all individuals within its territory and subject to its jurisdiction the rights recognized in the present Covenant, without distinction of any kind, such as race, colour, sex, language, religion, political or other opinion, national or social origin, birth or other status.

Article 3

The States Parties to the present Covenant undertake to respect and to ensure the equal right of men and women to the enjoyment of all civil and political rights set forth in the present Covenant.

Article 23

1. The family is the natural and fundamental group unit of society and is entitled to protection by society and the State.
2. The right of men and women of marriageable age to marry and to found a family shall be recognized.
3. No marriage shall be entered into without the free and full consent of the intending spouses.
4. States Parties to the present Covenant shall take appropriate steps to ensure equality of rights and responsibilities of spouses as to marriage, during marriage and at its dissolution. In case of dissolution, provision shall be made for the necessary protection of any children.

Article 24(1)

Every child shall have, without discrimination as to race, colour, sex, language, religion, national or social origin, property or birth, the right to such measures of protection as are required by his status as a minor, on the part of the family, society and the State.

Article 25

Every citizen shall have the right and the opportunity, without any of the distinctions mentioned in Article 2 and without unreasonable restrictions:
a. to take part in the conduct of public affairs, directly or through freely chosen representatives;
b. to vote and to be elected at genuine periodic elections which shall be by universal and equal suffrage and shall be held by secret ballot, guaranteeing the free expression of the will of the electors;
c. to have access, on general terms of equality, to public service in his country.

Article 26

All persons are equal before the law and are entitled without any discrimination to the equal protection of the law. In this respect, the law shall prohibit any discrimination and guarantee to all persons equal and effective protection against discrimination on any ground such as race, colour, sex, language, religion, political or other opinion, national or social origin, property, birth or other status.

The International Covenant on Economic, Social and Cultural Rights

Preamble

The States Parties to the Present Covenant,
Considering that, in accordance with the principles proclaimed in the Charter of the United Nations, recognition of the inherent dignity and of the equal and inalienable rights of all members of the human family is the foundation of freedom, justice and peace in the world,
Recognizing that these rights derive from the inherent dignity of the human person,
Recognizing that, in accordance with the Universal Declaration of Human Rights, the ideal of free human beings enjoying freedom from

fear and want can only be achieved if conditions are created whereby everyone may enjoy his economic, social and cultural rights, as well as his civil and political rights,

Considering the obligation of States under the Charter of the United Nations to promote universal respect for, and observance of, human rights and freedoms,

Realizing that the individual, having duties to other individuals and to the community to which he belongs, is under a responsibility to strive for the promotion and observance of the rights recognized in the present Covenant,

Agree upon the following articles:

Article 2(2)

The States Parties to the present Covenant undertake to guarantee that the rights enunciated in the present Covenant will be exercised without discrimination of any kind as to race, colour, sex, language, religion, political or other opinion, national or social origin, property, birth or other status.

Article 3

The States Parties to the present Covenant undertake to ensure the equal right of men and women to the enjoyment of all economic, social and cultural rights set forth in the present Covenant.

Article 7

The States Parties to the present Covenant recognize the right of everyone to the enjoyment of just and favorable conditions of work which ensure, in particular:

(a) Remuneration which provides workers, as a minimum, with:

(i) fair wages and equal remuneration for work of equal value without distinction of any kind, in particular women being guaranteed conditions of work not inferior to those enjoyed by men, with equal pay for equal work;

(ii) a decent living for themselves and their families in accordance with the provisions of the present Covenant;

(b) Safe and healthy working conditions;

(c) Equal opportunity for everyone to be promoted in his employment to an appropriate higher level, subject to no considerations other than those of seniority and competence.

Article 10

The States Parties to the present Covenant recognize that:

1. The widest possible protection and assistance should be accorded to the family, which is the natural and fundamental group unit of society, particularly for its establishment and while it is responsible for the care and education of dependent children. Marriage must be entered into with the free consent of the intending spouses.
2. Special protection should be accorded mothers during a reasonable period before and after childbirth. During such period working mothers should be accorded paid leave or leave with adequate social security benefits.

Convention (No. 103)
Concerning Maternity Protection
(adopted by the ILO in 1919; revised in 1952; came into force in 1955)

The International Labour Organization (ILO) adopted the Convention Concerning Maternity Protection in 1952, after they realized that the Convention Concerning the Employment of Women Before and After Childbirth, adopted in 1919, had to be updated. Excerpts are provided below.

Article 1

1. This Convention applies to women employed in industrial and agricultural occupations, including women wage earners working at home.
2. For the purpose of this Convention, the term "industrial undertaking" comprises public and private undertaking and any branch thereof and includes particularly—
(a) mines, quarries, and other works for the extraction of minerals from the earth;
(b) undertakings in which articles are manufactured, altered, cleaned, repaired, ornamented, finished, adapted for sale, broken up or demolished, or in which materials are transformed, including undertakings engaged in ship-building, or in the generation, transformation or transmission of electricity or motive power of any kind;
(c) undertakings engaged in building and civil engineering work, including constructional, repair, maintenance, alteration and demolition work;
(d) undertakings engaged in the transport of passengers or goods by road, rail, sea, inland waterway or air, including the handling of goods at docks, quays, wharves, warehouses or airports.
3. For the purpose of this Convention, the term "non-industrial occupations" includes all occupations which are carried on in or in connection with the following undertakings or services, whether public or private:

(a) commercial establishments;
(b) postal and telecommunication services;
(c) establishments and administrative services in which the persons employed are mainly engaged in clerical work;
(d) newspaper undertakings;
(e) hotels, boarding houses, restaurants, clubs, cafes and other refreshment houses;
(f) establishments for the treatment and care of the sick, infirm or destitute and of orphans;
(g) theatres and places of public entertainment;
(h) domestic work for wages in private households;
and any other non-industrial occupations to which the competent authority may decide to apply the provisions of the Convention.
4. For the purpose of this Convention, the term "agricultural occupations" includes all occupations carried on in agricultural undertakings, including plantations and large-scale industrialized agricultural undertakings. . . .
6. National laws or regulations may exempt from the application of this Convention, undertakings in which only members of the employer's family, as defined by national laws or regulations, are employed.

Article 2

For the purpose of this Convention, the term "woman" means any female person, irrespective of age, nationality, race or creed, whether married or unmarried, and the term "child" means any child whether born of marriage or not.

Article 3

1. A woman to whom this Convention applies shall, on the production of a medical certificate stating the presumed date of her confinement, be entitled to a period of maternity leave.
2. The period of maternity leave shall be at least twelve weeks, and shall include a period of compulsory leave after confinement.
3. The period of compulsory leave after confinement shall be prescribed by national laws or regulations, but shall in no case be less than six weeks; the remainder of the total period of maternity leave may be provided before the presumed date of confinement or following expiration of the compulsory leave period or partly before the presumed date of confinement and partly following the expiration of the compulsory leave period as may be prescribed by national laws or regulations.
4. The leave before the presumed date of confinement shall be extended by any period elapsing between the presumed date of confinement and the actual date of confinement and the period of compulsory leave to be taken after confinement shall not be reduced on that account.

5. In case of illness medically certified arising out of pregnancy, national laws or regulations shall provide for additional leave before confinement, the maximum duration of which may be fixed by the competent authority.

6. In case of illness medically certified arising out of confinement, the woman shall be entitled to an extension of the leave after confinement, the maximum duration of which may be fixed by the competent authority.

Article 4

1. While absent from work on maternity leave in accordance with the provisions of Article 3, the woman shall be entitled to receive cash and medical benefits.

2. The rates of cash benefit shall be fixed by national laws or regulations so as to ensure benefits sufficient for the full and healthy maintenance of herself and her child in accordance with a suitable standard of living.

3. Medical benefits shall include pre-natal, confinement and post-natal care by qualified midwives or medical practitioners as well as hospitalization care where necessary; freedom of choice of doctor and freedom of choice between a public and private hospital shall be respected.

4. The cash and medical benefits shall be provided either by means of compulsory social insurance or by means of public funds; in either case they shall be provided as a matter of right to all women who comply with the prescribed conditions.

5. Women who fail to qualify for benefits provided as a matter of right shall be entitled, subject to the means test required for social assistance, to adequate benefits out of social assistance funds.

6. Where cash benefits provided under compulsory social insurance are based on previous earnings, they shall be at a rate of not less than two-thirds of the woman's previous earnings taken into account for the purpose of computing benefits.

7. Any contribution due under a compulsory social insurance scheme providing maternity benefits and any tax based upon payrolls which is raised for the purpose of providing such benefits shall, whether paid both by the employer and the employees or by the employer, be paid in respect of the total number of men and women employed by the undertakings concerned, without distinction of sex.

8. In no case shall the employer be individually liable for the cost of such benefits due to women employed by him.

Article 5

1. If a woman is nursing her child she shall be entitled to interrupt her work for this purpose at a time or times to be prescribed by national laws or regulations.

2. Interruptions of work for the purpose of nursing are to be counted as working hours and remunerated accordingly in cases in which the matter is governed by or in accordance with laws and regulations; in cases in which the matter is governed by collective agreement, the position shall be as determined by the relevant agreement.

Article 6

While a woman is absent from work on maternity leave in accordance with the provisions of Article 3 of this Convention, it shall not be lawful for her employer to give her notice of dismissal during such absence, or to give her notice of dismissal at such a time that the notice would expire during such absence.

Article 7

1. Any Member of the International Labour Organization which ratifies this Convention may, by a declaration accompanying its ratification, provide for exceptions from the application of the Convention in respect of—
(a) certain categories of non-industrial occupations;
(b) occupations carried on in agricultural undertakings, other than plantations;
(c) domestic work for wages in private households;
(d) women wage earners working at home;
(e) undertakings engaged in the transport of passengers or goods by sea.
2. The categories of occupations or undertakings in respect of which the Member proposes to have recourse to the provisions of Paragraph 1 of this Article shall be specified in the declaration accompanying its ratification.

Convention Concerning the Employment of Women on Underground Work in Mines of All Kinds
(adopted in 1935; came into force in 1937)

Article 1

For the purposes of this Convention, the term "mine" includes any undertaking, whether public or private, for the extraction of any substance from under the surface of the earth.

Article 2

No female, whatever her age, shall be employed on underground work in any mine.

Article 3

National laws or regulations may exempt from the above prohibition—
(a) females holding positions of management who do not perform manual work;
(b) females employed in health and welfare services;
(c) females who, in the course of their studies, spend a period of training in the underground parts of a mine; and
(d) any other females who may occasionally have to enter the underground parts of a mine for the purpose of a non-manual occupation.

Article 5

1. This Convention shall be binding only upon those Members of the International Labour Organization whose ratifications have been registered with the Director-General.

Convention Concerning Equal Remuneration for Men and Women Workers for Work of Equal Value
(adopted in 1951; came into force in 1953)

Preamble

The General Conference of the International Labour Organization,
Having been convened at Geneva by the Governing Body of the International Labour Office and having met in its thirty-fourth session on 6 June 1951, and
Having decided upon the adoption of certain proposals with regard to the principle of equal remuneration for men and women workers for work of equal value, which is the seventh item on the agenda of the session, and
Having determined that these proposals shall take the form of an international Convention,
adopts this twenty-ninth day of June of the year one thousand nine hundred and fifty-one the following Convention, which may be cited as the Equal Remuneration Convention, 1951:

Article 1

For the purpose of this Convention:
(a) the term "remuneration" includes the ordinary, basic or minimum wage or salary and any additional emoluments whatsoever payable directly or indirectly, whether in cash or in kind, by the employer to the worker and arising out of the workers' employment;
(b) the term "equal remuneration for men and women workers for work of equal value" refers to rates of remuneration established without discrimination based on sex.

Article 2

1. Each member shall, by means appropriate to the methods in operation for determining rates of remuneration, promote and, in so far as is consistent with such methods, ensure the application to all workers of the principle of equal remuneration for men and women workers for work of equal value.
2. This principle may be applied by means of—
(a) national laws or regulations;
(b) legally established or recognized machinery for wage determination;
(c) collective agreements between employers and workers; or
(d) a combination of these various means.

Article 3

1. Where such action will assist in giving effect to the provisions of this Convention, measures shall be taken to promote objective appraisal of jobs on the basis of the work to be performed.
2. The methods to be followed in this appraisal may be decided upon by the authorities responsible for the determination of rates of remuneration, or, where such rates are determined by collective agreements, by the parties thereto.
3. Differential rates between workers, which correspond, without regard to sex, to differences, as determined by such objective appraisal, in the work to be performed shall not be considered as being contrary to the principle of equal remuneration for men and women workers for work of equal value.

Article 4

Each Member shall cooperate as appropriate with the employers' and workers' organizations concerned for the purpose of giving effect to the provisions of this Convention.

Convention Concerning Night Work of Women Employed in Industry
(ILO; revised 1948; came into force in 1951)

General Provisions, Article 1

1. For the purpose of this Convention, the term "industrial undertaking" includes particularly—
(a) mines, quarries, and other works for the extraction of minerals from the earth,
(b) undertakings in which articles are manufactured, altered, cleaned, repaired, ornamented, finished, adopted for sale, broken up or demolished, or in which materials are transformed, including undertakings engaged in shipbuilding or in the generation, transformation or transmission of electricity or motive power of any kind;
(c) undertakings engaged in building and civil engineering work, including constructional, repair, maintenance, alteration and demolition work.
2. The competent authority shall define the line of division which separates industry from agriculture, commerce and other nonindustrial occupations.

Article 2

For the purpose of this Convention the term "night" signifies a period of at least eleven consecutive hours, including an interval prescribed by the competent authority of at least seven consecutive hours falling between ten o' clock in the evening and seven o' clock in the morning; the competent authority may prescribe different intervals for different areas, industries, undertakings or branches of industries or undertakings, but shall consult the employers' and workers' organizations concerned before prescribing an interval beginning after eleven o' clock in the evening.

Article 3

Women without distinction of age shall not be employed during the night in any public or private industrial undertaking, or in any branch thereof, other than an undertaking in which only members of the same family are employed.

Article 4

Article 3 shall not apply—
(a) in cases of force majeure, when in any undertaking there occurs an interruption of work which was impossible to foresee, and which is not of a recurring character;

(b) in cases where the work has to do with raw materials or materials in course of treatment which are subject to rapid deterioration when such night work is necessary to preserve the said materials from certain loss.

Article 5

1. The prohibition of night work for women may be suspended by the government, after consultation with the employers' and workers' organizations concerned, when in case of serious emergency the national interest demands it.
2. Such suspension shall be notified by the government concerned to the Director-General of the International Labour Office in its annual report on the application of the Convention.

Article 6

In industrial undertakings which are influenced by the seasons and in all cases where exceptional circumstances demand it, the night period may be reduced to ten hours on sixty days of the year.

Article 7

In countries where the climate renders work by day particularly trying, the night period may be shorter than that prescribed in the above Articles if compensatory rest is accorded during the day.

Article 8

This Convention does not apply to—
(a) women holding responsible positions of a managerial or technical character; and
(b) women employed in health and welfare services who are not ordinarily engaged in manual work.

Article 9

In those countries where no government regulation as yet applies to the employment of women in industrial undertakings during the night, the term "night" may provisionally, and for a maximum period of three years, be declared by the government to signify a period of only ten hours, including an interval prescribed by the competent authority of at least seven consecutive hours falling between ten o' clock in the evening and seven o' clock in the morning.

Article 10

1. The provisions of this Convention shall apply to India subject to the modifications set forth in this Article.
2. The said provisions shall apply to all territories in respect of which the Indian legislature has jurisdiction to apply them.
3. The term "industrial undertaking" shall include—
(a) factories as defined in the Indian Factories Act; and
(b) mines to which the Indian Mines Act applies.

Article 11

1. The provisions of this Convention shall apply to Pakistan subject to the modifications set forth in this Article.
2. The said provisions shall apply to all territories in respect of which the Pakistan legislature has jurisdiction to apply them.
3. The term "industrial undertaking" shall include—
(a) factories as defined in the Factories Act.
(b) mines to which the Mines Act applies.

Discrimination (Employment and Occupation) Convention
(adopted in 1958; came into force in 1960)

Preamble

The General Conference of the International Labour Organization,
   Having decided upon the adoption of certain proposals with regard to discrimination in the field of employment and occupation . . . ,
   Considering that the Declaration of Philadelphia affirms that all human beings, irrespective of race, creed or sex, have the right to pursue both their material well-being and their spiritual development in conditions of freedom and dignity, of economic security and equal opportunity, and
   Considering further that discrimination constitutes a violation of rights enunciated by the Universal Declaration of Human Rights,
   adopts . . . the following Convention, which may be cited as the Discrimination (Employment and Occupation) Convention, 1958:

Article 1

1. For the purpose of this Convention the term "discrimination" includes—
(a) any distinction, exclusion or preference made on the basis of race, color, sex, religion, political opinion, national extraction or social origin,

which has the effect of nullifying or impairing equality of opportunity or treatment in employment or occupation;

(b) such other distinction, exclusion or preference which has the effect of nullifying or impairing equality of opportunity or treatment in employment or occupation as may be determined by the Member concerned after consultation with representative employers' and workers' organizations, where such exist, and with other appropriate bodies.

2. Any distinction, exclusion or preference in respect of a particular job based on the inherent requirements thereof shall not be deemed to be discrimination.

3. For the purpose of this Convention the terms "employment" and "occupation" include access to vocational training, access to employment and to particular occupations, and terms and conditions of employment.

Article 2

Each Member for which this Convention is in force undertakes to declare and pursue a national policy designed to promote, by methods appropriate to national conditions and practice, equality of opportunity and treatment in respect of employment and occupation, with a view to eliminating any discrimination in respect thereof.

Article 3

Each member for which this Convention is in force undertakes, by methods appropriate to national conditions and practice—

(a) to seek the cooperation of employers' and workers' organizations and other appropriate bodies in promoting the acceptance and observance of this policy;

(b) to enact such legislation and to promote such educational programs as may be calculated to secure the acceptance and observance of the policy;

(c) to repeal any statutory provisions and modify any administrative instructions or practices which are inconsistent with the policy;

(d) to pursue the policy in respect of employment under the direct control of a national authority;

(e) to ensure observance of the policy in the activities of vocational guidance, vocational training and placement services under the direction of a national authority;

(f) to indicate in its annual reports on the application of the Convention the action taken in pursuance of the policy and the results secured by such action.

Convention against Discrimination in Education
(adopted in 1960; came into force in 1962)

Preamble

The General Conference of the United Nations Educational, Scientific and Cultural Organization, meeting in Paris from 14 November to 15 December 1960 . . .

Recalling that the Universal Declaration of Human Rights asserts the principle of non-discrimination and proclaims that every person has the right to education,

Considering that, under the terms of its Constitution, the United Nations Educational, Scientific and Cultural Organization has the purpose of instituting collaboration among the nations with a view to furthering for all universal respect for human rights and equality of educational opportunity,

Recognizing that, consequently, the United Nations Educational, Scientific and Cultural Organization, while respecting the diversity of national educational systems has the duty not only to proscribe any form of discrimination in education but also to promote equality of opportunity and treatment for all in education,

Having before it proposals concerning the different aspects of discrimination in education . . .

Having decided at its tenth session that this question should be made the subject of an international convention as well as of recommendations to Member States,

Adopts this Convention on the fourteenth day of December 1960.

Article 1

1. For the purposes of this Convention, the term "discrimination" includes any distinction, exclusion, limitation or preference which, being based on race, colour, sex, language, religion, political or other opinion, national or social origin, economic condition or birth, has the purpose or effect of nullifying or impairing equality of treatment in education and in particular:
(a) of depriving any person or group of persons of access to education of any type or at any level;
(b) Of limiting any person or group of persons to education of an inferior standard;
(c) Subject to the provisions of Article 2 of this Convention, of establishing or maintaining separate educational systems or institutions for persons or groups of persons; or
(d) Of inflicting on any person or group of persons conditions which are incompatible with the dignity of man.

2. For the purposes of this Convention, the term "education" refers to all types and levels of education, and includes access to education, the standard and quality of education, and the conditions under which it is given.

Article 2

When permitted in a State, the following situations shall not be deemed to constitute discrimination, within the meaning of Article 1 of this Convention:

(a) The establishment or maintenance of separate educational systems or institutions for pupils of the two sexes, if these systems or institutions offer equivalent access to education, provide a teaching staff with qualifications of the same standard as well as school premises and equipment of the same quality, and afford the opportunity to take the same or equivalent courses of study;

(b) The establishment or maintenance, for religious or linguistic reasons, of separate educational systems or institutions offering an education which is in keeping with the wishes of the pupil's parents or legal guardians, if participation in such systems or attendance at such institutions is optional and if the education provided conforms to such standards as may be laid down or approved by the competent authorities, in particular for education of the same level;

(c) The establishment or maintenance of private educational institutions, if the object of the institutions is not to secure the exclusion of any group but to provide educational facilities in addition to those provided by the public authorities, if the institutions are conducted in accordance with that object, and if the education provided conforms with such standards as may be laid down or approved by the competent authorities, in particular for education of the same level.

Article 3

In order to eliminate and prevent discrimination within the meaning of this Convention, the States Parties thereto undertake:

(a) To abrogate any statutory provisions and any administrative instructions and to discontinue any administrative practices which involve discrimination in education;

(b) To ensure, by legislation where necessary, that there is no discrimination in the admission of pupils to educational institutions;

(c) Not to allow any differences of treatment by the public authorities between nationals, except on the basis of merit or need, in the matter of school fees and the grant of scholarships or other forms of assistance to pupils and necessary permits and facilities for the pursuit of studies in foreign countries;

(d) Not to allow, in any form of assistance granted by the public

authorities to educational institutions, any restrictions or preference based solely on the ground that pupils belong to a particular group;
(e) To give foreign nationals resident within their territory the same access to education as that given to their own nationals.

Article 4

The States Parties to this Convention undertake furthermore to formulate, develop and apply a national policy which, by methods appropriate to the circumstances and to national usage, will tend to promote equality of opportunity and of treatment in the matter of education and in particular:
(a) To make primary education free and compulsory; make secondary education in its different forms generally available and accessible to all; make higher education equally accessible to all on the basis of individual capacity; assure compliance by all with the obligation to attend school prescribed by law;
(b) To ensure that the standards of education are equivalent in all public educational institutions of the same level, and that the conditions relating to the quality of the education provided are also equivalent;
(c) To encourage and intensify by appropriate methods the education of persons who have not received any primary education or who have not completed the entire primary education course and the continuation of their education on the basis of individual capacity;
(d) To provide training for the teaching profession without discrimination.

Article 5

1. The States Parties to this Convention agree that:
(a) Education shall be directed to the full development of the human personality and to the strengthening of respect for human rights and fundamental freedoms; it shall promote understanding, tolerance and friendship among all nations, racial or religious groups, and shall further the activities of the United Nations for the maintenance of peace;
(b) It is essential to respect the liberty of parents and, where applicable, of legal guardians, firstly to choose for their children institutions other than those maintained by the public authorities but conforming to such minimum educational standards as may be laid down or approved by the competent authorities and, secondly, to ensure in a manner consistent with the procedures followed in the State for the application of its legislation, the religious and moral education of the children in conformity with their own convictions; and no person or group of persons should be compelled to receive religious instruction inconsistent with his or their conviction;
(c) It is essential to recognize the right of members of national minorities

to carry on their own educational activities, including the maintenance of schools and, depending on the educational policy of each State, the use or the teaching of their own language, provided however:

(i) That this right is not exercised in a manner which prevents the members of these minorities from understanding the culture and language of the community as a whole and from participating in its activities, or which prejudices national sovereignty;

(ii) That the standard of education is not lower than the general standard laid down or approved by the competent authorities; and

(iii) That attendance at such schools is optional.

2. The State Parties to this Convention undertake to take all necessary measures to ensure the application of the principles enunciated in paragraph 1 of this Article.

Convention on Consent to Marriage, Minimum Age for Marriage, and Registration of Marriages (1962)

Preamble

The Contracting States,

Desiring, in conformity with the Charter of the United Nations, to promote universal respect for, and observance of, human rights and fundamental freedoms for all, without distinction as to race, sex, language or religion,

Recalling that article 16 of the Universal Declaration of Human Rights states that:

"(1) Men and women of full age, without any limitation due to race, nationality or religion, have the right to marry and to found a family. They are entitled to equal rights as to marriage, during marriage and at its dissolution.

"(2) Marriage shall be entered into only with the free and full consent of the intending spouses."

Recalling further that the General Assembly of the United Nations declared, by resolution 843(IX) of 17 December 1954, that certain customs, ancient laws and practices relating to marriage and the family were inconsistent with the principles set forth in the Charter of the United Nations and in the Universal Declaration of Human Rights,

Reaffirming that all States, including those which have or assume responsibility for the administration of Non-Self-Governing and Trust Territories until their achievement of independence, should take all appropriate laws and practices by ensuring, inter alia, complete freedom in the choice of a spouse, eliminating completely child marriages and the betrothal of young girls before the age of puberty, establishing appropriate penalties where necessary and establishing a civil or other register in which all marriages will be recorded,

Hereby agrees as hereinafter provided:

Article 1

1. No marriage shall be legally entered into without the full and free consent of both parties, such consent to be expressed by them in person after due publicity and in the presence of the authority competent to solemnize the marriage and of witnesses, as prescribed by law.
2. Notwithstanding anything in paragraph 1 above, it shall not be necessary for one of the parties to be present when the competent authority is satisfied that the circumstances are exceptional and that the party has, before a competent authority and in such manner as may be prescribed by law, expressed and not withdrawn consent.

Article 2

States parties to the present Convention shall take legislative action to specify a minimum age for marriage. No marriage shall be legally entered into by any person under this age, except where a competent authority has granted a dispensation as to age, for serious reasons, in the interest of the intending spouses.

Article 3

All marriages shall be registered in an appropriate official register by the competent authority.

Convention on the Nationality of Married Women
(adopted in 1957; came into force in 1958)

Preamble

The Contracting States,

Recognizing that conflicts in law and in practice with reference to nationality arise as a result of provisions concerning the loss of acquisition of nationality by women as a result of marriage, of its dissolution, or of the change of nationality by the husband during marriage,

Recognizing that, in article 15 of the Universal Declaration of Human Rights, the General Assembly of the United Nations has proclaimed that "everyone has the right to a nationality" and that "no one shall be arbitrarily deprived of his nationality nor denied the right to change his nationality,"

Desiring to cooperate with the United Nations in promoting universal respect for, and observance of, human rights and fundamental freedoms for all without distinction as to sex,

Hereby agree as hereinafter provided:

Article 1

Each Contracting State agrees that neither the celebration nor the dissolution of a marriage between one of its nationals and an alien, nor the change of nationality by the husband during marriage, shall automatically affect the nationality of the wife.

Article 2

Each Contracting State agrees that neither the voluntary acquisition of the nationality of another State nor the renunciation of its nationality by one of its nationals shall prevent the retention of its nationality by the wife of such national.

Article 3

1. Each Contracting State agrees that the alien wife of one of its nationals may, at her request, acquire the nationality of her husband through specially privileged naturalization procedures; the grant of such nationality may be subject to such limitations as may be imposed in the interests of national security or public policy.
2. Each Contracting State agrees that the present Convention shall not be construed as affecting any legislation or judicial practice by which the alien wife of one of its nationals may, at her request, acquire her husband's nationality as a matter of right.

Convention on the Political Rights of Women
(adopted in 1952; came into force in 1954)

Preamble

The Contracting Parties,

Desiring to implement the principle of equality of rights for men and women contained in the Charter of the United Nations,

Recognizing that everyone has the right to take part in the government of his country, directly or indirectly through freely chosen representatives, and has the right to equal access to public service in his country, and desiring to equalize the status of men and women in the enjoyment and exercise of political rights, in accordance with the provisions of the Charter of the United Nations and of the Universal Declaration of Human Rights,

Having resolved to conclude a Convention for this purpose,

Hereby agree as hereinafter provided:

Article 1

Women shall be entitled to vote in all elections on equal terms with men, without any discrimination.

Article 2

Women shall be eligible for election to all publicly elected bodies, established by national law, on equal terms with men, without any discrimination.

Article 3

Women shall be entitled to hold public office and to exercise all public functions, established by national law, on equal terms with men without any discrimination.

Convention for the Suppression of the Traffic in Persons and of the Exploitation of the Prostitution of Others
(adopted in 1949; came into force in 1951)

Preamble

Whereas prostitution and the accompanying evil of the traffic in persons for the purpose of prostitution are incompatible with the dignity and worth of the human person and endanger the welfare of the individual, the family and the community.

Whereas, with respect to the suppression of the traffic in women and children, the following international instruments are in force

1. International Agreement of 18 May 1904 for the Suppression of the White Slave Traffic, as amended by the Protocol approved by the General Assembly of the United Nations on 3 December 1948

2. International Convention of 4 May 1910 for the Suppression of the White Slave Traffic, as amended by the above-mentioned Protocol,

3. International Convention of 30 September 1921 for the Suppression of the Traffic in Women and Children, as amended by the Protocol approved by the General Assembly of the United Nations on 20 October 1947.

4. International Convention of 11 October 1933 for the Suppression of the Traffic in Women of Full Age, as amended by the aforesaid Protocol,

Whereas the League of Nations in 1937 prepared a draft Convention extending the scope of the above-mentioned instruments, and

Whereas developments since 1937 make feasible the conclusion of a convention consolidating the above-mentioned instruments and embodying the substance of the 1937 draft Convention as well as desirable alterations therein:

Now therefore,

The Contracting Parties hereby agree as hereinafter provided:

Article 1

The Parties to the present Convention agree to punish any person who, to gratify the passions of another:

1. Procures, entices or leads away, for purposes of prostitution, another person, even with the consent of that person;

2. Exploits the prostitution of another person, even with the consent of that person.

Article 2

The Parties to the present Convention further agree to punish any person who:

1. Keeps or manages, or knowingly finances or takes part in the financing of a brothel;

2. Knowingly lets or rents a building or other place or any part thereof for the purpose of the prostitution of others.

Article 3

To the extent permitted by domestic law, attempts to commit any of the offenses referred to in articles 1 and 2, and acts preparatory to the commission thereof, shall also be punished.

Article 4

To the extent permitted by domestic law, international participation in the acts referred to in articles 1 and 2 above shall also be punishable.

To the extent permitted by domestic law, acts of participation shall be treated as separate offenses whenever this is necessary to prevent impunity.

Article 5

In cases where injured persons are entitled under domestic law to be parties to proceedings in respect of any of the offenses referred to in the present Convention, aliens shall be so entitled upon the same terms as nationals.

Article 6

Each Party to the present Convention agrees to take all the necessary measures to repeal or abolish any existing law, regulation or administrative provision by virtue of which persons who engage in or are suspected of engaging in prostitution are subject either to special registration or to possession of a special document or to any exceptional requirements for supervision or notification.

Article 7

Previous convictions pronounced in foreign States for offenses referred to in the present Convention shall, to the extent permitted by domestic law, be taken into account for the purpose of:
1. Establishing recidivism;
2. Disqualifying the offender from the exercise of civil rights.

Article 16

The Parties to the present Convention agree to take or to encourage, through their public and private educational, health, social, economic and other related services, measures for the prevention of prostitution and for the rehabilitation and social adjustment of the victims of prostitution and of the offenses referred to in the present Convention.

Article 17

The Parties to the present Convention undertake, in connection with immigration and emigration, to adopt or maintain such measures as are required, in terms of their obligations under the present Convention, to check the traffic in persons of either sex for the purpose of prostitution.
In particular they undertake:
1. To make sure regulations as are necessary for the protection of immigrants or emigrants, and in particular, women and children, both at the place of arrival and departure and while en route;
2. To arrange for appropriate publicity warning the public of the dangers of the aforesaid traffic;
3. To take appropriate measures to ensure supervision of railway stations, airports, seaports and en route, and of other public places, in order to prevent international traffic in persons for the purpose of prostitution;
4. To take appropriate measures in order that the appropriate authori-

ties be informed of the arrival of persons who appear . . . to be the principals and accomplices in or victims of such traffic.

Article 20

The Parties to the present Convention shall, if they have not already done so, take the necessary measures for the supervision of employment agencies in order to prevent persons seeking employment, in particular women and children, from being exposed to the danger of prostitution.

International Convention for the Suppression of the Traffic in Women of Full Age
(as amended 1947)

Article 1

Whoever, in order to gratify the passions of another person, has procured, enticed or led away even with her consent, a woman or girl of full age for immoral purposes notwithstanding that the various acts constituting the offense may have been committed in different countries.

Attempted offenses, and within the legal limits, acts preparatory to the offenses in question, shall also be punishable.

Article 2

The High Contracting Parties whose laws are at present inadequate to deal with the offenses specified in the preceding Article agree to take the necessary steps to ensure that these offenses shall be punished in accordance with their gravity.

Article 3

The High Contracting Parties undertake to communicate to each other in regard to any person of either sex who has committed or attempted to commit any of the offenses referred to in the present Convention or in the Conventions of 1910 and 1921 on the Suppression of the Traffic in Women and Children, the various constituent acts of which were, or were to have been, accomplished in different countries, the following information (or similar information which it may be possible to supply under the laws and regulations of the country concerned):
(a) Records of convictions, together with any useful and available information with regard to the offender, such as his civil status, description, fingerprints, photography and police record, his methods of operations, etc.

(b) Particulars of any measures of refusal of admission or of expulsion which may have been applied to him.

These documents and information shall be sent direct and without delay to the authorities of the countries concerned in each particular case. . . .

Convention on the Elimination of Discrimination against Women (1967)

The General Assembly,

Considering that the peoples of the United Nations have, in the Charter, reaffirmed their faith in fundamental human rights, in the dignity and worth of the human person and in the equal rights of men and women,

Considering that the Universal Declaration on Human Rights asserts the principle of non-discrimination and proclaims that all human beings are born free and equal in dignity and rights and that everyone is entitled to all the rights and freedoms set forth therein without distinction of any kind, including any distinction as to sex,

Taking into account the resolutions, declarations, conventions and recommendations of the United Nations and the specialized agencies designed to eliminate all forms of discrimination and to promote equal rights for men and women,

Concerned that, despite the Charter of the United Nations, the Universal Declaration of Human Rights, the International Covenants on Human Rights and other instruments of the United Nations and the specialized agencies and despite the progress made in the matter of equality of rights, there continues to exist considerable discrimination against women,

Considering that discrimination against women is incompatible with human dignity and with the welfare of the family and of society, prevents their participation, on equal terms with men, in the political, social, economic and cultural life of their countries and is an obstacle to the full development of the potentialities of women in the service of their countries and of humanity,

Bearing in mind the great contribution made by women in social, political, economic and cultural life and the part they play in the family and particularly in the rearing of children,

Convinced that the full and complete development of a country, the welfare of the world and the cause of peace require the maximum participation of women as well as men in all fields,

Considering that it is necessary to ensure the universal recognition in law and in fact of the principle of equality of men and women,

Solemnly proclaim this Declaration:

Article 1

Discrimination against women, denying or limiting as it does their equality of rights with men, is fundamentally unjust and constitutes an offense against human dignity.

Article 2

All appropriate measures shall be taken to abolish existing laws, customs, regulations and practices which are discriminatory against women, and to establish adequate legal protection for equal rights of men and women, in particular

(a) The principle of equality of rights shall be embodied in the constitution or otherwise guaranteed by law;

(b) The international instruments of the United Nations and the specialized agencies relating to the elimination of discrimination against women shall be ratified or acceded to and fully implemented as soon as practicable.

Article 3

All appropriate measures shall be taken to educate public opinion and to direct national aspirations towards the eradication of prejudice and the abolition of customary and all other practices which are based on the idea of the inferiority of women.

Article 4

All appropriate measures shall be taken to ensure to women on equal terms with men, without any discrimination:

(a) The right to vote in all elections and be eligible for election to all publicly elected bodies;

(b) The right to vote in all public referenda;

(c) The right to hold public office and to exercise all public functions.

Such rights shall be guaranteed by legislation.

Article 5

Women shall have the same rights as men to acquire, change or retain their nationality. Marriage to an alien shall not automatically affect the nationality of the wife either by rendering her stateless or by forcing upon her the nationality of her husband.

Article 6

1. Without prejudice to the safeguarding of the unity and the harmony of the family, which remains the basic unit of any society, all appropriate measures, particularly legislative measures, shall be taken to ensure to women, married or unmarried, equal rights with men in the field of civil law, and in particular:

(a) The right to acquire, administer, enjoy, dispose of and inherit property, including property acquired during marriage;

(b) The right to equality in legal capacity and the exercise thereof;

(c) The same rights as men with regard to the law on the movement of persons.

2. All appropriate measures shall be taken to ensure the principle of equality of status of the husband and wife, and in particular:

(a) Women shall have the same right as men to free choice of a spouse and to enter into marriage only with their free and full consent;

(b) Women shall have equal rights with men during marriage and at its dissolution. In all cases the interest of the children shall be paramount;

(c) Parents shall have equal rights and duties in matters relating to their children. In all cases the interest of the children shall be paramount.

3. Child marriage and the betrothal of young girls before puberty shall be prohibited, and effective action, including legislation, shall be taken to specify a minimum age for marriage and to make the registration of marriages in an official registry compulsory.

Article 7

All provisions of penal codes which constitute discrimination against women shall be repealed.

Article 8

All appropriate measures, including legislation, shall be taken to combat all forms of traffic in women and exploitation of prostitution of women.

Article 9

All appropriate measures shall be taken to ensure to girls and women, married or unmarried, equal rights with men in education at all levels, and in particular:

(a) Equal conditions of access to, and study in, educational institutions of all types, including universities and vocational, technical and professional schools;

(b) The same choice of curricula, the same examinations, teaching staff with qualifications of the same standards, and school premises and equipment of the same quality, whether the institutions are co-educational or not;

(c) Equal opportunities to benefit from scholarships and other study grants;

(d) Equal opportunities for access to programmes of continuing education, including adult literacy programmes;

(e) Access to educational information to help in ensuring the health and well-being of families.

Article 10

1. All appropriate measures shall be taken to ensure to women, married or unmarried, equal rights with men in the field of economic and social life, and in particular:

(a) The right, without discrimination on grounds of marital status or any other grounds, to receive vocational training, to work, to free choice of profession and employment, and to professional and vocational advancement;

(b) The right to equal remuneration with men and to equality of treatment in respect of work of equal value;

(c) The right to leave with pay, retirement privileges and provision for security in respect of unemployment, sickness, old age or other incapacity to work;

(d) The right to receive family allowances on equal terms with men.

2. In order to prevent discrimination against women on account of marriage or maternity and to ensure their effective right to work, measures shall be taken to prevent their dismissal in the event of marriage or maternity and to provide paid maternity leave, with the guarantee of returning to former employment, and to provide the necessary social services, including childcare facilities.

3. Measures taken to protect women in certain types of work, for reasons inherent in their physical nature, shall not be regarded as discriminatory.

Article 11

1. The principle of equality of rights of men and women demands implementation in all States in accordance with the principles of the Charter of the United Nations and of the Universal Declaration of Human Rights.

2. Governments, nongovernmental organizations and individuals are urged, therefore, to do all in their power to promote the implementation of the principles contained in this Declaration.

Convention on the Elimination of All Forms of Discrimination against Women (1979)

The States Parties to the present Convention,

Noting that the Charter of the United Nations reaffirms faith in fundamental human rights, in the dignity and worth of the human person and in the equal rights of men and women,

Noting that the Universal Declaration of Human Rights affirms the principle of the inadmissibility of discrimination and proclaims that all human beings are born free and equal in dignity and rights and that everyone is entitled to all the rights and freedoms set forth therein, without distinction of any kind, including distinction based on sex,

Considering the international conventions concluded under the auspices of the United Nations and the specialized agencies promoting equality of rights of men and women,

Noting also the resolutions, declarations and recommendations adopted by the United Nations and the specialized agencies promoting equality of rights of men and women,

Concerned, however, that despite these various instruments extensive discrimination against women continues to exist,

Recalling that discrimination against women violates the principles of equality of rights and respect for human dignity, is an obstacle to the participation of women, on equal terms with men, in the political, social, economic and cultural life of their countries, hampers the growth of the prosperity of society and the family and makes more difficult the full development of the potentialities of women in the service of their countries and of humanity,

Concerned that in situations of poverty women have the least access to food, health, education, training and opportunities for employment and other needs,

Convinced that the establishment of the new international economic order based on equity and justice will contribute significantly towards the promotion of equality between men and women,

Emphasizing that the eradication of apartheid, of all forms of racism, racial discrimination, colonialism, neo-colonialism, aggression, foreign occupation and domination and interference in the internal affairs of States is essential to the full enjoyment of the rights of men and women,

Affirming that the strengthening of international peace and security, relaxation of international tension, mutual co-operation among all States irrespective of their social and economic systems, general and complete disarmament, and in particular nuclear disarmament under strict and effective international control, the affirmation of the principles of justice, equality and mutual benefit in relations among countries and the realization of the right of peoples under alien and colonial

domination and foreign occupation to self-determination and independence, as well as respect for national sovereignty and territorial in-
tegrity, will promote social progress and development and as a
consequence will contribute to the attainment of full equality between
men and women,

Convinced that the full and complete development of a country,
the welfare of the world and the cause of peace require the maximum
participation of women on equal terms with men in all fields,

Bearing in mind the great contribution of women to the welfare of
the family and to the development of society, so far not fully recognized, the social significance of maternity and the role of both parents
in the family and in the upbringing of children, and aware that the role
of women in procreation should not be a basis for discrimination but
that the upbringing of children requires a sharing of responsibility between men and women and society as a whole,

Aware that a change in the traditional role of men as well as the
role of women in society and in the family is needed to achieve full
equality between men and women,

Determined to implement the principles set forth in the Declaration on the Elimination of Discrimination against Women and, for that
purpose, to adopt the measures required for the elimination of such
discrimination in all its forms and manifestations,

Have agreed on the following:

Article 1

For the purpose of the present Convention, the term "discrimination
against women" shall mean any distinction, exclusion or restriction
made on the basis of sex which has the effect or purpose of impairing
or nullifying the recognition, enjoyment or exercise by women, irrespective of their marital status, on the basis of equality of men and
women, of human rights and fundamental freedoms in the political,
economic, social, cultural, civil or any other field.

Article 2

States Parties condemn discrimination against women in all its forms,
agree to pursue by all appropriate means and without delay a policy of
eliminating discrimination against women and, to this end, undertake:
(a) To embody the principle of the equality of men and women in their
national constitutions or other appropriate legislation if not yet incorporated therein and to ensure, through law and other appropriate
means, the practical realization of this principle;
(b) To adopt appropriate legislative and other measures, including
sanctions where appropriate, prohibiting all discrimination against
women;

(c) To establish legal protection of the rights of women on an equal basis with men and to ensure through competent national tribunals and other public institutions the effective protection of women against any act of discrimination;

(d) To refrain from engaging in any act or practice of discrimination against women and to ensure that public authorities and institutions shall act in conformity with this obligation;

(e) To take all appropriate measures to eliminate discrimination against women by any person, organization or enterprise;

(f) To take all appropriate measures, including legislation, to modify or abolish existing laws, regulations, customs and practices which constitute discrimination against women;

(g) To repeal all national penal provisions which constitute discrimination against women.

Article 3

States Parties shall take in all fields, in particular in the political, social, economic and cultural fields, all appropriate measures, including legislation, to ensure the full development and advancement of women, for the purpose of guaranteeing them the exercise and enjoyment of human rights and fundamental freedoms on a basis of equality with men.

Article 4

1. Adoption by States Parties of temporary special measures aimed at accelerating de facto equality between men and women shall not be considered discrimination as defined in the present Convention, but shall in no way entail as a consequence the maintenance of unequal or separate standards; these measures shall be discontinued when the objectives of equality of opportunity and treatment have been achieved.

2. Adoption by States Parties of special measures, including those measures contained in the present Convention, aimed at protecting maternity shall not be considered discriminatory.

Article 5

States Parties shall take all appropriate measures:

(a) To modify the social and cultural patterns of conduct of men and women, with a view to achieving the elimination of prejudices and customary and all other practices which are based on the idea of the inferiority or the superiority of either of the sexes or on stereotyped roles for men and women;

(b) To ensure that family education includes a proper understanding of maternity as a social function and the recognition of the common responsibility of men and women in the upbringing and development of their children, it being understood that the interest of the children is the primordial consideration in all cases.

Article 6

States Parties shall take all appropriate measures, including legislation, to suppress all forms of traffic in women and exploitation of prostitution of women.

Article 7

States Parties shall take all appropriate measures to eliminate discrimination against women in the political and public life of the country and, in particular, shall ensure to women, on equal terms with men, the right:
(a) To vote in all elections and public referenda and to be eligible for election to all publicly elected bodies;
(b) To participate in the formulation of government policy and the implementation thereof and to hold public office and perform all public functions at all levels of government;
(c) To participate in non-governmental organizations and associations concerned with the public and political life of the country.

Article 8

States Parties shall take all appropriate measures to ensure to women, on equal terms with men and without any discrimination, the opportunity to represent their Governments at the international level and to participate in the work of international organizations.

Article 9

1. States Parties shall grant women equal rights with men to acquire, change or retain their nationality. They shall ensure in particular that neither marriage to an alien nor change of nationality by the husband during marriage shall automatically change the nationality of the wife, render her stateless or force upon her the nationality of the husband.
2. States Parties shall grant women equal rights with men with respect to the nationality of their children.

Article 10

States Parties shall take all appropriate measures to eliminate discrimination against women in order to ensure to them equal rights with men in the field of education and in particular to ensure, on a basis of equality of men and women:

(a) The same conditions for career and vocational guidance, for access to studies and for the achievement of diplomas in educational establishments of all categories in rural as well as in urban areas; this equality shall be ensured in pre-school, general, technical, professional and higher technical education, as well as in all types of vocational training;
(b) Access to the same curricula, the same examinations, teaching staff with qualifications of the same standard and school premises and equipment of the same quality;
(c) The elimination of any stereotyped concept of the roles of men and women at all levels and in all forms of education by encouraging coeducation and other types of education which will help to achieve this aim and, in particular, by the revision of textbooks and school programmes and the adaptation of teaching methods;
(d) The same opportunities to benefit from scholarships and other study grants;
(e) The same opportunities for access to programmes of continuing education, including adult and functional literacy programmes, particularly those aimed at reducing, at the earliest possible time, any gap in education existing between men and women;
(f) The reduction of female student drop-out rates and the organization of programmes for girls and women who have left school prematurely;
(g) The same opportunities to participate actively in sports and physical education;
(h) Access to specific educational information to help to ensure the health and well-being of families, including information and advice on family planning.

Article 11

1. States Parties shall take all appropriate measures to eliminate discrimination against women in the field of employment in order to ensure, on a basis of equality of men and women, the same rights, in particular:
(a) The right to work as an inalienable right of all human beings;
(b) The right to the same employment opportunities, including the application of the same criteria for selection in matters of employment;
(c) The right to free choice of profession and employment, the right to promotion, job security and all benefits and conditions of service and the right to receive vocational training and retraining, including apprenticeships, advanced vocational training and recurrent training;
(d) The right to equal remuneration, including benefits, and to equal treatment in respect of work of equal value, as well as equality of treatment in the evaluation of the quality of work;
(e) The right to social security, particularly in cases of retirement, unemployment, sickness, invalidity and old age and other incapacity to work, as well as the right to paid leave;

(f) The right to protection of health and to safety in working conditions, including the safeguarding of the function of reproduction;
2. In order to prevent discrimination against women on the grounds of marriage or maternity and to ensure their effective right to work, States Parties shall take appropriate measures:
(a) To prohibit, subject to the imposition of sanctions, dismissal on the grounds of pregnancy or of maternity leave and discrimination in dismissals on the basis of marital status;
(b) To introduce maternity leave with pay or with comparable social benefits without loss of former employment, seniority or social allowances;
(c) To encourage the provision of the necessary supporting social services to enable parents to combine family obligations with work responsibilities and participation in public life, in particular through promoting the establishment and development of a network of child-care facilities;
(d) To provide special protection to women during pregnancy in types of work proved to be harmful to them.
3. Protective legislation relating to matters covered in this article shall be reviewed periodically in the light of scientific and technological knowledge and shall be revised, repealed or extended as necessary.

Article 12

1. States Parties shall take all appropriate measures to eliminate discrimination against women in the field of health care in order to ensure, on a basis of equality of men and women, access to health care services, including those related to family planning.
2. Notwithstanding the provisions of paragraph 1 of this article, States Parties shall ensure to women appropriate services in connection with pregnancy, confinement and the post-natal period, granting free services where necessary, as well as adequate nutrition during pregnancy and lactation.

Article 13

1. States Parties shall take all appropriate measures to eliminate discrimination against women in other areas of economic and social life in order to ensure, on a basis of equality of men and women, the same rights, in particular:
(a) The right to family benefits;
(b) The right to bank loans, mortgages and other forms of financial credit;
(c) The right to participate in recreational activities, sports and all aspects of cultural life.

Article 14

1. States Parties shall take into account the particular problems faced by rural women and the significant roles which rural women play in the economic survival of their families, including their work in the non-monetized sectors of the economy, and shall take all appropriate measures to ensure the application of the provisions of this Convention to women in rural areas.

2. States Parties shall take all appropriate measures to eliminate discrimination against women in rural areas in order to ensure, on a basis of equality of men and women, that they participate in and benefit from rural development and, in particular, shall ensure to such women the right:

(a) To participate in the elaboration and implementation of development planning at all levels;

(b) To have access to adequate health care facilities, including information, counseling and services in family planning;

(c) To benefit directly from social security programmes;

(d) To obtain all types of training and education, formal and non-formal, including that relating to functional literacy, as well as, inter alia, the benefit of all community and extension services, in order to increase their technical proficiency;

(e) To organize self-help groups and co-operatives in order to obtain equal access to economic opportunities through employment or self-employment;

(f) To participate in all community activities;

(g) To have access to agricultural credit and loans, marketing facilities, appropriate technology and equal treatment in land and agrarian reform as well as in land resettlement schemes;

(h) To enjoy adequate living conditions, particularly in relation to housing, sanitation, electricity and water supply, transport and communications.

Article 15

1. States Parties shall accord to women equality with men before the law.

2. States Parties shall accord to women, in civil matters, a legal capacity identical to that of men and the same opportunities to exercise that capacity. In particular, they shall give women equal rights to conclude contracts and to administer property and shall treat them equally in all stages of procedure in courts and tribunals.

3. States Parties agree that all contracts and all other private instruments of any kind with a legal effect which is directed at restricting the legal capacity of women shall be deemed null and void.

4. States Parties shall accord to men and women the same rights with regard to the law relating to the movement of persons and the freedom to choose their residence and domicile.

Article 16

1. States Parties shall take all appropriate measures to eliminate discrimination against women in all matters relating to marriage and family relations and in particular shall ensure, on a basis of equality of men and women:
(a) The same right to enter into marriage;
(b) The same right freely to choose a spouse and to enter into marriage only with their free and full consent;
(c) The same rights and responsibilities during marriage and at its dissolution;
(d) The same rights and responsibilities as parents, irrespective of their marital status, in matters relating to their children; in all cases the interests of the children shall be paramount;
(e) The same rights to decide freely and responsibly on the number and spacing of their children and to have access to the information, education and means to enable them to exercise these rights;
(f) The same rights and responsibilities with regard to guardianship, wardship, trusteeship and adoption of children, or similar institutions where these concepts exist in national legislation; in all cases the interests of the children shall be paramount;
(g) The same personal rights as husband and wife, including the right to choose a family name, a profession and an occupation;
(h) The same rights for both spouses in respect of the ownership, acquisition, management, administration, enjoyment and disposition of property, whether free of charge or for a valuable consideration;
2. The betrothal and the marriage of a child shall have no legal effect, and all necessary action, including legislation, shall be taken to specify a minimum age for marriage and to make the registration of marriages in an official registry compulsory.

Article 17

1. For the purpose of considering the progress made in the implementation of the present Convention, there shall be established a Committee on the Elimination of Discrimination against Women (hereinafter referred to as the Committee) consisting, at the time of entry into force of the Convention, of eighteen and, after ratification of or accession to the Convention by the thirty-fifth State Party, of twenty-three experts of high moral standing and competence in the field covered by the Convention. The experts shall be elected by States Parties from among their nationals and shall serve in their personal capacity, consideration being given to equitable geographical distribution and to the representation of the different forms of civilization as well as the principle legal systems.
2. The members of the Committee shall be elected by secret ballot from

a list of persons nominated by States Parties. Each State Party may nominate one person from among its own nationals.

Article 18

1. States Parties undertake to submit to the Secretary-General of the United Nations, for consideration by the Committee, a report on the legislative, judicial, administrative or other measures which they have adopted to give effect to the provisions of the present Convention and on the progress made in this respect:
(a) Within a year after the entry into force for the State concerned; and
(b) Thereafter at least every four years and further whenever the Committee so requests.
2. Reports may indicate factors and difficulties affecting the degree of fulfillment of obligations under the present Convention.

Article 21

1. The Committee shall, through the Economic and Social Council, report annually to the General Assembly of the United Nations on its activities and may make suggestions and general recommendations based on the examination of reports and information received from the States Parties. Such suggestions and general recommendations shall be included in the report of the Committee together with comments, if any, from States Parties.
2. The Secretary-General shall transmit the reports of the Committee to the Commission on the States of Women for its information.

Article 23

Nothing in this Convention shall affect any provisions that are more conducive to the achievement of equality between men and women which may be contained:
(a) In the legislation of a State Party; or
(b) In any other international convention, treaty or agreement in force for that State.

Article 24

States Parties undertake to adopt all necessary measures at the national level aimed at achieving the full realization of the rights recognized in the present Convention.

United Nations High Commissioner for Refugees (UNHCR) Policy on Refugee Women

Introduction

1. The Executive Committee has adopted four general conclusions relating specifically to refugee women:

• During its thirty-sixth session in 1985, the Executive Committee adopted conclusion No. 39, entitled "Refugee Women and International Protection," in which it stressed the need for UNHCR and host governments to give particular attention to the international protection of refugee women.

• At its thirty-eighth session in 1987, the Executive Committee in its "General Conclusions on International Protection" noted that refugee women had protection and assistance needs which necessitated special attention in order to improve existing protection and assistance programmes, and called on all States and concerned agencies to support the efforts of the Office in this regard. It also recognized the need for reliable information and statistics about refugee women in order to increase awareness about their situation.

• In 1988, at its thirty-ninth session, the Executive Committee adopted a conclusion entitled "Refugee Women" which elaborates further on the special vulnerability of refugee women and the particular problems that they face, notably in the area of physical security, and noted the need to promote the participation of refugee women as agents as well as beneficiaries of programmes on their behalf. The conclusion also stressed the need for "an active senior-level steering committee" on refugee women to coordinate, integrate and oversee the assessment, reorientation and strengthening of existing policies and programmes in favour of refugee women, whilst ensuring that such efforts were culturally appropriate and resulted in the full integration of the women concerned. There was also emphasis on the necessity for public information on the issue of refugee women and the need for the development of training modules on the subject, in order to increase awareness of the specific needs of refugee women and the practical means of addressing these needs.

• At its fortieth session in 1989, the Executive Committee adopted a conclusion on refugee women reiterating concern about physical safety and sexual exploitation. It also called for a policy framework for the next stages in mainstreaming women's issues within the organization with particular attention to the need for female field workers to facilitate the participation of refugee women. It reaffirmed the conclusions of the thirty-ninth session regarding refugee women, called for expanded training and the development of a methodology to systematically address gender issues in refugee programmes.

• In addition to the Executive Committee conclusion, UNHCR, as a United Nations agency, is obliged to implement the Nairobi Forward Looking Strategies for the Advancement of Women. Both the above noted conclusions and the strategies reflect the international community's recognition that programmes which are planned or implemented without the consultation or participation of half the target population (the women) cannot be effective and could, inadvertently, have a negative impact on their socio-economic situation. This paper draws together the various Executive Committee conclusions and applicable United Nations resolutions into a policy framework for future action aimed at improving the situation of refugee women.

2. UNHCR's unique functions of providing protection to refugees and helping find durable solutions to their problems imply specific obligations with regard to programmes for refugee women who represent, with their dependents, over 80 percent of the beneficiaries of UNHCR's assistance programmes. The present paper sets out the policy framework for the elaboration of an organizational work plan for the integration of refugee women into programming and project activities. The Office's international protection activities on behalf of refugee women are considered in more detail in a separate paper, document EC/SCP/59, which also discusses some of the considerations in the area of protection and assistance on which the formulations of the present paper are based. The Executive Committee's conclusions on this paper will be incorporated into the organizational work plan.

3. The present paper introduces, in Part III, the underlying principles of the policy. These are the integration of the resources and needs of refugee women into all aspects of programming, rather than creating special women's projects, and the need for each staff member to ensure that this takes place in his or her area of competence. In Part IV, the paper outlines the organizational goals for refugee women, that is, the activities which UNHCR is required to carry out in this connection under its mandate. In Part V are outlined the policy objectives, that is, the interpretation of the organizational goals at the policy level. Finally, Part VI sets out the operational objectives of the policy, that is, a series of activities at the project level to ensure the practical implementation of the policy. These objectives are based on the Nairobi Forward Looking Strategies for the Advancement of Women and the conclusions adopted by the Executive Committee since its thirty-ninth session.

II. General

4. The policy set out in this document is premised on the recognition that becoming a refugee affects men and women differently and that effective programming must recognize these differences. Furthermore, to understand fully the protection needs and assistance resources of the refugee population, and to encourage dignity and self-sufficiency, refugee women themselves must participate in planning and imple-

menting projects. Socio-cultural and economic roles can, to a great extent, determine the pattern of such participation. Traditional roles are often disrupted and then either undermined or reinforced by the refugee situation. It is, therefore, essential that organizations working with refugees recognize that special initiatives must often be taken to ensure that all refugees have the opportunity to contribute to the activities planned for them.

III. The Basic Principle: Mainstreaming/Integration

5. It is the intention of UNHCR to integrate the resources and needs of refugee women in all aspects of programme planning and implementation. This does not mean that separate 'women's' projects are to be initiated or added on to existing general programme activities. Nor does it mean that responsibility for this process will rest with one work unit. It is the responsibility of each staff member to ensure that it takes place within his or her area of competence. The following terms and definitions are useful in understanding this concept.

What are programmes or projects which mainstream/integrate refugee women?

6. Any intervention, emergency, mid- or long-term, will have a different impact on men, women and children. Protection and assistance programmes or projects which mainstream/integrate refugee women are based on an explicit recognition of this fact. In activities which mainstream refugee women, action is taken to enable refugee women to participate and make a positive contribution.

7. Planning for such projects includes more than women's social role as daughter/wife/mother. It highlights a woman's economic role as income-earner for herself and her family, producer and/or manager of food, provider of fuel and water, and her religious, cultural and political activities. These roles, and, even more importantly, the change in these roles created by the refugee situation are frequently overlooked by planners. Consequently, interventions which do not take these factors into consideration may be inappropriate to women, tend to isolate them from mainstream project activities, further reinforce their dependency, and force them into unaccustomed social or economic roles.

8. The concept of mainstreaming refugee women arose from a better understanding of the implications of the division of labour between women and men. A programme which integrates refugee women will have taken into consideration factors influenced by the male/female roles in a society and included these in the planned activity with a view to benefiting the whole target population, not marginalizing a portion of it. Refugee women are emphasized because, inadvertently, planners have often overlooked them. Until needs assessment and par-

ticipation of all segments of a target group are integral to good planning, attention must be consistently drawn to refugee women. This will ensure that they are included in mainstream activities, not made peripheral to them or segregated into "women's projects."

Projects that focus on refugee women as a target group are not necessarily mainstreaming/integrating projects.

9. The provision of goods to refugee women, that is, when women are passive recipients of shelter or food aid, is not in itself integrating refugee women. Neither is the provision of services to refugee women and their families necessarily an integrating activity. However, the provision of goods and services to refugee women may be part of a project or programme which mainstreams or integrates women. For example, if women as well as men are consulted on the type of shelter required and the resources available to set up and maintain this shelter, then they have been integrated in the overall project. If women are asked about traditional diet, food preparation, and participate in the distribution and allocation of food, then they have been integrated into this activity.

10. By interpreting UNHCR's policy and operational objectives, the meaning of mainstreaming in a project becomes clearer. For example, projects may:

- identify constraints to women's participation related to project delivery procedures;
- respond to the initiatives of refugee women to improve their own situation;
- make available appropriate technologies that alleviate time and energy demands on refugee women;
- collect statistics indicating the male/female breakdown of the population and prepare baseline case studies in order to identify and to eliminate unintentional discrimination in delivering goods and services and thereby improve planning of future activities.

11. In its broadest sense, a UNHCR programme or project which mainstreams refugee women should attempt to:

- achieve greater involvement of refugee women both as participants and beneficiaries in the social and economic activities of the project;
- increase their status and participation in the community/society;
- provide a catalyst through which they can have access to better employment, education, services and opportunities in their society;
- take into account the particular social relationship between the refugee women and their families.

Underlying these broad definitions is the assumption that refugee women are participating or should participate at all levels of project and programme development, from the initial identification of resources and needs to the evaluation stage.

IV. Organizational Goals

12. The organizational goals of UNHCR regarding refugee women are:
a) to provide protection appropriate to their specific needs;
b) to identify an appropriate durable solution;
c) to provide assistance which will encourage the realization of their full potential and encourage their participation in preparing for the durable solution.

V. Policy Objectives

13. The policy objectives which support the overall organizational goals are
a) to recognize that refugee women represent, either as single women or with their dependents, approximately 80 percent of UNHCR's target population and that programmes can be effective only if they are planned with an adequate understanding of, and consultation with, this group;
b) to ensure that the specific protection needs and the legal rights of refugee women are understood and that adequate measures are taken to respond;
c) to support the efforts of refugee women by recognizing their needs and resources and ensuring their participation in UNHCR's protection and assistance activities;
d) to ensure that the differing needs and resources of refugee women and refugee men are considered in programme activities and, where necessary for cultural or social reasons, undertake special efforts to develop specific activities to ensure women benefit equally from programmes;
e) to place particular emphasis on strategies to protect and assist refugee women, recognizing that becoming a refugee can result not only in an unaccustomed social role such as becoming a single head of household or being without extended family support but also in [a] substantially increased physical workload in building and maintaining the future of the entire family;
f) to ensure that refugee women are equitably represented in resettlement programmes;
g) to encourage staff members of UNHCR and implementing partners to ensure that the integration of refugee women's resources/needs takes place in his/her area of competence.

VI. Operational Objectives

14. Operational objectives provide the basis for the development of appropriate activities and work plans to support implementation of UNHCR's Policy on Refugee Women. These are:

a) to develop mechanisms to ensure that the resources and needs of refugee women are addressed in all stages of programme (protection and assistance) planning, management and evaluation systems;

b) to cooperate with implementing partners, other United Nations institutions, governments and development agencies with a view to benefiting from their experience in women in development activities and, where appropriate, adapting these to UNHCR's specific programming requirements, sharing with them the long-term development implications specific to the situation of refugee women and appropriate methods of incorporating their specific needs and resources into programming activities;

c) to develop communication strategies to call attention to the situation of refugee women of the public, NGOs, other United Nations agencies, donors, and host countries;

d) to develop specific plans for each organizational work unit within UNHCR which will encourage and facilitate consultation and participation of refugee women, and serve as a means of monitoring and maintaining this consultation and participation;

e) to develop training courses for staff of UNHCR and implementing partners to assist them in identifying opportunities for increased participation of refugee women in their areas of competence;

f) to improve the efficiency and effectiveness of protection and assistance programmes by ensuring that adequate attention is given to the needs and resources of all members of the target population;

g) to review and, where necessary, amend existing policies to ensure that they adequately take into consideration the situation and participation of all members of the target population;

h) to improve data collection and needs assessment in order to have a more accurate representation of the refugee population in order to target programmes more effectively to specific social groups;

i) to ensure that there are adequate female field staff to work with refugee women, and, accordingly, to review staffing and recruitment policies to ensure that there is an equitable representation of female staff and that this is adequately reflected in appointments, posting and promotion activities by UNHCR.

j) to review present operational activities and identify means of improving them in order to facilitate participation of refugee women, and achieve a greater understanding of their needs and resources.

References

Del Frate, A. A., U. Zvekic, and J. J. M. van Dijk, eds. 1993. *Understanding Crime—Experiences of Crime and Crime Control.* Acts of the International Conference. Rome, 18–20 November 1992. New York: United Nations.

European Community. N.d. "Report to European Community Foreign Ministers of the Investigative Mission into the Treatment of Muslim Women in the Former Yugoslavia." Denmark: European Community.

Human Rights Watch. 1995. *The Human Rights Watch Global Report on Women's Human Rights.* New York: Human Rights Watch.

————. 1993. *A Modern Form of Slavery: Trafficking of Burmese Women and Girls into Brothels in Thailand.* New York: Human Rights Watch.

Jejeebhoy, Shireen J. 1995. *Women's Education, Autonomy, and Reproductive Behavior: Experience from Developing Countries.* Oxford: Clarendon Press.

Martin, Susan Forbes. 1991. *Refugee Women.* Atlantic Highlands, NJ: Zed Books.

Middle East Watch. 1992. "Punishing the Victim: Rape and Mistreatment of Asian Maids in Kuwait." *A Human Rights Watch Short Report,* Volume 4, Issue 8, August.

Philippines, government of. 1994. "Trafficking of Women in Migration: Perspective from the Philippines." Paper presented at the Eleventh IOM Seminar on Migration: International Response to Trafficking in Migrants and the Safeguarding of Migrant Rights. Geneva, 26–28 October.

Reid, Elizabeth, and Michael Bailey. 1993. "Young Women: Silence, Susceptibility and the HIV Epidemic." United Nations Development Programme, HIV and Development Programme, Issues Paper 12. New York: United Nations Development Programme.

Swiss, Shana, and Joan E. Giller. 1993. "Rape as a Crime of War: Medical Perspective." *Journal of the American Medical Association* 270(5): 612–615.

United Nations. 1996. "The International Migration of Women: An Overview." In *International Migration Policies and the Status of Female Migrants: Proceedings of the United Nations Expert Group Meeting on International Migration Policies and the Status of Female Migration.* San Miniato, Italy, 28–31 March 1990.

————. 1995. *The World's Women 1995: Trends and Statistics.* New York: United Nations.

————. 1994a. *AIDS and the Demography of Africa.* New York: United Nations.

————. 1994b. *World Contraceptive Use.* Wall chart. New York: United Nations.

————. 1992a. *Age Patterns of Fertility 1990–1995.* 1992 revision. Data base on diskettes.

————. 1992b. *Demographic Yearbook 1992.* New York: United Nations.

————. 1992c. "Final Report of the Commission of Experts Established

Pursuant to Security Council Resolution 780." New York: United Nations.

———. 1992d. *The Sex and Age Distribution of the World Populations.* 1992 revision. New York: United Nations.

———. 1992e. *Women's Indicators and Statistics Database* (Wistat). Version 3, CD-ROM.

———. 1989. *Violence against Women in the Family.* New York: United Nations.

———. 1985. "Some Aspects of Family Planning Programmes and Fertility in Selected ECA Member States." *African Population Study Series,* No. 9. New York: United Nations.

United Nations High Commissioner for Refugees. 1994. "Populations of Concern to UNHCR: A Statistical Review, 1993." Report prepared by the Food and Statistical Unit, Division of Programmes and Operational Support, May.

World Health Organization. 1994. "The HIV-AIDS Pandemic: 1994 Overview." Geneva: World Health Organization.

———. 1993. "Coverage of Maternity Care: Tabulation of Available Information." 3d ed. Geneva: World Health Organization.

———. 1991. "Maternal Mortality: Ratios and Rates, a Tabulation of Available Information." 3d ed. Geneva: World Health Organization.

———. 1989. "Youth and Reproductive Health." In *The Health of Youth: Facts for Action,* No. 6. Geneva: World Health Organization.

Directory of Organizations 5

The total number of nongovernmental organizations (NGOs) throughout the Third World is estimated to be in the hundreds of thousands (Fisher 1993). Some sources estimate that women's and women-related organizations worldwide number in the tens of thousands. NGOs are organizations that provide development, relief, education, and advocacy services in countries throughout the world. Two types of NGOs are grassroots support organizations (GRSOs) and grassroots organizations (GROs). GRSOs, usually national or regional in focus, are groups that provide development assistance and international funding to GROs at the local level. Fisher (1993) estimates that there are between 30,000 and 35,000 active GRSOs in the Third World, many of them providing services to women.

This chapter describes organizations, listed alphabetically, that are involved in working with women in the Third World. Some of these groups operate at the international or regional level, some are national in scope, and some provide services in local communities. Several governments have established women's bureaus to serve the particular needs of women. The organizations mentioned here are but a small part of the total number of organizations working on behalf of women, including women in developing countries.

Information contained in this chapter focuses on international organizations, with several regional, national, and local organizations included as a sample of the types of services provided, which include health, welfare, domestic violence, reproductive rights, AIDS, divorce, education, and training. Women's professional and business associations and sports associations are found throughout the world. Other groups provide information on project design, teaching aids, educational sources, health services, financial services, and other information that helps women participate fully in their families, communities, and national activities. References at the end of the chapter include resources where information on additional programs can be found.

African Centre for Women
c/o Economic Commission for Africa
P.O. Box 3001
Addis Ababa, Ethiopia
447000, 447200

Formerly known as the African Training and Research Centre for Women, the African Centre for Women was the first woman's center established as an integral component of a United Nations institution. The center offers a variety of services, including public awareness activities, research, and networking. Publications include *Women and Development: An Annotated Bibliography* (1978).

African Women's Task Force (FEMNET)
Africa Women's Development and Communications Network
P.O. Box 54562
Nairobi, Kenya
(254) 2-15441555

As a multinational organization, the primary purpose of the African Women's Task Force is to increase public awareness concerning the needs of African women. The task force offers a wide range of information services and provides contacts to help women in Africa improve their lives and status.

Alan Guttmacher Institute
120 Wall Street
New York, NY 10005 USA

(212) 248-1111
Fax: (212) 248-1951
e-mail: info@agi-usa.org

The Alan Guttmacher Institute (AGI) works to protect and expand the reproductive choices of all women and men, by ensuring that everyone has access to information and services necessary to make informed decisions concerning sexual activity, reproduction, and family formation. The program goals are to encourage the prevention of unwanted pregnancies; guarantee every woman's freedom to terminate an unwanted pregnancy; protect reproductive capacity and encourage wanted pregnancies; promote women's health before, during, and after pregnancy and childbirth; and promote the birth of healthy babies. Publications include *Today's Adolescents, Tomorrow's Parents: A Portrait of the Americas* and *Clandestine Abortion: A Latin American Reality.*

Arab Women's Solidarity Association
25 Murad Street
Giza 12211, Egypt
(20) 2-5723976
Fax: (20) 2-5738350

Founded in 1982 by Egypt's Dr. Nawal el Saadawi, the Arab Women's Solidarity Association (AWSA) is a multinational organization that focuses on improving the conditions for women in Arab countries. The association works to promote the interests of Arab women and to empower them to raise their consciousness, coordinates activities, and disseminates information. AWSA organizes conferences that examine the status and needs of women throughout the Arab world. Research and educational programs are organized and the association produces materials by and for women in the fields of science, culture, art, and literature. AWSA also works to increase literacy rates throughout the region.

Asia Pacific Forum on Women, Law, and Development
P.O. Box 12224
50770 Kuala Lumpur, Malaysia
(60) 3-2550648
Fax: (60) 2541371
Telex: MA 31655 MPS

As a multinational organization, the Asia Pacific Forum on Women, Law, and Development (APWLD) is composed of women's activists, lawyers, human rights activists, and other interested individuals. APWLD's major emphasis is on enabling women in the Asia Pacific region to use the law effectively to help empower them in their struggles for justice and equality. Women's development in family, society, economics, politics, and national arenas are promoted. The organization encourages the exchange of information among members. It also advocates for basic human rights and lobbies Asian-Pacific governments to ratify the United Nations Convention on the Elimination of All Forms of Discrimination against Women.

Asia Women's Institute
Association of Kinnaird College for Women
93 Jail Road
Lahore, Pakistan
(92) 42-487165
Cable: AWINSTI

The Asia Women's Institute has a multinational focus. Its members include Christian universities and colleges that offer baccalaureate degrees and women's studies programs. Staff members assist Asian women in leading fuller lives and gaining self-confidence by encouraging the development of women and their communities through research, social action, and communication. Continuing education programs and career services for women are offered. Research is conducted on issues of concern to women.

Asian Women's Human Rights Council
P.O. Box 190
Manila 1099, Philippines
(63) 2-9246381
Fax: (63) 2-9246406

Regional Secretariat:
2124 1st A Cross
16 Main H.A.L. II Stage
Bangalore 660008, India
(91) 80-527-8628

Members of the Asian Women's Human Rights Council, a multinational organization, are female lawyers and feminist activists who are actively involved in promoting and defending basic human rights and women's rights. The council encourages the study of human rights and the cooperation and solidarity between women's groups and individuals advocating human rights recognition. Council staff members compile information on national policies throughout Asia that influence the provision of human rights for all citizens.

Asian-Pacific Resource and Research Centre for Women
Block F, 2d Floor
Anjung Felda, Jalan Maktab
54000 Kuala Lumpur, Malaysia
(602) 292-9913
Fax: (602) 292-9958
e-mail: arrow@po.jaring.my

The Asian-Pacific Resource and Research Centre for Women researches and analyzes women's issues and provides advice to governmental and legislative organizations on women's issues. The organization researches and evaluates media coverage of women's health issues and conducts programs to increase public awareness of population growth and reproductive health. Counseling services on women's development are provided. Staff members work to encourage and promote networking activities among women and women's organizations. They operate a database on women and health, conduct bibliographic searches, and provide other information and online services.

Associated Country Women of the World
(Union Mondiale des Femmes Rurales)
Vincent House
Vincent Square
London SW1P 2NB, England
(44) 171-8348635
Fax: (44) 171-2336205

As an organization with affiliates in 70 countries throughout the world, the Associated Country Women of the World (ACWW) focuses activities on rural areas and the problems that rural women face worldwide. Staff members work to promote friendly relations among member organizations and provide assistance in the economic, social, and cultural development of their members and countries. ACWW maintains consultative status with the United Nations Economic and Social Council (ECOSOC). Leadership training courses, nutrition education, and functional literacy programs are offered. The organization also serves as an information clearinghouse. Publications include *The Countrywoman*, a quarterly magazine.

Association for the Advancement of Women in Africa
P.O. Box 28083
Kitwe, Zambia

The Association for the Advancement of Women in Africa focuses activities on ways to enhance the social and economic status of women in Africa, through public awareness campaigns, networking, and support groups.

Association of African Women for Research and Development
BP 3304
Dakar, Senegal
(221) 259823
Fax: (221) 241289
Telex: 61339 CODES SG

The Association of African Women for Research and Development was founded in 1979 as a multinational association to encourage the study of women and women's issues throughout Africa. Members include African women in 42 countries who work in the field of social science, national research groups, and researchers and research groups outside of Africa. The association conducts research on issues relevant to women in developing nations, assists members by identifying necessary resources, and provides networking opportunities for African women researchers. Issues of major concern include labor, demographic, educational, political, professional, and ideological issues. The status and condition of women in developing countries is examined. The association sponsors seminars, training programs, and specialized research workshops, including the Working Group on Women and Reproduction in Africa.

AVSC International
79 Madison Avenue
New York, NY 10016 USA
(212) 561-8000
Fax: (212) 779-9439
e-mail: info@avsc.org
Internet: http://www.igc.apc.org/avsc/

AVSC International works to provide access to family-planning services to women and men throughout the world. The program specializes in family-planning services provided in clinics and hospitals and works with government agencies, family-planning organizations, and health care professionals in over 60 countries to help develop, improve, and expand these services. Economic and technical aid is provided to local programs, training programs are supported, and staff members work with local health care providers to develop and implement service-delivery guidelines and to improve the quality of services. AVSC works globally to address major policy issues on both local and international levels and advocates for medical safety and informed choice and conducts clinical and programmatic research to improve the effectiveness of services. State-of-the-art information and research is provided to field programs and is published by AVSC. Regional offices are located in Bangkok, Thailand; Nairobi, Kenya; and Bogota, Colombia. Country office representatives are located in Bangladesh, the Dominican Republic, Egypt, Ghana, India, Indonesia, Mexico, Nepal, Nigeria, Pakistan, Peru, the Philippines, Russia, Turkey, and Yemen. Publications include *Family Planning Counseling: A Curriculum Prototype,* which is designed to improve counseling skills among health and family-planning workers; *Safe and Voluntary Surgical Contraception: Guidelines for Service Programs,* and *Quality Management for Family Planning Services: Practical Experience from Africa.*

Bangladesh Women's Health Coalition
113 46A Road 6A
D.R.A.
1209 Dhaka, Bangladesh
880 2 811134
Fax: 880 2 817969

The Bangladesh Women's Health Coalition began in 1980 as a single-purpose clinic that offered safe, legal menstrual regulation for low-income women; contraceptive and counseling services were added soon after opening for business.

Bina Swadaya
Jalan Gunung Sahari III/7
P.O. Box 1456
Jakarta Pusat 10610, Indonesia
(62-21) 420-4402
Fax: (62-21) 4201-8412

A well-known NGO, Bina Swadaya has been in operation for over 25 years. The program helps microentrepreneurs gain access to available resources in order to build community self-reliance. It supports approximately 700 workers and hundreds of self-help groups. Working in rural industries, such as agriculture, forestry, and area development, Bina Swadaya focuses on integrated area development, education and training, capital development, book publication, agribusiness development, and alternative tourism. Bina Swadaya promotes small enterprise development by providing training for female staff members of area NGOs, linking commercial banks and women's self-help groups to provide credit without collateral, promoting female leaders to operate microfinance institutions, and promoting social protection plans for women who are home-based workers.

Center for Women's Global Leadership
Douglass College, Rutgers University
27 Clifton Avenue
New Brunswick, NJ 08903 USA
(908) 932-8782
Fax: (908) 932-1180
e-mail: cwgl@igc.apc.org

The Center for Women's Global Leadership examines the ways in which gender affects leadership and power as well as the conduct of public policy throughout the world. The center's three major goals are building international linkages among local leaders who are women, promoting visibility of women in the making of public policy worldwide, and increasing women's participation in national and international governing bodies and processes. Abuses of women's human rights are watched, and the center works to expand understanding and implementation of international human rights policy. Working with local organizations and governments, the center holds governments accountable for ensuring the protection of women and their rights. Two-week intensive leadership institutes are held each year for women at grassroots and national levels to share experiences and work toward common goals. Programs are sponsored to bring women together to plan and coordinate specific strategies concerning women's rights. An annual global campaign, 16 Days of Activism against Gender Violence, highlights gender-based violence. Global tribunals, hearings, and conferences are conducted on women's human rights. Publications include *From Vienna to Beijing: The Global Tribunal on Ac-*

countability for Women's Human Rights, which focuses on 22 testimonies presented at the tribunal addressing women's human rights violations, *Bringing Women's Human Rights Home: Using Beijing Commitments to End Violence against Women,* and a quarterly newsletter.

Center for Women's Resources
2d Floor, Mar Santos Building
43 Roces Avenue
Quezon City, Philippines
632-99 27 55

Founded in 1982, the Center for Women's Resources promotes the full participation of Filipino women in the movement to achieve their full liberation. In collaboration with institutions and community and volunteer groups, the center responds to specific needs of women from different sectors of society. Education and training workshops are organized, research is conducted, and journals and articles on current issues are published. It is affiliated with the General Assembly Binding Women for Reforms, Equality, Leadership, and Action (GABRIELA) (see below). A public library is maintained and audio-visual materials are produced.

Centre for Development and Population Activities
1717 Massachusetts Avenue NW
Suite 2000
Washington, DC 20036 USA
(202) 667-1142
Fax: (202) 332-4496
e-mail: email@cedpa.org

Regional offices:

CEDPA/New Delhi
4/2 Shanti Niketan
New Delhi, India
011-91-11-672841
Fax: 011-91-11-688-5850

CEDPA/Nepal Country Office
GPO Box 5006
Bhatbotani, Kathmandu, Nepal
011-977-1-411-458
Fax: 011-977-1-410-831

CEDPA/Nairobi
P.O. Box 14996
Nairobi, Kenya
011-254-2-740-457
Fax: 011-254-2-740-382

CEDPA/Romania
St. Av Theodor Iliescu, nr 52
Ap 1 Sector 1
Bucharest, Romania
(40) 1-212-0415
Fax: (40) 1-212-2937

As an international nonprofit organization, the Centre for Development and Population Activities (CEDPA), works to empower women to take charge of their lives. Founded in 1975, CEDPA encourages positive change through partnership projects, training, and advocacy. Development strategies that CEDPA focuses on include supporting community-based reproductive health programs, training women leaders, advocating for women and girls, and promoting gender equity in development activities. Leadership training sessions, conducted in Washington, D.C., in English, French, Spanish, Arabic, and Russian, include women in management, institution building, youth leadership, and women's reproductive health. Partner organizations offer family planning and reproductive health services. In the Better Life Options for Girls and Young Women program, partner organizations conduct national and international advocacy to increase girls' access to education and health care. In health education, CEDPA provides education about sexually transmitted diseases, water and sanitation improvement, the prevention and treatment of diarrhea, training for maternal and child health workers, family planning, and health and nutrition education for young girls. Technical assistance is offered in strategic planning, management training, service delivery, curriculum design, training of trainers, and program design, management, and evaluation. Publications include a training manual series, a working papers series, and a quarterly newsletter.

Centre for Social Development and Humanitarian Affairs
Division for the Advancement of Women
United Nations Office at Vienna
Postfach 500
A-1400 Vienna, Austria
(43) 1-211315284
Fax: (43) 1-237495

The Centre for Social Development and Humanitarian Affairs monitors and evaluates advances in women's struggle for equality throughout the world. In an effort to eliminate all types of discrimination against women, the center conducts research on women's economic, social, and educational status, prepares reports, and recommends action that groups can take on women's issues. Bibliographic search services are provided in French, Spanish, and English. Publications include *Women 2000* (a magazine in French, Spanish, and English); *World Survey on the Role of*

Women in Development, and *National Machinery for the Advancement of Women: United Nations and UN Organizations Focal Points for the Advancement of Women.*

Change-International Reports: Women and Society
P.O. Box 824
London SEZ4 9JS, England
(44) 71-2776187

Change-International Reports: Women and Society is an international organization that conducts research and publishes reports concerning the status of women throughout the world. The program works to show that the suppression of women negatively affects economic and political processes in society. The organization believes that nongovernmental organizations should represent the need for change; reports should be written by women natives of the relevant country; and even though real economic inequalities exist, developed and developing countries should not be separated, in order to prevent patronizing attitudes. Activities include public education concerning the inequalities women experience through disseminating information, encouraging an international exchange of information, promoting recognition of women's human rights, and publishing abuses by governments, businesses, or individuals. The program contributes to campaigns, networks, and conferences throughout the world, offers gender training, and trains personnel in lobbying and advocacy activities. The staff maintains a reference library that is open to the public. Publications include *Economic Development and Women's Place: Women in Singapore, When Will Democracy Include Women?* and *Providence and Prostitution: Image and Reality for Women in Buddhist Thailand.*

Commission on the Status of Women
United Nations Vienna International Centre
Postfach 500
A-1400 Vienna, Austria
(43) 1-211315284
Fax: (43) 1-232156
Cable: UNATIONS VIENNA

Division for the Advancement of Women
United Nations, Room DC2-1220
P.O. Box 20

New York, NY 10017 USA
(212) 963-5086
Fax: (212) 963-3463

The Commission on the Status of Women (CSW) has 45 members and was established by the Economic and Social Council of the United Nations. Members are representatives from United Nations member countries. The commission promotes women's rights in political, economic, civil, social, and educational fields, encourages cooperation between organizations seeking to advance the status of women, and advises the United Nations and member states on situations requiring immediate attention.

Committee for Asian Women
57 Peking Road, 4th Floor
Kowloon, Hong Kong
(852) 72326150
Fax: (852) 3699895

The Committee for Asian Women works to promote the interests of women workers throughout Asia and to protect the rights of women. The committee provides financial support to needy local women's organizations. Educational training and workshops are organized. Research is conducted concerning the impact of industrial restructuring on women workers. The committee publishes in English the *Asian Women Workers Newsletter*.

Development Alternatives with Women for a New Era
Ain O Salish Kendra
55 Inner Circular Road
Shantinagar
Dacca, Bangladesh
880 2 835851
Fax: 880 2 833638

University of South Pacific
School of Social and Economic Development
Department of History and Politics
P.O. Box 1168
Suva, Fiji

Asia and Pacific Development Centre
Pesiaran Duta
P.O. Box 12224
50770 Kuala Lumpur, Malaysia

c/o IUPERJ
Rua da Matriz
82 Botafogo
22260 Rio de Janeiro, RJ, Brazil
55 21 2461830

Development Alternatives with Women for a New Era (DAWN) seeks to promote the positive image of women and the role of women in economic development. The program works to reduce the negative impact of development activities on women and the environment, conducts research, training, and advocacy programs to eliminate inequalities of gender, class, and race, and encourages and promotes communication and networking among women's movements. Other activities include protecting and defending women's reproductive rights.

Equality Now
P.O. Box 20646
Columbus Circle Station
New York, NY 10023 USA
(212) 586-0906
Fax: (212) 586-1611

Equality Now is an international human rights group working for the protection and promotion of women's rights. By adapting the research, organizational, and action techniques of the mainstream international human rights community, Equality Now addresses human rights issues of rape, trafficking in women, domestic violence, female infanticide, genital mutilation, reproductive rights, gender discrimination, political representation, sexual harassment, and pornography. A network of activists gathers information about specific abuses and ongoing violations throughout the world; appropriate actions and strategies are established in collaboration with local experts and are rapidly publicized and implemented through the network.

Facultad Latinoamericana de Ciencias Sociales—
Area de la Mujer
Iglesia Santa Teresita
Apartado 5429-1000
San Jose, Costa Rica
(506) 570533
Fax: (506) 215671
Telex: 2846 FLACSOCR

As a multinational organization, Facultad Latinoamericana de Ciencias Sociales—Area de la Mujer (FLACSO) conducts advocacy activities to make public and private institutes aware of women's problems and issues. The organization develops a wide variety of activities by and for women based on an examination and analysis of their needs. Surveys of organizations working with women and demographic studies of women are conducted and projects are organized concerning reproductive health, nutrition, rural women, and public policy. The program operates the Asociacion Andar to train women leaders throughout the region.

Family Care International
588 Broadway, 503
New York, NY 10012 USA
(212) 941-5300
Fax: (212) 941-5563
Telex: 210 474 FAMCAR UR
e-mail: fci@chelsea.ios.com

Africa Regional Office:
P.O. Box 45763
Nairobi, Kenya
(254-2) 446615
e-mail: fcinbi@arso.gn.apc.org

Family Care International (FCI) is a private, nonprofit organization dedicated to improving women's sexual and reproductive health in developing countries. Working with governments and NGOs, FCI explores the many factors that lead to poor reproductive health and develops collaborative programs. FCI develops tools and provides assistance to local agencies to design community-level programs based on women's needs and realities, with an emphasis on comprehensive care, high-quality services and counseling, education to help women take action on improving their health, and women's participation in program development and implementation. FCI has worked directly with governments and local organizations in many countries to develop national plans, model programs, and essential tools to address reproductive health needs. Publications include several resource documents for use in Africa including *Healthy Women, Healthy Mothers: An Information Guide* and *Getting the Message Out: Designing an Information Campaign on Women's Health.*

Family Planning International Assistance
Planned Parenthood Federation of America
810 Seventh Avenue
New York, NY 10019 USA
(212) 541-7800
Fax: (212) 247-6274
e-mail: fpia@ppfa.org

As the international service arm of Planned Parenthood, the Family Planning International Assistance (FPIA) program addresses the reproductive health needs of people around the world. Founded in 1971, FPIA has developed or assisted over 600 programs in over 70 countries. The program attempts to help hard-to-reach people in hard-to-reach places; the major goals include supporting reproductive health services in areas of unmet need, establishing new reproductive health service models, upgrading existing reproductive health services, supporting reproductive rights activities, and fostering continuation of service following the phaseout of FPIA support. Program support is provided through financial assistance for project operations, contraceptives and health-related supplies and materials, and technical assistance.

Federation of Asian Women's Associations
Centro Escolar University
Mendiola
Manila
Metro Manila, Philippines

This multinational program promotes awareness of women's issues and sponsors a variety of educational and research programs.

Feminist Center for Information and Action
(Centro Feminista de Informacion y Accion)
P.O. Box 5355
San Jose 1000, Costa Rica
(506) 225860
Fax: (506) 346875

The Feminist Center for Information and Action (CEFEMINA) has an international emphasis and focuses on improving the standard of living for women, eliminating obstacles to women's development, and increasing public awareness of women's issues.

The center provides education and training in home construction and organizes groups of women who design, plan, and construct new communities. Women are trained in health, legal, and economic issues. Support and assistance are provided to women who have been abused. Legal professionals are trained to understand the problems facing women today. Staff members assess and pursue women's legal cases. Environmental reconstruction and preservation projects are encouraged. The program promotes and organizes sports and other activities for women. Major issues concerning women are monitored, including housing, baby food, medical supplies, sexually transmitted diseases, and legal and governmental programs designed to help women. Efforts are coordinated with other international women's organizations.

Feminist International Radio Endeavor
P.O. Box 88
Santa Ana, Costa Rica
(506) 249-18-21

Founded in 1991, Feminist International Radio Endeavor (FIRE) is a women's radio project that broadcasts a two-hour daily program on the shortwave radio station Radio for Peace International in Costa Rica that is heard in over 100 countries throughout the world. One hour of the broadcast is in Spanish, the other in English. The project was inspired by the Women's Peace Tent in Nairobi in 1985. FIRE seeks to create a communications channel on shortwave where women's voices are heard by people throughout the world. The daily shows focus on diverse themes from a gender perspective, including structural adjustment, women's human rights, the environment, racism, militarism, sexuality, education, art, and culture.

50 Years Is Enough Campaign
1025 Vermont Avenue NW, Suite 300
Washington, DC 20005 USA
(202) 463-2265
Fax: (202) 879-3186
e-mail: wb50years@igc.apc.org

The 50 Years Is Enough Campaign was started in 1994 by a coalition of 34 NGOs seeking to draw attention to the development model promoted by the World Bank and the International Monetary Fund (IMF), a model that this organization feels has contributed to growing poverty and environmental degradation around the world. More than 160 U.S. organizations have joined the campaign, along with more than 170 NGOs from 50 countries. Most members are social, religious, development, student, or environmental organizations. A steering committee consists of representatives of active caucuses and regional coalitions; all caucuses and regional coalitions are required to recruit and involve women's organizations and to encourage member organizations to assign persons with a gendered perspective to leadership positions within the group. A guiding principle of the campaign is that affected women and men should participate fully in the design, implementation, monitoring, and evaluation of all aspects of World Bank and IMF projects, policies, and programs. The campaign believes that the World Bank and IMF must address the issue of gender and gender bias in their work, that many of the decisions of these institutions often affect women and men in different ways, and that women have been more negatively impacted than men in these decisions. The campaign works to change these attitudes of the World Bank and IMF.

FINCA International
1101 14th Street NW, 11th Floor
Washington, DC 20005 USA
(202) 682-1510
Fax: (202) 682-1535
e-mail: 76215.1034@compuserve.com

Founded in 1984, FINCA International is a nonprofit organization with a network of 14 affiliated agencies in 12 countries. The program's goal is to support the economic and human development of families who are trapped in severe poverty. Self-employment loans of between $50 and $300 are provided to women with no collateral required and a reasonable interest rate; women are also offered a safe and profitable place to accumulate savings, a plan to develop $300 of their own working capital within three years, and group support for personal empowerment. Program affiliates currently provide services to over 42,000 borrowers through more than 1,600 village banks.

General Arab Women Federation
Hay al-Maghreb
Mahaela 304
Baghdad, Iraq
(964) 1-4227117

This organization unites the activities of national women's federations in Arab countries. It lobbies for the liberation of occupied Arab territories, the liberation of Palestine, the establishment of Arab unity, the development of Arab society, and the defeat of colonialism throughout the area, with a specific focus on the status of Arab women. Program activities include attempting to unify the Arab women's movement throughout the world; reinforcing solidarity among Arab women; and encouraging and explaining the important role of Arab women in the growth of their society. Staff members work to make Arab women aware of their rights and how to assert them and they attempt to integrate women into Arab society. Educational opportunities are provided and include courses and training for governmental responsibilities. The program coordinates social and health services such as family planning and the care of children, the elderly, and the disabled, sponsors research, maintains biographical archives, compiles statistics, and operates placement services. Publications include *Arab Women*, a semiannual journal.

General Assembly Binding Women for Reforms, Equality, Leadership, and Action
35 Scout Delgado
Roxas District
Quezon City, Philippines
632-998034

Founded in 1984 in the Philippines, the General Assembly Binding Women for Reforms, Equality, Leadership, and Action (GABRIELA) is a progressive and nationalist organization with over 100 institutions, organizations, and programs that represent approximately 30,000 women. Its purpose is to mobilize all women to work for a just, equal, and democratic society. Activities include income-generating and community development programs; campaigning and lobbying for women's rights and services, including maternal health care facilities, maternity benefits, contraception, and abortion rights; vocational training; and educational programs. Staff members conduct feminist research and campaigns are organized to protest against sexual harassment and gender-based discrimination, prostitution, female boxing, militarization, and the presence of military bases.

Global Fund for Women
425 Sherman Avenue, Suite 300

Palo Alto, CA 94306-1823 USA
(415) 853-8305
Fax: (415) 328-0384
e-mail: gfw@igc.apc.org

The Global Fund for Women was founded in 1987 and focuses worldwide on improving the lives of women by listening to the concerns of women's groups, providing women's groups with financial and other resources, developing increased support for women's efforts, developing and strengthening connections among women's groups, and increasing awareness of women's needs and strengths. The fund is committed to providing flexible and timely support to women's groups throughout the world that focus on emerging, controversial, or difficult issues. Grants are provided to organizations that work for female human rights, women's access to communications and the media, and the economic autonomy of women. The staff also assists groups throughout the world that want to establish philanthropic organizations to benefit women. Publications include *A Woman's Fundraising Handbook, The United Nations Fourth World Conference on Women and Non-Governmental Forum,* and *Poverty, Women's Rights, and the Global Economy.*

Grameen Bank
Mirpur Two
Dhaka 1216, Bangladesh
(880-2) 801691
Fax: (880-2) 803559

Founded in 1976, the Grameen Bank provides access to credit to the landless poor in rural Bangladesh. One of the best-known banks that provide small loans to women entrepreneurs, by 1994 the bank had distributed $385 million in loans, averaging slightly over $180 per loan, primarily to poor women. By 1995, over $1,435 million in loans had been distributed. Using peer support and an incremental loan structure as incentives for repayment, Grameen Bank has proven that the poor can be good credit risks and that collateral is not needed to secure loans. The bank has over 1,000 branch offices that serve 35,000 villages and 2,000,000 customers; 94 percent of the customers are women. This approach has been replicated in over 55 countries throughout the world, including Cambodia, China, India, Malaysia, Sri Lanka, and the United States.

Grassroots Organizations Operating Together in Sisterhood
c/o Ms. Jaya Arunachalam
55 Bhimsena Garden Road
Madras 600 004, India
91 44 4992853
Fax: 91 44 4992853

Founded in 1978, Grassroots Organizations Operating Together in Sisterhood (GROOTS) promotes the social and financial independence of women in India by encouraging small enterprise development. The program shows women how to influence public policy through collective action, advances the legal rights and social standing of women, and opposes traditional definitions of dowry, rape, and divorce. GROOTS organizes health care projects to provide members with health care, nutrition education, and family planning assistance; encourages women to learn marketable skills in the health care field; and distributes information about current health care programs. The program encourages and helps women gain economic independence through a credit program that provides low-interest loans to neighborhood groups of women. Publications include *Towards Sustainable Development; Empowerment of Poor Women* and *Working Women's Forum: A Counter-Culture by Poor Women.*

Habitat International Coalition—Women and Shelter Network
c/o Mazingira International
P.O. Box 14564
Nairobi, Kenya
(254) 2-443219
Fax: (254) 2-444643

The Women and Shelter Network of the Habitat International Coalition consists of individuals and NGOs who work to provide adequate shelter for women in developing regions of Africa. The network provides a forum for the exchange of information on housing issues for women throughout the world. Research is conducted on the connections between housing and gender issues.

Institute for Women's Studies in the Arab World
Beirut University College
P.O. Box 13-5053
Beirut, Lebanon

961 867618
Telex: BUC 23389 LE

Organized in 1973, the Institute for Women's Studies in the Arab World encourages and evaluates research on the history, status, and rights of women in the Arab world. The institute promotes a better understanding of Arab women by providing education and assistance to them. Training projects include an in-service training for social work, basic living skills for illiterate and semi-literate women, and preschool teachers' training. A network of women's organizations, universities, and research centers has been developed for the exchange of information.

Inter-African Committee on Traditional Practices Affecting the Health of Women and Children
P.O. Box 30001
Addis Ababa, Ethiopia

The Inter-African Committee on Traditional Practices Affecting the Health of Women and Children, a multinational organization, focuses on eliminating the practice of female genital mutilation through educational programs and informational seminars, lobbying activities encouraging government agencies to prohibit this practice, research, and information provided to television and radio stations for broadcast.

Inter-American Commission of Women
Organization of American States
1889 F Street NW, Suite 880
Washington, DC 20006 USA
(202) 458-6084
Fax: (202) 458-6094

Established in 1928, the Inter-American Commission of Women (CIM) is a specialized agency of the Organization of American States (OAS). CIM was the first official intergovernmental agency created specifically to ensure the civil and political rights of women in the Americas. The functions of the commission include formulating strategies that enable the role of men and women in society to be seen as that of two beings equally responsible for the face of humanity; analyzing the problems of women of the Americas; promoting, mobilizing, training, and organizing women for continuing and effective participation in the process of development; and promoting access of all women to education. A limited seed fund is available to help develop or improve small projects in member countries. The group sponsors activities that focus on leadership training to enable women to enter politics, legislative reform concerning equal rights, appropriate technologies, training to establish small businesses, training in nontraditional skills, the role of women in development, and women in prisons. Publications include *Strategic Plan of Action of the Inter-American Commission of Women (CIM)*, a document presented at the Fourth World Conference on Women in Beijing, China, in 1995.

International Alliance of Women
(AIF) (Alliance Internationale des Femmes)
1 Lycavittou Street
GR-106 72 Athens, Greece
(30) 1-3626111
Fax: (30) 1-3622454

Members of the International Alliance of Women include women's organizations and individuals in 85 countries. The program advocates for reforms that are necessary to establish a real equality of liberties, status, and opportunities between men and women and urges women to use their rights and influence in public life to ensure that the status of every individual shall be based on the respect for human personality and not on sex, race, or creed. Staff members promote the exchange of views and experiences. Seminars, conferences, workshops, and study tours are conducted with special emphasis on developing countries. Publications include *International Women's News Journal* (in English and French), a quarterly journal.

International Center for Research on Women
1717 Massachusetts Avenue NW
Suite 302
Washington, DC 20036 USA
(202) 797-0007
Fax: (202) 797-0020
e-mail: icrw@igc.apc.org

The International Center for Research on Women (ICRW) is a private, nonprofit organization focusing on promoting social and economic development with the full participation of women. Working with policymakers, practitioners, and researchers throughout Africa, Asia, and Latin America, ICRW helps formulate policy and action concerning the economic, social, and health status of women in developing countries. Women's critical contributions to development are emphasized, including their dual productive and reproductive roles. The program focuses on economic policies, family and household structure, health and nutrition, agriculture, and the environment. Services provided include policy-oriented research, program support and analysis services, and communications forums. Policy research focuses on economic policies, family structure, health and nutrition, and the environment. The communications program consists of discussion forums, a conference center in Washington, D.C., a resource center that maintains over 15,000 published and unpublished materials on women in development, and a series of publications. Publications include *Investing in Women; Women, Poverty and Environment in Latin America;* and *Integrating Women into Development Programs: A Guide for Latin America and the Caribbean.*

International Confederation of Midwives
(CISF) (Confederation Internationale des Sages-Femmes)
10 Barley Mow Passage
Chiswick
London W4 4PH, England
(44) 81-9946477
Fax: (44) 81-9941533

The membership of the International Confederation of Midwives consists of national midwives' associations in 47 countries. The program advocates for the improvement of standards of care provided to mothers, babies, and the family. Advocacy activities promote midwifery education and the dissemination of information about the art and science of midwifery. Workshops and seminars on midwifery and safe motherhood are provided.

International Council for Women
(CIF) (Conseil International des Femmes)
13, rue Caumartin
F-75009 Paris, France
(33) 1-47421940
Fax: (33) 1-42662623

Members of the International Council for Women include national councils of women composed of national and local women's organizations. The council encourages consultation among women on actions necessary to promote human welfare. Women are provided with information concerning their rights and their civic, social, and political responsibilities. The council advocates for the equal legal status of women and for the removal of all restrictions on women and supports international peace and arbitration. Areas of interest include the advancement of women, education, human rights, literacy, and the role of women in economic and social development. The council maintains consultative status with the Economic and Social Council of the United Nations, United Nations Educational, Scientific and Cultural Organization, United Nations Children's Fund, the World Health Organization, and the Council of Europe.

International Federation for Family Health
(Federasi Keschatan Keluarga Internasional)
Jalan Makmur 24
Bandung, Indonesia
(62) 22-52902
Cable: IFFH BANDUNG

Members of the International Federation for Family Health include national fertility research programs that evaluate family planning projects designed to improve the quality of life in the Third World. The primary objectives are to promote family health care, to exchange ideas, and to share problems and experiences resulting from project activities within member countries. The organization works to reduce maternal and perinatal mortality and to encourage acceptance of family planning counseling.

International Planned Parenthood Federation
(Federation Internationale pour la Planification Familiale)
Regent's College
Inner Circle
Regent's Park
London NW1 4NS, England
(44) 71-4860741
Fax: (44) 71-4877950
Cable: IPEPEE G LONDON

African Regional Office:
P.O. Box 30234
Nairobi, Kenya
(254) 2-720280
Fax: (254) 2-726596

Telex: 22703 INFED
Cable: INFED NAIROBI

The International Planned Parenthood Federation (IPPF) helps to initiate and support family planning services throughout the world and increase government and public awareness of the population problems of local communities throughout the world. Planned Parenthood promotes effective family planning services and is concerned about the efficacy and safety of various methods of contraception. Program goals include the creation of strong volunteer participation, promotion of family planning as a basic human right, improvement of family planning services, meeting the needs of young people, improvement in the status of women, increasing male involvement in family planning, development of human financial and material resources, stimulation of research on subjects related to human fertility and dissemination of the findings of such research, and the development of training programs for the federation's professional workers. Programs concentrate on family life, population, and sex education. Workshops and seminars are sponsored. Publications include *AIDS Watch* (in English and French), a quarterly newsletter; *Earthwatch/Eco-Monde* (in English and French), a quarterly magazine; and *IPPF Directory of Contraceptives: Research in Reproduction*, a quarterly magazine.

**International Research and Training Institute
for the Advancement of Women**
Calle Cesar Nicolas Penson 102-A
Apartado Postal 21747
Santo Domingo, Dominican Republic
(809) 685-2111
Fax: (809) 685-2117

Liaison Office:
Room DC1-1106
One United Nations Plaza
New York, NY 10017 USA
(212) 963-5684
Fax: (212) 963-2978

The International Research and Training Institute for the Advancement of Women (INSTRAW) is an autonomous institute within the framework of the United Nations. INSTRAW undertakes research, training, and information activities in order to develop new methods for enhancing women's contribution to development as well as their empowerment and for making the overall development process more attuned to the needs and concerns of women. Major activities are focused on four major areas: (1) economic and political empowerment of women; (2) women, the environment, and sustainable development; (3) women, communications, and media; and (4) statistics and indicators on gender issues. INSTRAW works closely with other UN agencies, governments, and NGOs. Publications include research studies and training materials from its own work programs as well as other public information materials, and *INSTRAW News,* a twice yearly newsletter published in English, French, and Spanish.

International Wages for Housework Campaign
King's Cross Women's Centre
71 Tonbridge Street
London WC1H 9DZ, England
(44) 71-8377509
Fax: (44) 71-8334817

The International Wages for Housework Campaign (IWFHC) is an international network of women in developing and industrialized countries who campaign for compensation for housework. Believing that women's unpaid work is the foundation of every nation's economy and profit, the network actively campaigns for women's wages to be paid through the dismantling of the military-industrial complex. IWFHC lobbies for legislation for compensation for housework at the national level and distributes information regarding the organization's objectives. Publications include *The Power of Women and the Subversion of the Community; Black Women and the Peace Movement;* and *Women, the Unions and Work.*

International Women's Development Agency
P.O. Box 1680
Collingwood, NSW 3066, Australia
(61) 3-4193004
Fax (61) 3-4160519

The International Women's Development Agency (IWDA) is a multinational organization that focuses on actively involving women in development projects. Believing that many traditional development projects fail because they neglect to seek and consider women's input, the IWDA provides skill training programs, encourages communication among development workers, organizes informational forums, and conducts educational courses. The agency publishes a quarterly newsletter, *International Women's Development Agency Report to Associates and Friends.*

International Women's Health Coalition
24 East 21st Street
New York, NY 10010 USA
(212) 979-8500
Fax: (212) 979-9009
e-mail: iwhc@igc.apc.org

Founded in 1980, the International Women's Health Coalition (IWHC) is a nonprofit organization that works with women and men from countries in Asia, Africa, and Latin America to secure women's reproductive and sexual health and rights. The coalition works to build national and international women's health movements to create conditions necessary for more caring, respectful, and responsible sexual relationships. IWHC also acts directly to influence the work of population and health professionals, national governments, and international agencies. The coalition's goals are to enable women to manage their own fertility safely and effectively; to experience a healthy sexual life that is free of disease, violence, disability, fear, pain, or death; and to bear and raise healthy children as and when they desire to do so. The coalition supports innovative reproductive health programs and services, fosters leadership and alliances among women worldwide, promotes dialogues between women's health advocates and health and population policymakers and researchers, educates decision makers, and advocates policies that will secure sexual and reproductive health and rights for women, girls, and men everywhere. In order to support program goals, the coaltion makes grants, publishes books and essays, maintains a global network, and convenes meetings.

International Women's Rights Action Watch
Humphrey Institute of Public Affairs
University of Minnesota
301 19th Avenue South
Minneapolis, MN 55455 USA
(612) 625-5093
Fax: (612) 624-0068
e-mail: iwraw@hhh.umn.edu

The International Women's Rights Action Watch (IWRAW) consists of an international network of activists, scholars, and organizations that focuses on advancement of women's human rights. Organized in 1985 at the World Conference on Women in Nairobi, IWRAW monitors implementation of the Convention on the Elimination of All Forms of Discrimination against Women. This convention was adopted by the United Nations in 1979 and carries legal weight. Countries that ratify the convention agree to the legal obligation to take all appropriate measures to improve the status of women and to change customs and laws that impede women's advancement. NGOs are supported by IWRAW, especially in efforts to change law, culture, and society to help women fully participate in their society. The work of the UN Committee on the Elimination of Discrimination against Women (CEDAW), a 23-member group that reviews reports from countries that have ratified the convention, is publicized by IWRAW. Publications include *Women's Watch* newsletter, *Assessing the Status of Women,* and other special reports on the status of women.

International Women's Tribune Centre
777 United Nations Plaza
New York, NY 10017 USA
(212) 687-8633
Fax: (212) 661-2704
e-mail: iwtc@igc.apc.org

The International Women's Tribune Centre, an NGO, began as a result of the International Women's Year Tribune that was held at the same time as the United Nation's first world conference on women in Mexico City. The Tribune, an NGO forum, was attended by over 6,000 women. The organization facilitates the exchange of skills, experiences, and ideas among all groups that promote an active and equitable role for women. Major activities focus on information dissemination, education, communication, and organizing activities. The organization provides information, technical assistance, and training in four areas: information, communication, and networking; science, technology, and environment; community economic development; and women organizing for change. An information resource center contains over 3,000 selected monographs and 800 periodicals of interest to women. Informative materials include training manuals, directories, resource books, posters, postcards, *Computer NewsNote,* and a funding newsletter focusing on funding sources for women's projects. The center publishes audio-visual materials and a quarterly newsletter.

IPAS
303 E. Main Street
P.O. Box 999
Carrboro, NC 27510 USA
(919) 967-7052; (800) 334-8446
Fax: (919)929-0258
e-mail: ipas@ipas.org

Founded in 1973, IPAS is a nonprofit, nongovernmental organization dedicated to improving women's health through a focus on reproductive health care. Specifically, IPAS concentrates on preventing unsafe abortions, treating complications from abortions, reducing the consequences of abortion, and increasing women's access to a broad range of reproductive health services. Staff members work with governmental officials, health care providers and administrators, and NGO representatives worldwide in the development and implementation of high quality, sustainable programs in reproductive health and abortion-related care. Publications include *Initiatives in Reproductive Health Policy* and *Preventing Unwanted Pregnancy: Management Strategies;* many publications are available in both English and Spanish.

ISIS International
P.O. Box 1837
Quezon City Main
Quezon City 1100, Philippines
63 2 967297
Fax: 63 2 9241065
e-mail: isis@phil.gn.apc.org

ISIS International provides information and communication services; encourages and facilitates global communication among women; disseminates information and materials produced by women and women's groups; and examines issues such as women's role in development, health, education, food and nutrition, media, prostitution and violence against women, employment, and theories of feminism. The organization provides technical assistance in communication skills and information management and works to mobilize support and solidarity among women on an international scale. ISIS is currently developing the Asia-Pacific Women's Health Network to coordinate the exchange of information between women and health organizations. Biographical archives, a documentation center, and a library of 800 women's serials and 700 volumes on women's issues are maintained. Publications include the ISIS International "Women's Book Series," published semiannually; *Women in Action,* a quarterly journal; and *Directory of Third World's Women's Publications: Women in Development Resource Guide.*

ISIS Women's International Cross-Cultural Exchange
3, chemin des Campanules
Aire
CH-1219 Geneva, Switzerland
(41) 22-7964437
Fax: (41) 22-7960603

ISIS Women's International Cross-Cultural Exchange (ISIS-WICCE) is a resource center organized to exchange information on women's issues. The program works to improve the lives of women through information and communication networks; promotes ideas and actions that help women combat sex discrimination and injustice; offers information services on topics including food, health, violence against women, development, and communication; responds to written and telephone requests for information; offers training and technical assistance in communication and information management; and organizes internships for women activists working in fields involving women's issues. The program sponsors a three-month exchange program for women working on women's projects in various Third World countries. ISIS-WICCE supports the International Feminist Network which coordinates campaigns on women's issues of justice, peace, sex discrimination, and violence. Publications include *Women in Development: A Resource Guide for Organization and Action* (in English and French).

JHPIEGO Corporation
1615 Thames Street, Suite 200
Baltimore, MD 21231-3447 USA
(410) 955-8558
Fax: (410) 955-6199
e-mail: info@wpo.jhpiego.org
Internet: http://www.jhpiego.jhu.edu

Affiliated with Johns Hopkins University, the JHPIEGO Corporation is a nonprofit organization dedicated to improving the health of women and families throughout the world. Started in 1973, the program's goal is to increase the availability of high quality reproductive health services, with an emphasis on family planning services. Staff members train health care providers throughout the world to meet this goal. Over the past 20 years, over 83,000 health professionals representing over 5,000 institutions located in 128 countries have been trained. Each year, the program funds an average of 62 projects in 29 countries. The corporation works to help host countries develop their own training programs for health care professionals in order to provide quality family planning services, to meet short-term national family planning needs, to increase access and quality of reproductive health services, to improve the effectiveness and efficiency of reproductive health training, and to expand international reproductive health training resources and systems. Publications include many training packages and materials, including videos, on a wide variety of topics such as genital tract infections, infection prevention, training skills, post-abortion care, IUDs, Norplant implants, and the training of trainers.

Latin American and Caribbean Women's Health Network
Casilla 2067
Correa Central
Santiago, Chile
56 2-44150
Fax: 56 2-490271

The Latin American and Caribbean Women's Health Network, an international organization, includes groups and organizations that work directly or indirectly in fields related to women's health. The program works to establish contacts among women and organizations active in women's health issues at the local, regional, and national levels; to encourage the sharing of information, experiences, and ideas through the development of communication networks; to coordinate activities that focus on women's health; and to encourage public awareness campaigns on such subjects as reproductive rights, medicine, the environment, and other health topics of interest to women. Members participate in conferences, seminars, and meetings. Computer services are available and include a data base and bibliographic information on health-related groups and organizations in Latin America, the Caribbean, and other regions. Publications include *Revista de Salud*, a quarterly magazine, and *Women's Health Journal*, published quarterly.

**Latin American Association for Human Rights—
Women's Rights Area**
(Asociacion Latinoamericana para los Derechos Humanos—Area
Derechos de la Mujer—ALDHU)
Concha y Toro 17, Segundo Piso
Santiago, Chile
(56) 2-6716815
Fax: (56) 2-6723038

A multinational organization, the Latin American Association for
Human Rights—Women's Rights Area promotes and defends
women's human rights; conducts research on women's social,
cultural, sexual, reproductive, and political rights; and conducts
workshops to educate women about their rights. Programs and
policies are developed on domestic violence, sexual and reproductive rights, and sociopolitical participation of women to help
politicians understand the problems that women face and to help
them improve their lives.

**Latin American Association for the Development
and Integration of Women**
(ALADIM) (Asociacion Latinoamericana para el Desarollo y la
Integracion de la Mujer)
Estado 115, Oficina 703
Casilla 9540
Santiago, Chile
(56) 2-332491

The Latin American Association for the Development and Integration of Women is composed of individuals interested in the
defense of women's rights. The program disseminates legal information related to the rights of women; advises and helps protect women who have been physically or psychologically abused;
works against all discrimination; and improves the status of
women toward mental and economic independence. The program is working to establish a home for abused women; it produces films and radio programs, conducts research, fosters
educational programs, and compiles statistics on women in the
workforce, female delinquency, and domestic violence. The organization sponsors lectures and seminars. Publications include *Information Bulletin* (in English and Spanish), published
semiannually, and *The Chilean Women: Their Cooperation in the Social Development*.

Latin American Committee for the
Defense of the Rights of the Woman
(CLADEM) (Comite Latinoamericano para la Defensa de los
Derechos de la Mujer)
Apartado Postal 11-0470
Lima 11, Peru
[Tel]: (51-14) 639237
Fax: (51-14) 424585
e-mail: cladem@cladem.org.pe

The Latin American Committee for the Defense of the Rights of
the Woman is a regional network with offices in 15 countries that
works for the protection of gender rights, promotion of women's
political participation, provision of legal education, and the elimination of discriminatory legislation. Advocacy efforts have produced major legislative reform in Peru and a few other countries.
CLADEM also works locally with community legal educators
and participates in regional and international campaigns concerning issues of importance to women.

Latin American Council of Catholic Women
(Consejo Latinoamericano de Mujeres Catolicas)
c/o Dr. Elena Cumella
Gelly y Obes 2213
1425 Buenos Aires, Argentina
(54) 1-8034901

Members of the Latin American Council of Catholic Women include Catholic women's organizations in 23 Latin American
countries. The program focuses on ways to advance women in
Latin America and Latin American societies, to strengthen the
family unit through the woman, to promote Catholicism, and to
communicate with female religious and Christian organizations.
The council operates the Centro de Estudios para la Promocion
Integral, which offers programs on family and women's issues,
adult education, and Christian faith. Training centers in under-
developed communities are maintained. The program also monitors international events, conducts religious discussion groups,
holds seminars, and works in conjunction with Catholic church
authorities. Liaisons are maintained with the United Nations, the
United Nations Educational, Scientific and Cultural Organization, and the Food and Agriculture Organization of the United
Nations.

Marie Stopes International
62 Grafton Way
London W1P 5LO, England
(44) 71-3883740
Fax: (44) 71-3881946

The Marie Stopes International program encourages and maintains mother and child health care services, family planning clinics, and educational programs in developing countries. The program works to prevent unwanted births by promoting population control policies and disseminating information. The program cooperates with NGOs that have similar goals.

Medical Women's International Association
Herbert-Lewin-Strasse 1
50931 Cologne, Germany
49 221 4004558
Fax: 49 221 4004557
Telex: 08882161 BAEK

Founded in 1919, the Medical Women's International Association has over 20,000 members from 70 countries. Members include women involved in or interested in medicine. The association provides women with an opportunity to exchange information about medical problems with worldwide implications, promotes friendships among women, encourages women to enter the field of medicine and allied sciences, and advocates for an end to discrimination against female physicians. The association also helps women in developing countries obtain fellowships and grants for research and travel. Publications include a semiannual newsletter and *Women Physicians of the World*.

MotherCare Project
John Snow, Inc.
1616 North Fort Myer Drive, 11th Floor
Arlington, VA 22209 USA
(703) 528-7474
Fax: (703) 528-7480
Telex: 272896 JSI WUR

The MotherCare Project focuses on improving the maternal and neonatal health of women and their children throughout the world. The program uses an integrated reproductive health approach and focuses on community-based approaches to maternal and perinatal mortality reduction, prevention and control of sexually transmitted diseases, improved nutrition through education and distribution of iron-folate tablets, special newborn care, and family planning. The program is funded by the Agency for International Development, U.S. Department of State. It was created to assist countries, communities, and individuals in identifying and implementing solutions to the many problems affecting women's reproductive health and the health of newborns. Country assessment visits are conducted and support is provided for long-term projects geared to develop and test strategies for improving reproductive health care; short-term technical assistance and training activities are provided; planning and assessment activities are provided; reproductive health services are enhanced; indigenous organizations, associations, and networks are identified and strengthened; programs are evaluated; and applied research is conducted.

National Clearinghouse on Women in Development
c/o National Population and Family Development Board
Prime Minister's Department
P.O. Box 10416
Kuala Lumpur, Malaysia
03-2937555

Founded in 1983, the National Clearinghouse on Women in Development works to enhance awareness of the role of and need to include women in the overall development process. The clearinghouse promotes awareness of women's concerns and their role in national development, ensures the future participation of women in development processes, and provides a resource base to support national programs and encourage women's participation in development projects.

National Council of Women's Societies
Plot PC 14 Ahmed Oribudo Street
Off Idowu Taylor Street
Victoria Island
Lagos, Nigeria

Founded in 1959, the National Council of Women's Societies is the largest organization of Nigerian women. The program promotes women's participation in social and community affairs, supports the interests of women living in rural areas of Nigeria, develops public awareness campaigns on women's issues, and conducts research.

NGO Women's Forum
Arbeitsstelle Frauenforschung des FB 4
Universität Frankfurt, Senckenberganlage 13-17
60054 Frankfurt am Main, Germany
49 69 79828493
Fax: 49 69 79828493

The NGO Women's Forum was founded in 1989 as an international organization composed of NGOs focusing on women's issues throughout Africa, Asia, and Latin America. The forum promotes women's interests in development areas and raises public awareness of gender issues. It works to improve women's working conditions and employment opportunities. Cooperation and information exchange is fostered between women's groups and development programs.

Office of Women in Development
U.S. Agency for International Development
320 21st Street NW
Washington, DC 20523 USA
(202) 647-3992

The Office of Women in Development, a U.S. government program, focuses on ways to include women in the development of their countries. Program staff conduct research, organize conferences and community projects, and offer training programs in development skills. They maintain a public resource center on women's issues and a reference library that is open to the public.

Opportunities for Women
Centre Two
Ossian Mews
London N4 4DX, England
(44) 81-3489458
Fax: (44) 81-3403975

Opportunities for Women advocates for improving the status of women in developing countries. This international organization supports programs and services that promote self-dependency and personal growth among women of developing countries, including income-generation projects, literacy and training programs, and health care counseling. Program staff also conduct research and compile information on issues of importance to women.

Pacific Institute for Women's Health
2999 Overland Avenue, Suite 111
Los Angeles, CA 90064 USA
(310) 842-6828
Fax: (310) 280-0600
e-mail: piwh@aol.com

Founded in 1993, the Pacific Institute for Women's Health is a nonprofit organization dedicated to improving women's health locally and globally. The institute builds bridges between ideas and action locally and around the world as well as across disciplines to improve women's health. Creating worldwide partnerships with community groups, policymakers, researchers, service providers, and clients is one of the program's major goals. In the area of reproductive health and rights, the institute helps expand reproductive choice, improve contraceptive safety, and promote respect for women's reproductive rights. In the area of adolescent health linkages, a holistic approach is taken to create innovative programs that benefit the health of adolescents. To encourage women's rights and empowerment, the institute is working to ensure that women's voices are heard in discussions of policy on human rights issues. The program works to build links between domestic and international women's health programs and activities.

Pacific Women's Resource Bureau
(Bureau Technique des Femmes du Pacifique)
c/o South Pacific Commission
BP D5
Noumea Cedex, New Caledonia
(687) 262000
Fax: (687) 263818
Telex: 3139 NMSOPACOM
Cable: SOUTHPACOM NOUMEA

The Pacific Women's Resource Bureau supports the activities of Pacific island women. The bureau promotes the study of women and women's issues, supports and offers assistance to national women's organizations to help with women's development issues in the Pacific region, disseminates information to women throughout the Pacific islands, and conducts conferences, meetings, training, and workshops. The bureau maintains a reference library that is open to the public.

Pan American Medical Women's Alliance
c/o Dr. Juana Diaz de Ruiz
Apartado Postal 6-9414
Panama City, Panama
(507) 604518

The Pan American Medical Women's Alliance is composed of female doctors in the Caribbean and North, South, and Central America. The alliance promotes friendship among women physicians and encourages the exchange of ideas and information on improved methods of treatment and social and economic services related to women in medicine. Other activities include the provision of assistance to physicians in obtaining residencies in specialties and the maintenance of a travel fund to help members attend congresses and international meetings.

Pan American Office of Health—World Health Organization—Regional Office of Women, Health and Development
(Oficina Panamericana de la Salud—
Organizacion Mundial de la Salud—
Programa Regional Mujer, Salud y Desarrollo
[OPS/OMS-MSD])
Ministerio de Salud, piso 3
Apartado 3745-1000
San Jose, Costa Rica
(506) 337354
Fax: (506) 338061

This international organization promotes and supports the improvement of women's health status in Central America. Program staff members coordinate and organize activities with similar organizations; conduct research on women's health legislation and social, political, and economic status; conduct public awareness campaigns to increase knowledge of women's concerns; provide assistance and education for women on health care; and encourage women to organize and participate in community development and health projects. Other program activities include advising government and private organizations on women's health issues and advocating for changes in laws relating to women and health. Staff members train workers for the health ministry, conduct workshops on self-help medical procedures, disseminate information about women's health issues, and encourage formation of women's groups.

Pan Pacific and South-East Asia Women's Association
Office of the President
2234 New Petchburi Road
Bangkok 10310, Thailand
(66) 2-3144316

Members of the Pan Pacific and South-East Asia Women's Association include women from 18 countries who are united for the purpose of strengthening the bonds of peace by fostering better understanding and friendship among Pacific and Southeast Asian women. The group promotes cooperation among women in these regions in order to study and work to improve the social welfare of women throughout the region.

Pathfinder International
Nine Galen Street, Suite 217
Watertown, MA 02172-4501 USA
(617) 924-7200
Fax: (617) 924-3833
Telex: 681-7095 PFBOS

Regional Offices:

Fuente del Amor 31
Fracc. Fuentes del Pedregal
Tlalpan, Mexico DF 14140
Mexico
52-5-652-5176
Fax: 52-5-568-0611

P.O. Box 48147
Nairobi, Kenya
254-2-224-154
Fax: 254-2-214-890

Bagdat Caddesi No. 225/6
Ciftehavuzlar-Istanbul
Turkey
90-216-355-1173
Fax: 90-216-363-5961

Pathfinder International works with organizations and governments in developing countries to improve the accessibility and quality of family planning and related reproductive health services for women and men. The program is funded by private foundations, the U.S. Agency for International Development (USAID), and individual donations. Pathfinder supports local institutions that provide family planning and related services in over 60 countries in Latin America, Africa, Asia, and the Near East. Activities focus on developing comprehensive national family planning programs, expanding and improving the quality of existing programs, reaching underserved client groups, addressing emerging reproductive health concerns, testing and implementing creative approaches for service delivery, and increasing the sustainability and impact of well-established programs. Pathfinder has three regional offices—in Mexico, Kenya, and Turkey—and country offices in Bolivia, Brazil, Mexico, Peru, Ethiopia, Nigeria, Swaziland, Uganda, Bangladesh, Egypt, Indonesia, Jordan, Pakistan, and Vietnam.

Population Action International
1120 19th Street NW, Suite 550
Washington, DC 20036 USA
(202) 659-1833
Fax: (202) 293-1795
e-mail: pai@popact.org

Population Action International (PAI) is a private, nonprofit organization that attempts to enhance the long-term well-being of individuals, families, and nations by promoting stabilization of the world's population. PAI advocates for family planning and related health services, for education of girls, and for economic opportunities for women. The program works with other development, reproductive health, and environmental organizations in support of effective population policies. Publications include *India's Family Planning Challenge* and *Women's Well-Being: Health and Education.*

Population Communications International
777 United Nations Plaza
New York, NY 100171-3521 USA
(212) 687-3366
Fax: (212) 661-4188
Telex: MCI 66560 UN
e-mail: pci@together.org

Population Communications International (PCI) focuses on the need for information and motivation to encourage use of family planning and the adoption of small-family ideals worldwide. PCI works with the news media worldwide to encourage coverage of population and related environmental issues. The organization has used entertainment serial dramas on radio and television in six countries to develop characters as role models for elevating the status of women and encouraging the use of family planning. Entertainment/education programs have been developed and are used successfully in Tanzania, Kenya, Madagascar, Ethiopia, Namibia, China, the Philippines, India, Pakistan, Brazil, and St. Lucia. Publications include a monthly newsletter that includes broadcast-ready stories on population-related news for distribution to 3,000 news organizations and NGOs in developing countries as well as over 7,000 newsrooms in the United States. As the secretariat for the Population Task Force of NGOs at United Nations headquarters, PCI holds regular briefings on population issues.

Population Council
One Dag Hammarskjold Plaza
New York, NY 10017 USA
(212) 339-0500
Fax: (212) 755-6052
Telex: 9102900660 POPCO
Internet: http://www.popcouncil.com

Regional Offices:

Ground Floor, Zone 5A
India Habitat Centre
Lodi Road
New Delhi 110 003, India
(91)(11) 464-2901, 464-2902
Fax: (91)(11) 464-2903

P.O. Box 115
Dokki, Cairo, Egypt
(20)(2) 5738277
Fax: (20)(2) 5701804

The Chancery Building
Valley Road
P.O. Box 17643
Nairobi, Kenya
(254)(2) 713-480, 713-481
Fax: (254)(2) 713-479

Apartado Postal 105-152
11560 Mexico, DF, Mexico
(52)(5) 280-1725, 280-1475
Fax: (52)(5) 281-0702

The Population Council is a nonprofit, nongovernmental research organization devoted to improving the reproductive health and well-being of women and men throughout the world. The council studies population issues and trends, conducts social and reproductive sciences research, works with government and private organizations to improve family planning and related health services, helps governments implement effective population policies, reports research results to a wide audience, and helps strengthen professional resources in developing countries. The council's Gender, Family, and Development (GFD) Program seeks to bring to bear a sophisticated understanding of gender dynamics, determinants of women's status, and family factors on population, reproductive health, and development programs. The GFD program focuses on four major areas, including broadening population policy beyond family planning; promoting greater attention by policymakers to the extensiveness and conditions of nontraditional families; describing and supporting an active and responsible role for men as partners and fathers; and seeking the means to assist young girls in their transition to a meaningful adulthood. The council publishes two journals, *Population and Development Review,* a quarterly journal examining population dynamics and socioeconomic change, and *Studies in Family Planning,* a bi-monthly journal examining all aspects of family planning. A variety of booklets provides information on Population Council research; family planning programs noted for quality of care; innovative projects that support and enhance women's productive roles and economic empowerment; contraception; and breastfeeding. Four regional offices are located in India, Egypt, Kenya, and Mexico, and country offices are located in Bangladesh, Indonesia, Pakistan, Philippines, Thailand, Vietnam, Burkina Faso, Mali, Senegal, Tanzania, Brazil, Guatemala, Haiti, Honduras, and Peru.

Population Institute
107 Second Street NE
Washington, DC 20002 USA
(202) 544-3300
Fax: (202) 544-0068
e-mail: Popline@Primanet.com
Internet: http://www.populationinstitute.org

As a population advocacy organization, the Population Institute provides leadership in creating national and international awareness of the social, economic, and environmental implications of rapid population growth. Dedicated to bringing about global population stabilization, the institute has members in 160 countries. Publications include *Popline,* a bi-monthly newspaper covering global population issues, and *Half the Sky: Women and Development.*

Population Reference Bureau
1875 Connecticut Avenue NW, Suite 520
Washington, DC 20009-5728 USA
(202) 483-1100

Fax: (202) 328-3937
e-mail: popref@prb.org
Internet: http://www.prb.org/prb

The Population Reference Bureau (PRB) was founded in 1929 and is a nonprofit educational organization. The program works with public and private sector partners to increase the amount, accuracy, and usefulness of information concerning changes in population and the impact these changes may have on society. Staff members gather, interpret, and disseminate information in a variety of publications, information services, seminars, and workshops. PRB maintains a developing country database and files that contain information on population trends, programs, and policy issues affecting these countries. PRB develops briefing packages and analyses for USAID, cooperating agencies, other government agencies, and NGOs. Through a cooperative agreement with USAID, the bureau makes population, family planning, and reproductive health information available to policymakers in developing countries and the donor community. Publications include a wide variety of relevant documents, including *Conveying Concerns: Women Write on Reproductive Health, International Migration: A Global Challenge, The Challenge of World Health, The International Family Planning Movement,* and *Contraceptive Safety: Rumors and Realities.*

Program for Appropriate Technology in Health
4 Nickerson Street
Seattle, WA 98109 USA
(206) 285-3500
Fax: (206) 285-6619
e-mail: info@path.org
Internet: http://www.path.org

Field offices:
8/F Arwan Building
1339 Pracharat 1 Road, Bangsue
Bangkok 10800, Thailand
(66-2) 587-2001, 587-2002
Fax: (66-2) 587-5125
Internet: pathbkk@mozart.inet.co.th

P.O. Box 76634
30 Ole Odume Road
Nairobi, Kenya

(254-2) 569331, 569357
Internet: path@ken.healthnet.org

Tifa Building, 11th Floor
Suite 1102
Jl. Kuningan Barat No. 26
Jakarta 12710, Indonesia
(62-21) 520-0737, 520-0065
Fax: (62-21) 520-0621
Internet: path@pathjkt.klwarta.or.id

Project offices:
3/4 Malaya Zhitominskaya Street
Apt. 13
Kiev 252009, Ukraine
380-44-229-87-84
Fax: 380-44-229-87-84

Jl. Pendidikan No. 56
Mataram 83125
Lombok, Indonesia
(62-364) 34330
Fax: (62-364) 31055
Internet: lombokmgr@pactok.peg.apc.org

Thomas Jefferson Cultural Center Building
395 Sen. Gil J. Puyat Avenue
Makati, Metro Manila, Philippines
(63-2) 895-3201, 899-1580
Fax: (63-2) 899-5561
Internet: path@phil.gn.apc.org

The Program for Appropriate Technology in Health (PATH) is a
nonprofit, nongovernmental, international organization focusing
on improving health, especially the health of women and children. Staff members seek solutions to public health problems,
specifically in the areas of reproductive health and widespread
communicable diseases. Knowledge, skills, and technologies are
exchanged with governments and private organizations
throughout the world. Activities include assessing reproductive
and primary health care needs, developing ways to meet these
needs, building partnerships with public and private organizations to introduce health products, strengthening local capabili-

ties to implement and evaluate educational activities, designing culturally appropriate training programs, educational materials, and media programs with the help of local personnel, and building innovative interventions into health programs. Publications include *Developing Health and Family Planning Print Materials for Low-Literate Audiences: A Guide.*

Regional Information Network on Arab Women
c/o Social Research Center
American University in Cairo
P.O. Box 2511
113 Sharia Kasr El-Aini
Cairo, Egypt

The multinational Regional Information Network provides information concerning the major issues that affect Arab women. Information is compiled on the status, role, culture, and achievements of Arab women.

Self-Employed Women's Association
Opp. Lok Manya Tilak Bagh
Ahmedabad 380001, India

Founded in 1972, the Self-Employed Women's Association (SEWA) organizes women who are self-employed, increases their access to credit and assets, improves their status, and advocates for working women. The program started the SEWA Mahila Trust, which provides banking, credit, and other financial facilities for poor women wanting to start their own businesses or expand existing services or products. The trust offers training courses, technical information, legal aid, maternity benefits, death and widowhood benefits, health services, insurance, and other services. Producer cooperatives are organized to ensure that women have greater control over the products of their labors. Development of income-generating opportunities in rural areas is encouraged. Staff members advocate for women through campaigns, lobbying efforts, and negotiations.

Third World Movement against the Exploitation of Women
41 Rajah Matanda
Project 4
Quezon City, Metro Manila 1109, Philippines
(63) 2-786469
Fax: (63) 2-9215662

Members of the Third World Movement against the Exploitation of Women (TW-MAE-W) include women's groups and individuals in 45 countries concerned with organizing to combat female sexual slavery and exploitation. The program encourages a transnational approach to women's issues as an effective means for women to liberate themselves. Serving as a networking organization, TW-MAE-W focuses on activities that affect women— marriage bureaus, migrant labor, international beauty contests, child prostitution, Islamic oppression of women, and the importation of Third World entertainers. Members have protested against organized Japanese sex tours and launched CAMP International, the Campaign against Military Prostitution, which draws attention to prostitution occurring near military bases. Centers for prostitutes and a transition home for those prostitutes seeking an alternative livelihood are operated; AIDS prevention and care programs among sex workers are offered. A speakers' bureau is maintained; program staff conduct research on issues concerning women, such as labor, self-determination, and the role of the media and sex tourism in prostitution. Workshops and charitable and educational programs are provided.

United Nations Development Fund for Women
304 East 45th Street, 6th Floor
New York, NY 10017 USA
(212) 906-6400
Fax: (212) 906-6705

Apartado Postal 4540-1000
San Jose, Costa Rica
(506) 553311
Fax: (506) 553778
Telex: 2339

The United Nations Development Fund for Women (UNIFEM) seeks to promote the economic and political empowerment of women in developing countries by providing direct technical and financial support to women's programs. Encouraging the participation of women in all levels of development planning, UNIFEM acts as a catalyst within the United Nations system to link the needs and concerns of women to all issues on global agendas. Created in 1976 as the Voluntary Fund for the UN Decade for Women, UNIFEM became an organization in autonomous association with the UN Development Programme (UNDP) in 1985. UNIFEM works to help women in developing countries by strengthening the local, national, and international organizations as well as helping to encourage links and partnerships at every level. The organization's economic empowerment program ensures that women have access to and control over economic resources, assets, and opportunities. The political empowerment program works to strengthen the role of women in government and decision making at all levels, ensuring that women have control over their lives both within and outside the household. In 1991, UNIFEM's publishing program was established and in its first four years has produced 12 books and occasional papers, such as *A Commitment to the World's Women* and *Financing Women's Enterprises: Beyond Barriers and Bias.* UNIFEM has regional program advisers located in Nigeria, Senegal, Zimbabwe, India, Jordan, Thailand, Barbados, Brazil, Ecuador, and Mexico.

United Nations Program for Development
(Programa de las Naciones Unidas Para el Desarrollo)
Apartado Postal 114
San Salvador, El Salvador
(503) 234466
(503) 240957

The international Programa de las Naciones Unidas Para el Desarrollo focuses on improving the quality of life for families by involving women in development projects. Program staff members work to make women aware that they can overcome the problems of poverty through organization. Productive projects are developed through a combination of available resources and application of suitable technology. The program trains women in organization and administration duties to carry out projects and provides technical assistance and training. Other activities include the investigation and documentation of activities of Salvadoran women and the provision of technical assistance to other women-oriented organizations.

Women and Development
(KULU) (Kuindernes u Landsudvalg)
Landgreven 7, 3 tv.
DK-1301 Copenhagen K, Denmark
(45) 33157870
Fax: (45) 33325330

Members of Women and Development include regional organizations, women's groups, and individuals. This international organization supports the rights of women in developing countries and attempts to influence national and international policies affecting their development. The organization monitors legislation dealing with feminist issues, disseminates information, encourages the creation of women's groups in developing countries, and lobbies for increased financial aid to assist in their formation.

Women and International Development Program
Michigan State University
202 Center for International Programs
East Lansing, MI 48824-1035 USA
(517) 353-5040
Fax: (517) 353-7254
e-mail: 22635mgr@msu.edu; 22635mgr@msu.bitnet

The Women and International Development (WID) Program was established in 1978 to encourage recognition that international development creates costs and benefits that are not provided equally to men and women of different nationalities, races, classes, and ethnicities. The program was designated as a National Resource Center by the U.S. Department of Education in 1994. The program cooperates with a wide spectrum of departments and groups across the Michigan State University campus and encourages both graduate and undergraduate teaching and research on gender and global transformation. The application of knowledge on women from a comparative perspective is promoted through a monograph series. An active outreach program offers training, resources, seminars, and briefings to other schools, colleges, the media, and the general public. Publications include the *WID Bulletin*, a guide to resources, including scholarships, conferences, and employment opportunities, that is published three times each year; the *Women and International Development Annual*, published in cooperation with Westview Press, which explores women's experiences worldwide; the WID Forum, a series of brief papers that describe research projects and development programs and review current policy issues; and the *Working Papers on Women and International Development*, which feature journal-length articles concerning relevant research, theoretical analyses, and evaluations of development programs and policy.

Women in Law and Development in Africa
P.O. Box 4622
Harare, Zimbabwe

The Women in Law and Development in Africa (WILDAF) organization is an international program that focuses on empowering women through legal education, law reform, and legal services. WILDAF promotes training and educational programs on legal literacy, conducts research and disseminates information on legal issues affecting women, and coordinates activities with other organizations concerned with women and the law.

Women Living under Muslim Laws
Boite Postale 23
34790 Grabels, France

Coordination for Asia:
208, Scotch Corner
Upper Mall
Lahore, Pakistan

Set up in 1986 to break the isolation that women experience in Muslim countries, the Women Living under Muslim Laws program provides information, solidarity, and support. Links are created among women and women's groups within Muslim countries. The program works to increase women's knowledge about their common and diverse experiences throughout the Muslim world. Another objective is to create ways to support women in their struggles internationally from within Muslim countries and from other non-Muslim countries. The organization provides information to women and women's groups, disseminates information to other Muslim women, supports women's struggles and provides information concerning these struggles to the non-Muslim world, provides a channel of communication among all women, builds a network of information and solidarity, and facilitates exchanges of women and information.

Women to Women: Worldwide Living for Development
c/o OXFAM
274 Banbury Road
Oxford OX2 7DZ, England

The international Women to Women: Worldwide Living for Development program works with women from Brazil, Senegal, the Philippines, South Africa, Palestine, Mexico, Egypt, and India to encourage the networking of women and women's groups to exchange information on common struggles and strategies. Program staff work to formulate strategies and to promote the implementation of aid policies that can help create a just world for women.

Women's Development Association
(Nari Bikash Sangha)
Post Office
Jhilimili
Bankura 722 135, West Bengal, India

The Women's Development Association is an international association of rural women and organizations striving to increase the standard of living for women and children. The program coordinates the projects of local affiliates; provides child care, adult education, training, and raw materials; helps to market local groups' products; distributes food, clothes, and kerosene to the needy; and offers legal help to female victims of violence. Members communicate with development groups to encourage and promote similar projects. The association conducts workshops and seminars, encourages women to become self-sufficient, and participates in research.

Women's Feature Service
49 Golf Links
New Delhi 110 003
Delhi 9, India
(91) 11-4629886
Fax: (91) 11-4629886
Telex: 3161922 RAJAINN

20 West 20th Street
Suite 1103
New York, NY 10011 USA
(212) 807-9192
(212) 807-9331
e-mail: wfs@igc.apc.org
Internet: http://www.igc.apc.org/wfs

The Women's Feature Service is an international organization that promotes the interests of women on international, national, and local levels. The group disseminates information on women's development and works to change discrimination in the media's portrayal of women. The organization has a network of over 100 female journalists who produce approximately 500 articles each year, written from a women's perspective and with a special focus on developing countries. Stories focus on the political, social, economic, and cultural issues and trends that shape women's lives throughout the world. Some of the topics of interest include the environment, health, politics, economic development, traditional customs, human rights, women's movements, children, and immigration. Regional offices are located in the Philippines, Zimbabwe, Costa Rica, and the United States.

Women's Global Network for Reproductive Rights
NZ Voorburgwal 32
1012 RZ Amsterdam, Netherlands
3120-620-9672
Fax: 3120-622-2450
e-mail: wgnrr@antenna.nl

The Women's Global Network for Reproductive Rights is an international network of women's health groups, reproductive rights campaigns, clinics, health workers, and interested individuals. The program supports women's right to decide if and when to have children, and defends the right to safe, effective contraceptives, legal abortion, and freedom from sterilization abuse. Public awareness campaigns focus on issues including what the group considers the "dumping of dangerous contraceptives in the Third World," the lack of complete information to help women make informed decisions on spacing and controlling births, and the lack of availability of safe contraceptive methods to women who want them. The network focuses on raising public awareness of issues surrounding maternal mortality and illness and serves as an information clearinghouse for abortion; sterilization; research, testing, and distribution of contraceptives; and other reproductive health and services issues. The network operates a resource center and publishes a quarterly newsletter.

Women's Health Action Foundation
P.O. Box 94263
1009 AG Amsterdam, Netherlands
[Tel]: 31 20 6652002
Fax: 31 20 6653002
e-mail: 101526.250@compuserve.com

Founded in 1991, the Women's Health Action Foundation (WHAF) protects women's health by encouraging the rational use of pharmaceuticals, promoting the improvement of health services, and ensuring that women participate in formulating health services. Publications include *A Question of Control: Women's Perspectives on the Development and Use of Contraceptive Technologies; Guidelines for the Distribution and Use of Fertility Regulation Methods; Norplant: Under Her Skin; RU 486: The Abortion Pill;* and *Women and Pharmaceuticals Bulletin.*

Women's International League for Peace and Freedom
United States Section
1213 Race Street
Philadelphia, PA 19107-1691 USA
(215) 563-7110
Fax: (215) 563-5527
e-mail: wilpfnatl@igc.apc.org

International Office:
Centre International
1 rue de Varembe
1211 Geneva 20, Switzerland
[Tel]: 41-22-733-61-75
Fax: 41-22-740-10-63
e-mail: womensleague@gn.apc.org

Founded in 1915, the Women's International League for Peace and Freedom (WILPF) works through peaceful means for those political, economic, social, and psychological conditions throughout the world that can assure peace, freedom, and justice for all people. Jane Addams, the first U.S. woman to receive the Nobel Peace Prize, was elected WILPF's first president in 1919. WILPF works for political solutions to international conflicts, disarmament, the promotion of women to full and equal participation in all of society's activities, economic justice within and among states, the elimination of racism and all forms of discrimination and exploitation, the respect of fundamental human rights, and the right to development in a sustainable environment. Working at the international, national, and local levels, WILPF works to educate, inform, and mobilize women for action to achieve its goals. It organizes meetings, seminars, and conferences to study relevant issues and campaigns to promote disarmament. WILPF has consultative status with the Economic and Social Council of the United Nations (ECOSOC), the UN Educational, Scientific and Cultural Organization (UNESCO), and the UN Conference on Trade and Development (UNCTAD) and has established special relations with the UN Children's Emergency

Fund (UNICEF), the International Labour Organization (ILO), and the Food and Agriculture Organization (FAO). WILPF provides these organizations with information concerning conditions in the areas of its concerns and makes suggestions for action by them. Publications include *Justice Denied! Human Rights and the International Financial Institutions,* a book that explains how the global economic system works and how it harms people and the environment worldwide; and *Peace and Freedom,* a quarterly news magazine.

Women's International Network
187 Grant Street
Lexington, MA 02173 USA
(617) 862-9431
Fax: (617) 862-1734

The Women's International Network (WIN) is a nonprofit organization that works for women's health and development throughout the world and provides educational materials to members and other interested individuals and groups. The network focuses on encouraging cooperation and communication between women of all backgrounds, beliefs, nationalities, and age groups through the compilation and dissemination of information on women's development. Members contribute news and information on women and health, environment, media, violence, female genital mutilation, and United Nations events of concern to women. The network's Women and International Affairs Clearinghouse surveys career opportunities for women interested in working in international and development agencies. A newsletter, *WIN News,* is published four times a year.

**Women's Network of the Council for
Adult Education in Latin America**
(REPEM-CEAAL) (Red de Educacion Popular entre Mujeres Afilada al Consejo de Educacion de Adultos de America Latin)
Casilla 17-15-0123-C
Quito, Ecuador
(593) 2-571315
Fax: (593) 2-580112

Members of the Women's Network of the Council for Adult Education in Latin America include women's organizations and institutions. The network works to promote public education for women and seeks to develop a systematized educational theory and methodology for the education of women in Latin America. Staff members coordinate members' activities; participate in research; and conduct seminars, training programs, and educational courses.

Women's World Banking
8 West 40th Street
New York, NY 10018 USA
(212) 768-8513
Fax: (212) 768-8519

Women's World Banking (WWB) is a global nonprofit financial institution that advances and promotes the full participation of women in society. Established in 1979, WWB currently has over 50 affiliates in more than 40 countries. WWB's goals are to expand the economic participation of low income women by providing direct services and influencing government and bank policies; to support local initiatives to build affiliate organizations; to create innovative systems and relationships that give low income women entrepreneurs access to banking services, markets, and information; to nurture an active, global network of entrepreneurs, bankers, and community organizers; and to build networks of enterprises that add value and values. WWB encourages women to play an active economic and social role in their communities to decide the right mix of credit, savings, training, and commercial connections that will provide economic development. This program has provided financial and business development services to over 500,000 women in 40 countries. The repayment rate for the loans exceeds 95 percent—much better than most commercial banks. WWB makes small loans, averaging about $300 to micro and small businesswomen throughout the world.

Zonta International
557 West Randolph Street
Chicago, IL 60661-2206 USA
(312) 930-5848
Fax: (312) 930-0951

Zonta is a worldwide service organization composed of executives in business and the professions who work together to advance the status of women throughout the world. There are approximately 35,000 members in over 1,100 clubs in 68 countries. Members volunteer their time, talents, and energy to local and international service projects designed to advance the status of women. The organization supports women's education, leadership, and development through a series of international service projects in over 20 countries in cooperation with UNICEF, UNIFEM, and other organizations. Zonta's International Service Fund supports projects that improve the quality of life for women through developing women's leadership and economic skills; these projects are organized in conjunction with agencies of the United Nations.

References/Other Sources

Barrett, Jacqueline K., ed. 1993. *Encyclopedia of Women's Associations Worldwide: A Guide to over 3,400 National and Multinational Nonprofit Women's and Women-Related Organizations.* London: Gale Research International.

Fisher, Julie. 1993. *The Road from Rio: Sustainable Development and the Nongovernmental Movement in the Third World.* Westport, CT: Praeger.

Shreir, Sally, ed. 1988. *Women's Movements of the World.* United Kingdom: Longman.

Selected Print Resources 6

This chapter contains descriptions of books concerning women in the Third World. Because the literature in this field is so vast, the materials listed here are primarily recent books. In some cases, earlier books that are considered classics in the field of women and the Third World or that have had an impact in the field are included. Books listed are divided into three categories: general topics, region specific, and country specific. The chapter also includes a list of journals containing articles that focus on women in the Third World and bibliographic and other sources to help find other books and reports.

Books, General

Adler, Leonore Loeb, ed. 1993. *International Handbook on Gender Roles.* Westport, CT: Greenwood Press. 525 pages. Bibliography, index. ISBN 0-313-28336-2.

This book is a good resource for students who want to gain an understanding of the part that gender roles play in a variety of societies. Each chapter provides information on a specific country and consists of an introduction, overview, comparisons of men's and women's roles in various stages of the life cycle (infancy, early childhood, school years, young adulthood, adulthood, and old age), and a summary and conclusions. Countries represent six continents and include developed nations as well as developing countries.

Afshar, Haleh, ed. 1991. *Women, Development and Survival in the Third World.* New York: Longman. 325 pages. Bibliography, index. ISBN 0-582-03494-9.

Women play an important role in the economic development process of their countries. In this book, Afshar has collected the views of many experts in the field of women in development. A woman's position is based on her gender and on the economic and political organization of the country in which she lives. This book explores the myths and realities that shape women's lives in Asia, Africa, and Latin America, using case studies from China, India, Iran, Malaysia, Nicaragua, Nigeria, and Vietnam that describe constraints on women farmers in southern Africa, rice production in Malaysia, agricultural collectives in Vietnam, institutional credit in India, and women in manufacturing in India.

————, ed. 1987. *Women, State, and Ideology: Studies from Africa and Asia.* Albany: State University of New York Press. 245 pages. Glossary, index. ISBN 0-88706-393-4.

Many governments in the Third World encourage the domesticity of women and want to keep women working at home. Legislation passed by these governments is usually directed at controlling women and their fertility and encouraging continued subordination. Afshar has brought together the writings of several researchers in the field of gender and development to examine the position of women in Africa and Asia. Specific policies of African and Asian governments concerning women and sexuality, fertility, health, and paid employment are discussed. Individual chapters focus on fundamentalist views of women in Nigeria, Zimbabwe, Ghana, and Iran; family and state in the industrialization of Malaysia; gender and population in China; state responses to needs of males and females in British India; and midwifery, childbearing, and the state in rural north India. The final section discusses women and handicraft production in North India, sexual division of labor in the Israeli army, controlling women's access to political power in Andhra Pradesh, India, and continuity and change in the position of women in rural Vietnam.

Anker, Richard, and Catherine Hein, eds. 1986. *Sex Inequalities in Urban Employment in the Third World.* New York: St. Martin's Press. 378 pages. Index. ISBN 0-312-71341-X.

This book is a result of a research program on women's roles and demographic change sponsored by the International Labour Organization (ILO). The contributors include a variety of experts in the field of gender and development and include sociologists, economists, and social psychologists. The editors' goal is to examine the inequalities between males and females in nonagricultural employment within Third World countries. While the nonagricultural component of the economy is not large in most developing countries, this component is often the fastest-growing segment of the economy in many of these countries. Therefore, the ways in which women are treated differently from men are an important indication of the ways they are still seen and treated in many of these countries. Some of the issues the editors focus on include "the degree to which employment markets are segregated on the basis of workers' sex; inequalities in earnings between male and female workers; differences in recruitment, hiring, firing and promotion practices for men and women; [and] the effect of family responsibilities on career development and worker productivity" (page 1).

Aslanbeigui, Nahid, Steven Pressman, and Gale Summerfield, eds. 1994. *Women in the Age of Economic Transformation: Gender Impact of Reforms in Post-Socialist and Developing Countries.* New York: Routledge. 232 pages. Bibliography, index. ISBN 0-415-10422-X.

Economic reform and subsequent benefits and losses for people within individual countries vary between men and women. The editors of this volume found that women have been, overwhelmingly, the losers in countries undergoing economic transformation; it does not matter whether the country's economy improved, stagnated, or worsened. The authors found that "women's relative losses have been manifested in different ways, but in every country examined in this volume, economic transformation has led to fewer gains or greater losses for women" (page 2). Part 1 focuses on Eastern Europe and examines women's positions in East Germany, Poland, Romania, and Russia. The economic status of women in less-developed countries is described in Part 2, which covers Zambia and sub-Saharan Africa; China, Singapore, and South Korea; and Chile, Mexico, and Nicaragua. Government economic reforms, employment conditions, industrial restructuring, rural-urban interfaces, and political reforms are examined.

Ballara, Marcela. 1991. *Women and Literacy.* Atlantic Highlands, NJ: Zed Books. 84 pages. List of organizations, bibliography, index. ISBN 1-85649-980-9.

The education of women and young girls can play an important role in the economic development, improved health, and improved living conditions of all citizens. Ballara focuses on the impact that literate women and girls can have in key areas of development and reviews the necessary conditions that must be met for literacy programs to succeed. The book examines the links between various factors that affect gender-specific illiteracy, looks at the effect of women's and girls' illiteracy on society and on the development process, describes various approaches that countries and individual programs have taken to improve levels of women's literacy, provides an understanding of the problems that illiterate women and girls face, and supplies the reader with information on how to prepare teaching materials to support literacy activities. The author hopes to encourage individuals and groups to discuss and develop solutions to the problems facing illiterate women and girls. Appendices offer a guide to education and action activities and questions as well as a list of organizations that are working to reduce illiteracy among women and girls.

Bernard, Jessie. 1987. *The Female World from a Global Perspective.* Bloomington: Indiana University Press. 288 pages. Bibliography, index. ISBN 0-253-32167-0.

Jessie Bernard has been studying women for many years—she is a founder of feminist scholarship in the field of sociology. In this book, Bernard draws on her many rich experiences as a sociologist to discuss the status of women throughout the world. She describes the role that reproduction and productivity have played in the lives of women and she examines the role of work and the sexual division of labor that has divided men and women and affected their relationships. Part II discusses equitable relationships and integrating women into all aspects of society. The experience that women are gaining on a personal level as well as at national and international women's meetings and their progress using networks to communicate and develop political and personal power are examined in Part III, including the "ways the female world is discovering, cultivating, sharing, and using its own resources of talent and skill" (pages 124–125). Finally, the conference celebrating International Women's Year in Mexico City in June 1975, the International Decade for Women, the 1980 conference in Copenhagen, and the Nairobi conference in 1985 are discussed in Part IV. Appendices provide information on refugee women, migratory workers, and the female world of South Africa.

Blumberg, Rae Lesser, Cathy A. Rakowski, Irene Tinker, and Michael Monteon, eds. 1995. *EnGENDERing Wealth and Well-Being: Empowerment for Global Change.* Boulder, CO: Westview Press. 311 pages. Index. ISBN 0-8133-2106-9.

Blumberg and her colleagues explore the role of women in development and the significant contributions that women make toward the health, wealth, and well-being of their families. Trends and case studies provide valuable information from Islamic countries, Africa, China, Latin America, and Eastern Europe. The growth of studies concerning women's roles in development since 1970 is examined. Women's impact on contemporary economic change throughout the world is discussed. Historical and current trends related to economic crises in Latin America are described. The importance of understanding how access to income and resources influences decision making and state and national policies is discussed. The relationships among income, economic crisis, and the well-being of families are described. Suggestions are made concerning ways that women, along with men, can encourage positive economic change in their societies.

Boserup, Ester. 1970. *Women's Role in Economic Development.* New York: St. Martin's Press. 283 pages. References, author index, subject index. LC catalog card number 70-118569.

This book is one of the classic works on women in development. Boserup believed that women played an important role in their local and national economy and in this book she examined the role that women play in economic development throughout the world. As the field of agriculture became modernized and many families migrated to urban areas, the role of women in the economy expanded. If women are restricted in their productive activities, area economies suffer. Boserup points out the patterns of women's participation in the economy and explains the significance of these patterns in relation to development theory and policy. In Part I, work patterns in the village are examined, including male and female farming systems, the economics of polygamy, loss of status under European rule, and the casual worker. Part II examines work patterns in larger towns and includes discussions of women's work in the men's world, industry from the hut to the factory, the educated woman, and women in the urban hierarchy. The movement of the population from village to urban area is discussed in Part III and includes discussions of the lure of the towns, urban job opportunities for women, the unemployment scare, and the design of female education. Appendices provide many tables that offer statistical information to back up the earlier discussions.

Braidotti, Rosi, Ewa Charkiewicz, Sabine Hausler, and Saskia Wieringa. 1994. *Women, the Environment and Sustainable Development: Towards a Theoretical Synthesis.* Atlantic Highlands, NJ: Zed Books. 220 pages. Bibliography, index. ISBN 1-85649-183-8.

Based on a study of women, the environment, and sustainable development supported by INSTRAW (International Research and Training Institute for the Advancement of Women), this book provides an understanding of the role of women in sustainable development. Included is a discussion of development theory, feminist theories of development, environmental reforms and debates concerning sustainable development, and the impact that environmental destruction and sustainable development have on women and their families in developing countries.

Brydon, Lynne, and Sylvia Chant. 1989. *Women in the Third World: Gender Issues in Rural and Urban Areas.* New Brunswick, NJ: Rutgers University Press. 327 pages. Bibliography; author, place names, and subject indexes. ISBN 0-8135-1470-3.

Brydon and Chant provide an overview of the status and role of women in developing countries. They examine the role that gender discrimination and inequality plays in development activities and the ways that this inequality affects women's lives. Distinctions are made between women in urban and in rural settings. Major themes include gender issues related to households, production activities, reproduction, policy and planning, and migration. A 50-page bibliography provides a rich source of materials for further research.

Bullock, Susan. 1994. *Women and Work.* Atlantic Highlands, NJ: Zed Books. 160 pages. List of organizations, selected bibliography, index. ISBN 1-85649-117-X.

The role of women in the workforce has been examined by many researchers in recent years. Most researchers agree that women have always played an important role in the economy of communities as well as nations. Most often, their contribution has been minimized because much of their work is nonpaying. Bullock examines women's participation in the workforce, highlighting the "ideology and structures that limit and undervalue women's participation in the world of work" (page vii) and explores the steps that women themselves are taking to overcome this subordination. Individual chapters discuss issues related to general employment trends, women's employment trends, variables that affect women's productive and reproductive work, the role of women in agriculture, women in the informal sector of work, the ways that women are being integrated into the global workforce, the impact of industrialization, the positive and negative effects of education and training programs, international labor standards and other programs to encourage equal opportunities and treatment of women at work, and the ways that grassroots organization can contribute to strengthening the power of women.

Bunch, Charlotte, and Niamh Reilly. 1994. *Demanding Accountability: The Global Campaign and Vienna Tribunal for Women's Human Rights.* New Brunswick, NJ: Center for Women's Global Leadership, and New York: United Nations Development Fund for Women. 169 pages. ISBN 0-912917-29-6.

At the United Nations World Conference on Human Rights in Vienna in 1993, one issue that was widely covered was gender-based violence and women's human rights. This book documents women's organizing strategies at this world conference. The testimonies and other statements from the Global Tribunal on Violations of Women's Human Rights, held during the World Conference, are provided; these feature women from 25 countries who describe the large range of human rights abuses that they experienced. This book provides an illuminating history and analysis of this conference and its impact on the field of women's human rights.

Buvinic, Mayra, Catherine Gwin, and Lisa M. Bates. 1996. *Investing in Women: Progress and Prospects for the World Bank.* Washington, DC: Overseas Development Council in cooperation with the International Center for Research on Women. Distributed by the Johns Hopkins University Press. 115 pages. ISBN 1-56517-018-0.

In 1995, an internal review at the World Bank examined all bank projects between 1967 and 1993 and found that only 615 out of 4,955 projects (12 percent) included at least minimal attempts to specifically address the needs of women. In this study of the World Bank, the authors examine the bank's potential role in helping to break the cycle of deprivation that many women experience. Specific initiatives and projects are examined that focus on improving the lives of women throughout the world. The authors believe that the World Bank can and should work on ways to improve women's lives, and the book examines the ways that the bank can contribute to that improvement. Projects that have had a positive impact on women are examined, areas of relative neglect on the part of the bank are described, and several critical issues and challenges that face the bank are identified.

Chhachhi, Amrita, and Renée Pittin, eds. 1996. *Confronting State, Capital and Patriarchy: Women Organizing in the Process of Industrialization.* New York: St. Martin's Press. 369 pages. Index. ISBN 0-312-12980-7.

Chhachhi and Pittin have assembled the work of several researchers and activists in this book concerning a variety of women's and labor issues that are similar throughout the world. Contributors focus on the "methods, strategies and forms of organization elaborated by working women to confront the state, capital and patriarchy in the context of industrialization" (page 1). Currently accepted social and economic theories concerning development are examined. The relationship between the experiences of women workers and the restructuring of the world economy is explored. The relationship between capital and patriarchy is discussed. Three major sections focus on reconceptualizing industrialization and organization, trade unions and new organizational strategies, and organizing from home and community. Individual chapters focus on efforts to organize working women, Philippine trade unions, women organizing for change in Caribbean free zones, organizing women factory workers in Pakistan, Asian industrial women workers, struggles of women workers in Zimbabwe, and homeworking in South Korea.

Cook, Rebecca J., ed. 1994. *Human Rights of Women: National and International Perspectives.* Philadelphia: University of Pennsylvania Press. 636 pages. Index. ISBN 0-8122-3261-5.

Cook examines the Convention on the Elimination of All Forms of Discrimination against Women adopted by the United Nations General Assembly in 1979 and its impact on women's lives. She discusses the ways in which the convention can be used effectively to help women achieve "equality, protection, and individual dignity" (pages ix–x). Human rights law, feminist studies, and political science and how these can help women in the Third World alleviate the social inequities, legal discrimination, and economic disadvantages they often face are examined. Challenges to the human rights of women, international and regional approaches, national approaches, and strategies to guarantee human rights of particular significance to women are discussed.

Counts, Dorothy Ayers, Judith K. Brown, and Jacquelyn C. Campbell, eds. 1992. *Sanctions and Sanctuary: Cultural Perspectives on the Beating of Wives.* Boulder, CO: Westview Press. 268 pages. Index. ISBN 0-8133-7897-4.

The editors have gathered an experienced group of anthropologists, sociologists, psychologists, and other professionals to provide an intriguing examination of wife-beating and battering throughout the world. Through primarily anthropological accounts of their experiences, the contributors provide valuable information concerning the ways in which other societies view family violence, especially violence toward women. Individual chapters focus on the question of whether wife-beating has an evolutionary origin; men, women, and interpersonal aggression in an Australian aboriginal community; how !Kung women cope with men; wife-beating in Papua New Guinea; preventing violence against women in Belize; men's rights and domestic violence in Ecuador; variations of wife-beating in India; domestic violence among Indo-Fijians; wife abuse and the political system in Iran; wife abuse in the context of development and change in Taiwan; and cultural contexts of domestic violence versus Western social sciences.

Dandekar, Hemalata C., ed. 1993. *Shelter, Women, and Development: First and Third World Perspectives.* Ann Arbor, MI: George Wahr Publishing Company. 447 pages. ISBN 0-911586-96-2.

This extensive resource grew out of a conference of the same name held at the University of Michigan's College of Architecture and Urban Planning in 1992. The conference emphasized the importance of shelter for women's development in a multicultural and international context. The book is organized around nine major themes: (1) shelter policy; implications for women's development; (2) the structure of legal interventions; (3) shelter and women in crisis; (4) women's participation in the production of shelter; (5) shelter and income opportunities; (6) women and shelter-related services and infrastructure; (7) nontraditional living arrangements beyond the nuclear family; (8) design and creation of shelter for women; and (9) shelter options for elderly women.

Dixon-Mueller, Ruth. 1993. *Population Policy and Women's Rights: Transforming Reproductive Choice.* Westport, CT: Praeger. 289 pages. Bibliography, index. ISBN 0-275-94504-9.

This book is written by a "feminist demographer . . . who is passionately committed to the idea that a woman's ability to decide whether, when, if, and with whom to have sex and have children is a fundamental component of her rights as a woman and of her human dignity" (page xi). Dixon-Mueller has organized the book into four parts. Part One, Women's Rights as Human Rights, provides the basis for the discussion of population policies and women's rights that follows and includes the evolution of concepts of human rights in Western thought, identification of women's rights, and women's sexual and reproductive rights. Part Two, The Politics of Feminism and Birth Control/Population Control, examines birth control and population control as social movements. Part Three, Women's Rights, Women's Lives, looks at the conditions of women's lives and women's sexual and reproductive choices, using research findings from surveys and ethnographic research in developing countries. Part Four, Toward a Feminist Population Policy, suggests recommendations for a comprehensive policy agenda, based on the understanding that women's needs vary around the world—and their perception of their needs vary as well. These suggestions take into account the variety, depth, and breadth of women's experiences throughout the world.

Dwyer, Daisy J. and Judith Bruce, eds. 1988. *A Home Divided: Women and Income in the Third World.* Stanford: Stanford University Press. 290 pages. References. ISBN 0-8047-1485-1.

The authors discuss how women are perceived as having a less important role than men in generating and controlling family income. They describe the distinctive ways that men and women have access to money and other economic resources and the impact that this access has on the way they see their family and its survival. The goals that men and women have are often determined by institutionalized inequalities. This book examines the impact of reproductive failure in rural South Asia, sexual stratification in Taiwan, earning and managing money in Indonesia, women's contribution to household maintenance in South India, budgeting and financial household management in Egypt, methods of budgeting in Africa, income allocation and marriage options in Zambia, agrarian reform in Honduras, and patterns of money allocation and women's subordination in Mexico City.

El Saadawi, Nawal. 1980. *The Hidden Face of Eve.* Translated and edited by Dr. Sherif Hetata. London: Zed Press. 212 pages. ISBN 0-905762-51-7.

This book is the first book by Nawal el Saadawi (see Chapter 3) to be published in English. She describes her experiences growing up as a woman in an Islamic world. Topics discussed include sexual aggression against female children, prostitution, marriage, divorce, sexual relationships, and her own experience with female genital circumcision. Her experiences and relationships are described in relation to the larger societal context, specifically the chauvinist interpretation of Islam rather than the earlier egalitarian promises of Islam. This book is one of the first to vividly portray the oppression of women in Egypt and other Middle East, Islamic countries. By writing and publishing this book and others similar in focus, Nawal el Saadawi took a brave step in informing the world about the status and treatment of women; she made many enemies because of her views, including those in positions of power within the Egyptian government.

Foster, Catherine. 1989. *Women for All Seasons: The Story of the Women's International League for Peace and Freedom.* Athens: University of Georgia Press. 230 pages. Bibliography, index. ISBN 0-8203-1147-2.

The history of the Women's International League for Peace and Freedom (WILPF) is detailed in this fascinating account of the women's peace movement. Started in 1915 by a group of women from twelve countries who wanted to end all wars and stop the violence associated with war, WILPF continues to be a force in today's violent world. Foster describes the history of the organization, the women who founded it, and those who continue the antiwar activities to the present day. The author has convincingly captured their enthusiasm, their strong sense of peace and justice, and their attempts to bring peace to the world. She profiles 18 women involved in WILPF, including Mildred Scott Olmsted, a Quaker who was a founding member; Inga Thorsson, a politician from Sweden; Yvonne See, a French poet involved since World War II; Fujiko Isono, a Japanese scholar involved in WILPF for over 40 years; Ida Harsloff; Anissa Najjar; Kay Camp; Edith Ballantyne, known by many as the backbone of the organization; Ruth Gleissberg; Else Pickvance; Janet Bruin; Betty McIntosh; Marie-Therese Danielsson; Harriet Otterloo; Carlota Lopes da Silva; Irene Eckert; Olga Bianchi; and Angela Gethi.

Friedlander, Eva, ed. 1996. *Look at the World through Women's Eyes: Plenary Speeches from the NGO Forum on Women, Beijing '95.* New York: NGO Forum on Women, Beijing '95 Inc. Distributed by Women, Ink. 289 pages. ISBN 0-9651556-0-9.

This book is an excellent resource for the reader who wants an understanding of what happened at the NGO Forum held in Beijing in 1995 in parallel with the Fourth World Conference on Women. Speeches are provided from the opening plenary sessions, including a taped message from Aung San Suu Kyi and the keynote address by Winona LaDuke. Speeches from other sessions include regional perspectives; approaches to governance; obstacles to peace and human security; challenges posed by the globalization of the economy; the rise of conservatism in its various forms; media, culture, and communication; strategies for governance, citizenship, and political participation; violence against women; institutional mechanisms and financial arrangements; gender equity strategies of the United Nations agencies; NGO structures and accountability; and intergenerational dialogue.

Grant, Rebecca, and Kathleen Newland, eds. 1991. *Gender and International Relations.* Bloomington: Indiana University Press. 176 pages. Index. ISBN 0-253-32613-3.

For the most part, women and their opinions, knowledge, and

experience have been excluded from the theory and research related to international relations. "This exclusion has resulted in an academic field excessively focused on conflict and anarchy, and a way of practicing statecraft and formulating strategy that is excessively focused on competition and fear" (page 5). Grant and Newland chose writers and chapters for this book that represent research that is focused specifically on international relations and that is concerned with integrating women into the development process. Topics discussed include the origins of gender bias in international relations; the masculine bias found in the work of Hans Margenthau, a well-known influence in the field of international politics; the influence of socialist nations in promoting feminism; British thinking concerning women and international relations before World War II; the role that women play in economic development; the evolution of the growth of NGOs focusing on women in development; contradictions in feminist approaches to the issue of women in development; and the challenges of incorporating women and international relations into academic fields of study.

Henderson, Helen Kreider, with Ellen Hansen, eds. 1995. *Gender and Agricultural Development: Surveying the Field.* Tucson: University of Arizona Press. 161 pages. References, index. ISBN 0-8165-1542-5.

Women play a major role in agriculture in developing countries. This book discusses the major issues concerning women in development and agricultural planning. The editors show that women are prime actors in agriculture in developing countries and that materials on gender-related agricultural issues should be incorporated into development planning, research, and training activities. Henderson presents "various analytical approaches to gender issues in agriculture and indicates further resources for obtaining appropriate data" (page 120). The book is divided into two major parts: the first focuses on agricultural systems and the second on applying gender-related approaches to development activities. Topics discussed include the gender division of labor, time allocation, access to land, income-generating activities, credit, appropriate technology, agricultural extension, out-migration, livestock management, water management, and agroforestry.

Human Rights Watch Women's Rights Project. 1995. *The Human Rights Watch Global Report on Women's Human Rights.* New York: Human Rights Watch. 458 pages. ISBN 0-300-06546-9.

After five years of gathering evidence of the epidemic levels of violence against women and increasing sexual discrimination throughout the world, the Human Rights Watch has published this excellent report of what is happening to women around the world. The report focuses on the role that governments play in perpetrating, encouraging, condoning, and tolerating several types of abuse against women, including rape as a tactic of war and political repression; trafficking of women into forced prostitution; custodial violence against women; abuses against women workers; domestic violence; sexual abuse of refugee women; and human rights violations that are related to reproduction and female sexuality. Specific actions that governments and the international community can and should take to eliminate violence against women are provided.

Jejeebhoy, Shireen J. 1995. *Women's Education, Autonomy, and Reproductive Behavior: Experience from Developing Countries.* Oxford: Clarendon Press. 306 pages. Glossary, references, index. ISBN 0-19-829033-0.

At the International Conference on Population and Development in Cairo in 1994, the Programme of Action reaffirmed everyone's right to an education and gives particular attention to women and female children. Education is a key factor in quality of life and in empowering women. In this study, Jejeebhoy reviews current literature that is available from a variety of disciplines and regions of the world. The ways in which education affects women's lives and autonomy and the links between education and reproductive behavior are examined. The role that education plays in affecting a woman's age at marriage, specifically how education delays marriage, is explored. The fertility-enhancing effects of education are discussed. The ways in which education improves infant and child survival, family size preference, fertility regulation, and contraceptive practices are examined. The implications of these relationships for policymakers, families, and communities is discussed.

Kahne, Hilda, and Janet Z. Giele, eds. 1992. *Women's Work and Women's Lives: The Continuing Struggle Worldwide.* Boulder, CO: Westview Press. 324 pages. Index. ISBN 0-8133-0636-1.

The relationship between women and paid employment in industrialized as well as developing countries is explored by editors

Kahne and Giele and the impressive group of contributors to this book. In addition to the economic factors that play an important role in determining women's status within economic development, other noneconomic factors are analyzed. These factors include demographic factors, the social and cultural context in which women live and work, the political environment, and the level of economic development within each country. Specific chapters focus on women's work and women's lives in ten different countries or regions of the world. These chapters include topics on women in the economies of sub-Saharan Africa; development and changing gender roles in Latin America and the Caribbean; women, employment, and social change in the Middle East and North Africa; women and work in communist and post-communist central and eastern Europe; interaction of women's work and family roles in the former USSR; women's labor market experience in the two Germanys; women's work and lives in Great Britain; women's place in Japanese society; women and the welfare state in the Nordic countries; and work and family policies in the United States. Kahne, in the conclusion, pulls everything together and discusses the several common features in women's roles and status throughout the world.

Kelly, Gail P., ed. 1989. *International Handbook of Women's Education.* Westport, CT: Greenwood Press. 657 pages. Bibliography, index. ISBN 0-313-25638-1.

This is an excellent sourcebook on women and education throughout the world. Individual chapters focus on a specific country and include information on the history of women's education in that country, ideological and religious beliefs, cultural and political traditions, enrollment patterns, content of women's education, and outcomes of education for women in the workforce, the political system, and the family. Contemporary government policies that attempt to correct inequalities in education are provided. Because gathering information from every country would be a monumental task and require years to gather, the editor has chosen 23 countries that represent "a range of political, social and economic systems; levels of industrialization and wealth; historical contexts; and dominant ideologies about women's proper place" (page xii). Industrial nations include the United States, Japan, France, the German Democratic Republic, Great Britain, Sweden, the Soviet Union, and Canada. Poland, China, and Vietnam are included. Third World countries include

Botswana, Kenya, Nigeria, Senegal, and Zaire in Africa; India; Chile and Peru in Latin America; and Egypt, Iran, and Israel in the Middle East.

Koblinsky, Marge, Judith Timyan, and Jill Gay, eds. 1993. *The Health of Women: A Global Perspective.* Boulder, CO: Westview Press. 291 pages. Index. ISBN 0-8133-8500-8.

In 1991 the National Council for International Health sponsored a conference on "Women's Health: the Action Agenda" in Arlington, Virginia. Based on the information exchanged at that conference, this book reviews the factors that affect women's health, including low socioeconomic status, poor nutrition, infection, and economic conditions of the country in which each woman lives. An excellent resource for information on the major issues concerning women's health, topics discussed include an overview of major women's health issues, women's nutrition, social and medical realities of infection, family planning issues, abortion, women's mortality, violence against women, women's mental health, access to care, and quality of care.

Langley, Winston E. 1991. *Women's Rights in International Documents: A Sourcebook with Commentary.* Jefferson, NC: McFarland and Company. 192 pages. Index. ISBN 0-89950-548-1.

This book is an excellent resource on international documents that focus on or deal with women's rights. It includes the Charter of the United Nations, the Universal Declaration of Human Rights, the International Covenant on Civil and Political Rights, and the International Covenant of Economic, Social and Cultural Rights. Conventions and recommendations adopted by the United Nations or one of its six organs (the Security Council, the Trusteeship Council, the International Court of Justice, the Secretariat, the General Assembly, and the Economic and Social Council), the International Labour Organization, and the UN Educational, Scientific and Cultural Organization (UNESCO) are described and excerpted. International agreements cited focus on issues of employment, wages, education, nationality, marriage, family, children, prostitution, slavery, and political rights. The Convention on the Elimination of All Forms of Discrimination against Women and the Declaration on the Elimination of Discrimination against Women also are included.

Leonard, Ann, ed. 1995. *Seeds 2: Supporting Women's Work around the World.* New York: Feminist Press of the City University of New York. 243 pages. ISBN 1-55861-107-X.

This book is a sequel to *Seeds: Supporting Women's Work in the Third World* (see below) and includes nine case studies and four original essays that examine women's economic development from international and regional perspectives. Case studies focus on reaching out to female farmers in Western Zambia, supporting female farmers in the green zones of Mozambique, a small-scale enterprise program in Port Sudan, a women's dairy project in Thailand, wasteland development in India, self-employment as a means to women's economic self-sufficiency in the United States, and child care programs to meet the needs of working mothers in Nepal, Ecuador, and Ethiopia. The final essays focus on the transition from women in development to gender and development, mainstreaming women in development, women's income-generation activities in Latin America and the Caribbean, and mainstreaming gender development from the UN Children's Emergency Fund (UNICEF) perspective.

————, ed. 1989. *Seeds: Supporting Women's Work in the Third World.* New York: Feminist Press of the City University of New York. 242 pages. ISBN 0-935312-92-7.

This book grew out a series of pamphlets, called *Seeds,* that presented case studies about income-generating programs for women in all regions of the Third World. Nine case studies "document projects that are based on women's own initiatives and solidarity; that encourage broad changes in participants' socio-economic status and personal sense of worth; and that are economically viable" (page xi). These projects include village women who organize a community bus service in Kenya, a women's cooperative in Mali to help women find paid employment; a working women's forum in India organized for credit and change in Madras, India; developing noncraft employment in Bangladesh; forest conservation in Nepal; a women's credit program in Nicaragua; community management of waste recycling in Mexico; a women's construction collective in Kingston, Jamaica; and women and handicrafts throughout the world.

Liswood, Laura A. 1995. *Women World Leaders: Fifteen Great Politicians Tell Their Stories.* London: Pandora. 188 pages. Selected bibliography, index. ISBN 0-04-440904-4.

Laura Liswood interviewed 15 women who are, or have been, leaders of their countries, including Corazon Aquino (Philippines), Sirimavo Bandaranaike (Sri Lanka), Benazir Bhutto (Pakistan), Gro Harlem Brundtland (Norway), Violeta Chamorro (Nicaragua), Eugenia Charles (Dominica), Tansu Ciller (Turkey), Edith Cresson (France), Vigdis Finnbogadottir (Iceland), Maria Liberia-Peters (Netherlands Antilles), Kazimiera Prunskiene (Lithuania), Mary Robinson (Ireland), Hanna Suchocka (Poland), Margaret Thatcher (United Kingdom), and Khaleda Zia (Bangladesh). Short biographies of each leader are provided. Liswood discusses the commonalities in the backgrounds of these leaders, the role that their parents played in helping them develop confidence in themselves, the problems they faced as women trying to lead their countries, how they combine politics and motherhood, leadership styles, women's perceived lack of toughness as leaders, and advice to women leaders. Finally, Liswood provides a short description of each country represented in this book by these women, including population statistics and descriptions of the economy, politics, and attitudes toward women.

Lubin, Carol Riegelman, and Anne Winslow. 1990. *Social Justice for Women: The International Labor Organization and Women.* Durham: Duke University Press. 329 pages. Index. ISBN 0-8223-1062-7.

The International Labor Organization (ILO) was established in 1919 as an intergovernmental organization dedicated to promoting social justice as a precondition for universal peace. The ILO was one of the first organizations to promote the equality of women with men; one of its objectives is to promote the principle that men and women should receive equal pay for comparable work. This book examines the history of the ILO, the militant women, primarily in the U.S. and British labor movements, who played a prominent role in the early days of the ILO, the ILO's major activities that affect women, and the ILO's interaction with national and international women's movements. The role of the ILO in the United Nations Conference on International Organization is explored, along with the effect of emerging new women's organizations on the ILO's programs for women.

Martin, Susan Forbes. 1991. *Refugee Women.* Atlantic Highlands, NJ: Zed Books. 140 pages. List of international organizations, bibliography, index. ISBN 1-85649-000-9.

This book provides an excellent overview of the status of refugee and displaced women, their needs, and the contributions they make in improving their situations and to their new homeland. The steps that the United Nations, nongovernmental organizations, and governments are taking to respond to the needs of these women are discussed. Recommendations are made for further improvements. Individual chapters focus on the role of refugee women in their communities and in decision-making and programming activities; issues of physical and legal protection affecting these women; assistance issues, such as access to food, water, shelter, health care, education, and social services; economic activities; the search for enduring solutions to issues of repatriation and permanent settlement in countries of asylum; and the status of policy and programmatic actions at the international level that attempt to improve the lives of refugee and displaced women. Appendices provide information concerning suggestions for further study and activity, relevant United Nations documents, and a list of relevant international organizations involved in assisting refugees.

Momsen, Janet H. 1991. *Women and Development in the Third World.* New York: Routledge. Index. ISBN 0-415-01695-9.

All societies have a clear division of labor by sex, and modernization and a restructuring of traditional economies have changed this division of labor. Women have borne the brunt of these changes, including an increase in women's dependent status and in their workload. Momsen provides ten case studies to demonstrate the ways that women have been affected. Topics include the sex ratio in South Asia, migration, female-headed households, biological reproduction, education, housing, gender differences in time budgets, women in the plantation sector, women as rural traders, female marginalization, gender divisions of labor, barriers to women's participation in the urban modern sector, women in industry, women in the service sector, contemporary problems of development, community management, and development policies for women. Case studies focus on Bangladesh, Lesotho, Singapore, Trinidad, Sri Lanka, Peru, Colombia, Malaysia, Korea, and Kenya.

Momsen, Janet H., and Janet G. Townsend, eds. 1987. *Geography of Gender in the Third World.* Albany: State University of New York Press. 424 pages. Bibliography, index. ISBN 0-88706-441-8.

Momsen and Townsend explore the growing understanding of the relationship between geography and gender. No matter what the country, the socioeconomic class, or individual variations, the subordination of women is found in the study of the geography of gender. In this book, case studies from a variety of Third World countries are presented. An overview of the major issues in the study of gender in developing countries is provided. The sex ratio in South Asia, women as caretakers of health in Nepal, and malnutrition in Bangladesh are described as they relate to individual survival. The work of rural women and nutrition in sub-Saharan Africa, women farmers in Nigeria, the heavy burdens and few privileges of women in Tanzania, and peasant women in Bolivia's Lake Titicaca are discussed. The many aspects of women in the labor force are examined, including women and migration in Lesotho, rainforest colonization in Colombia, and female labor mobility in Thailand. Industrial changes and the division of labor are illustrated with descriptions of family structure and female labor in Mexico, gender and industrialization in Brazil, and women's issues and men's roles in Sri Lanka. Finally, the direction that research on gender issues is taking is described in chapters that focus on rural energy and the role of women, agricultural modernization in India, women's role in integrated development in Egypt, the feminization of agriculture in the Caribbean, structural change in the Malay family, and women workers and the creation of demand.

Moser, Caroline O. N. 1993. *Gender Planning and Development: Theory, Practice and Training.* New York: Routledge. 285 pages. Notes, bibliography, index. ISBN 0-415-05620-9.

Many current approaches to development and women in the Third World are beginning to focus on gender and development rather than women and development. Gender and development examines the social relationship between men and women and develops policies and programs based on these relationships while women in development activities have more often focused on the biological differences between men and women. The first part of this book discusses feminist theories, women in development theories, and gender and development theories and their relationship to gender planning. Fundamental misconceptions and assumptions are examined that have led development planners to exclude women from the development process or to discriminate against them. Some of these assumptions are related to family structure and division of labor within the household. The relationship between different economic development models and policy approaches concerning women in the Third World are discussed. In Part 2, characteristics of and major issues in the field of gender planning are discussed. Procedures for implementing gender policies, programs and projects, training strategies, and the political agenda of women's organizations are examined. An appendix offers a gender-planning training methodology.

Nelson, Barbara J., and Najma Chowdhury, eds. 1994. *Women and Politics Worldwide.* New Haven, CT: Yale University Press. 818 pages. Index. ISBN 0-300-05407-6.

This book provides an excellent overview and resource material concerning women and their involvement in politics throughout the world. The editors found that "in no country do women have political status, access, or influence equal to men's. The sweep of women's political subordination encompasses the great variety of cultures, economic arrangements, and regimes in which they live" (page 3). Women and the extent of their political involvement were studied in 43 countries, which represent a variety of political systems, regions of the world, and levels of economic development. The first chapter presents an overview of major issues concerning women's status and involvement in politics and covers topics such as international forces that affect women's participation in politics, including economic and religious forces; a global review of women's issues concerning violence, safety, reproductive rights, abortion, maternal and child health, access to education, employment, health care, and credit; and reasons for excluding women from politics, including patriarchy and fraternalism. A discussion is presented concerning the research design, the history of this project, and problems encountered in collecting data on women's experience. The next section, and the major portion of the book, offers chapters on each of the 43 countries and includes information on women's experiences in politics from the early 1960s to the early 1990s.

Newsom, Doug A., and Bob J. Carrell, eds. 1995. *Silent Voices.* Lanham, MD: University Press of America. 244 pages. Index. ISBN 0-8191-9854-4.

The editors chose to title this collection of papers *Silent Voices* to show that women are capable of voicing their opinions and ideas but that "women's voices have been 'silenced' indeed by cultural, social, economic, or political factors" (p. vii). This book provides versions of many of the papers presented at an international colloquium in 1993 organized to examine the global status of women. Topics covered include the positive effect on the world's agenda that women's voices can bring, a women's organization in El Salvador that sponsors women-owned and operated projects, gender-sensitive research strategies for planning development activities based on experience in the Philippines, a comparison of two rural women's organizations in Nigeria, and the problems faced by female development workers trying to fit into the male power structure. A section on cultural expectations contains articles concerning the problems women face in attempting to live up to social and cultural expectations in Nigeria, Muslim women in Malaysia working to improve their lives, and the effect that a patriarchal system has on the value placed on women's work. Finally, a section on struggling with stereotypes focuses on Hispanic female politicians trying to break the stereotypes of Hispanic women as fragile, the role of female journalists in the Philippines, female foreign news correspondents from developing countries who report from Washington, D.C., and the inability of news magazines to fairly represent women and their activities.

Nussbaum, Martha C., and Jonathan Glover, eds. 1995. *Women, Culture, and Development: A Study of Human Capabilities.* Oxford: Clarendon Press. 481 pages. Name, subject indexes. ISBN 0-19-828917-0.

This book is a result of a study prepared for the World Institute for Development Economics Research (WIDER), which was established in 1984 by the United Nations University as its first research and training center. It grew out of the need for an accurate assessment of the role of cultural traditions in determining the quality of life for community residents and the justice in such traditions. A case study on women's right to employment in India and Bangladesh as a matter of survival poignantly illustrates the problems that women face in trying to survive in an impossible situation—Metha Dai, a widow with two young children living in Rajasthan, India, is prohibited by her caste from working outside her home, but no one else will help feed her and her children. If she works, her in-laws will likely beat her and her children. Part II focuses on theoretical and methodological foundations and issues in studying women and development issues and dealing with cross-cultural standards of justice. In Part III, concrete issues of justice are discussed, including topics on the inequalities between the sexes in different cultural contexts, the issue of law and its impact on women, the question concerning the effect of women's emotions on their capabilities, and the value of gender identification. The final section presents an account of women's inequality in China, Mexico, and India and a discussion of the value of traditional gender roles in Nigeria.

Olsen, Kirstin. 1994. *Chronology of Women's History.* Westport, CT: Greenwood Press. 507 pages. Selected bibliography, index. ISBN 0-313-28803-8.

This is an excellent reference/resource book on women's history and includes information on activities and accomplishments of women throughout the world. Organized by year, entries are divided into a variety of categories, including general status and daily life; government, the military, and the law; literature and the visual arts; performing arts and entertainment; athletics and exploration; activism; business and industry; science and medicine; education and scholarship; and religion. Women's activities from prehistory to 1993 are included.

Ostergaard, Lise, ed. 1992. *Gender and Development: A Practical Guide.* New York: Routledge. 220 pages. References, index. ISBN 0-415-07131-3.

Understanding the role that gender plays in economic development is necessary to creating effective programs in economic development. This book discusses the reasons why using a gender perspective can lead to successful development efforts. Differences in the roles and opportunities afforded men and women in developing countries pervade all aspects of life in these countries. This book helps the reader understand the importance of gender by examining the concept of gender, traditional data-gathering methods that have distorted the economic role of women in development, gender-related issues that affect women in agriculture, employment, housing, and transportation; access to health and medical services; diversion of income and management of household resources; and guidelines on incorporating gender awareness in programs for economic development in developing countries.

Peters, Julie, and Andrea Wolper, eds. 1995. *Women's Rights, Human Rights: International Feminist Perspectives.* New York: Routledge. 372 pages. Index. ISBN 0-415-90995-3.

An excellent resource on the issues surrounding women's human rights, this book includes contributions by activists, journalists, lawyers, and scholars from 21 countries. Major topics covered include a background discussion of women's rights as human rights, regional reports, gendered law, cultural differences, violence and health, development and the socioeconomy, and persecuted women. Specific chapters focus on the women's rights movement, women's rights and the United Nations, violence against women in India and the former Yugoslavia, violations of women's human rights in Iran, gender discrimination in Kenya, the Convention on the Elimination of All Forms of Discrimination against Women, the public/private distinction in international human rights law, human rights of women in the family, the politics of gender, cultural particularism, gendered war crimes, AIDS and gender violence, female genital mutilation, women's reproductive rights and health, women's access to productive resources, women's rights and the right to development, human rights for refugee and displaced women, and women fleeing gender-based persecution.

Rowbotham, Sheila, and Swasti Mitter, eds. 1994. *Dignity and Daily Bread: New Forms of Economic Organizing among Poor Women in the Third World and the First.* New York: Routledge. 233 pages. Index. ISBN 0-415-09585-9.

The general condition of a country's economy has an impact on the well-being of women in that country. Rowbotham and Mitter have gathered the input of other scholars and researchers to examine this relationship and the ways that "gender relations interact with other social relationships" (page xi). Specific case studies are used to demonstrate the impact that government policies and market forces have on the lives of women, especially poor women. They show the growing ability of women to organize at the grassroots level to gain economic benefits. Specific topics discussed include an overview of organizing women in the Bombay cotton textile industry (1919–1940); women in free trade zones in Malaysia, the Philippines, and Sri Lanka; the Nineteenth of September National Union of Garment Workers in Mexico; the Self-Employed Women's Association of Gujarat, India; the growth of women's economic associations and networks in urban Tanzania; and strategies against sweated work in Britain (1820–1920).

Roy, Kartik C., Clement A. Tisdell, and Hans C. Blomqvist, eds. 1996. *Economic Development and Women in the World Community.* Westport, CT: Praeger. 247 pages. References, index. ISBN 0-275-95134-0.

Many researchers believe that women play a crucial role in economic development and as agents of change within their countries. Economic development requires a significant improvement in the socioeconomic status of women in many countries. This book examines the current socioeconomic status of women, the impact that economic changes have on women, and steps that many countries are taking to empower women in the economic development process. The editors present an overview of discrimination and changes in the status of women in relation to economic development. Individual chapters focus on women and development in Taiwan, China, Malaysia, Japan, South Asia, sub-Saharan Africa (Tanzania), Finland, Europe, the United States, Latin America, the Caribbean, and Australia.

Sachs, Carolyn E. 1996. *Gendered Fields: Rural Women, Agriculture, and Environment.* Boulder, CO: Westview Press. 205 pages. Bibliography, index. ISBN 0-8133-2519-6.

In *Gendered Fields,* Sachs works to incorporate an understanding of rural women into general feminist theory, which often focuses on the experiences of "white, Western, upper-middle-class, urban women" (page 3). Several questions are answered in an attempt to understand the lives of rural women. The answers to these questions focus on the relationship of women to the natural environment, the forms that patriarchal relations take in rural areas, the effect that global economic restructuring has on rural women, and the strategies that rural women employ to improve their lives. Feminist theory, rural women's connections to the land, women's work with plants and animals, women's roles on family farms, and global restructuring, including the impact of the growing amount of finance capital, industrial reorganization, and changes in the structure of labor markets, are examined.

Schuler, Margaret, ed. 1992. *Freedom from Violence: Women's Strategies from around the World.* New York: UNIFEM (United Nations Development Fund for Women). 354 pages. References, index. LC 92-80009. Books from UNIFEM are sold exclusively by Women, Ink: 777 United Nations Plaza, New York, NY 10017; (212) 687-8633; Fax: (212) 661-2704; e-mail: wink@igc.apc.org.

Schuler provides an overview of the major issues surrounding violence against women and the types of approaches that are used around the world to prevent this violence. Contemporary issues concerning the provision of services to women, the reform of legal systems, and education of women in ways to avoid violence are discussed. Contributors discuss the many approaches taken to combat violence against women in Sri Lanka, Pakistan, India, Malaysia, Thailand, Sudan, Zimbabwe, Mexico, Brazil, Bolivia, Chile, and the United States.

Sen, Gita, Adrienne Germain, and Lincoln C. Chen, eds. 1994. *Population Policies Reconsidered: Health, Empowerment, and Rights.* Boston: Harvard University Press. 280 pages. Index. ISBN 0-674-69003-6.

Contributors to this volume come from the fields of social activism, ethics and law, demography, social sciences, and health sciences to provide the reader with a comprehensive examination of population policies and family planning programs throughout the world. Chapters discuss current debates on population policies and are organized into four sections. Section One reexamines premises that population policies have historically been based on, including population and ethics; sexual and reproductive health and rights; women's rights versus population control; development, population, and the environment; and population, well-being, and freedom. Section Two, on human rights and reproductive rights, looks at the ways that human rights can be honored in population policies and reproductive and sexual rights. Gender and empowerment is the focus in Section Three, which includes a discussion of the meaning of women's empowerment; women's burdens; women's status, empowerment, and reproductive outcomes; and gender relations and household dynamics. The final section looks at reproductive and sexual health: individual chapters focus on reproductive and sexual health services; a reproductive health approach to the objectives and assessment of family planning programs; reaching young people; fertility control technology; and financing reproductive and sexual health services.

Sen, Gita, and Rachel C. Snow, eds. 1994. *Power and Decision: The Social Control of Reproduction.* Boston: Harvard University Press. 348 pages. Index, acronyms. ISBN 0-674-69533-X.

Sen and Snow have gathered a multidisciplinary group of researchers, in fields as diverse as economics, political science, public health, biology, sociology, pharmacy, and the law, to discuss the social implications of reproduction. Women's reproductive rights have improved in many countries over the last several years, with the acceptance of family planning activities in most of the United Nations member states, the improvement in contraceptives and their acceptance in many countries, and increasing advances in treating infertility. Divided into two major sections, this book covers policies and politics of reproduction and the new technologies in reproductive science. Topics concerning policies and politics include the feminist challenge to social policy concerning reproduction; the working world, day care, and other impacts on working mothers; the experiences of Thai women; religious doctrine and reproductive options in Islam; feminist policies and reproductive rights in Brazil; and abortion policies in Canada and the United States. The discussions of the new technologies include in-vitro fertilization, contraceptive vaccines, the use of Norplant, and improvements in diagnostic technologies. The authors explore how these new technologies can be used by women, their families, health professionals, communities, and societies to promote humane values. This is examined with the understanding "that these technologies themselves are not neutral tools being used or abused by society. Rather, they are chosen, designed, evaluated and promoted by select (and often different) political communities, and they manifest the values and interests of those communities" (page 148).

Shreir, Sally, ed. 1988. *Women's Movements of the World: An International Directory and Reference Guide.* Essex, UK: Longman. 384 pages. Bibliography. ISBN 0-582-00988-X.

This reference book provides a wealth of information on women's issues and organizations throughout the world, organized by country. Information on topics of interest to women (and men) is presented, including women's participation in the political process, in the workplace, and in education, the rights women have in marriage and divorce, and contraception and abortion. A listing of women's organizations offers national groups as well as many that operate on a local level; included are member organizations and those that focus on research, education, database and information services, and the provision of technical assistance. A bibliography of selected materials is also included.

Sparr, Pamela, ed. 1994. *Mortgaging Women's Lives: Feminist Critiques of Structural Adjustment.* Atlantic Highlands, NJ: Zed Books. 214 pages. Index. ISBN 1-85649-101-3.

In the early 1980s many developing countries were unable to find commercial banks willing or able to lend them money for development projects. Many of these countries found themselves in economic difficulty and were forced to seek help from institutions such as the World Bank and the International Monetary Fund. These institutions required that loan recipients correct many of their problems, such as severe inflation, stagnating output, trade deficits, and government budget deficits, through the application of structural adjustment policies. These policies allow market forces to operate freely. This book focuses on the impact that structural adjustment policies have had on women in developing countries. The editor explains what structural adjustment is and how it has affected women in general. Individual chapters provide analyses of structural adjustment policies and their impact on women in Ghana, Egypt, Turkey, Sri Lanka, the Philippines, Nigeria, and Jamaica. The final chapter suggests areas for further research, the direction that advocacy programs should take to improve the role of women in development activities, and relevant policy issues that should be discussed and resolved in order for women to benefit economically.

Steady, Fillomina Chioma, ed. 1993. *Women and Children First: Environment, Poverty, and Sustainable Development.* Rochester, VT: Schenkman Books. 475 pages. Bibliography. ISBN 0-87047-064-7.

Many of the chapters in this book are based on papers presented at the symposium "Women and Children First: The Impact of Poverty and Environmental Degradation on Women and Children," held in May 1991 in Geneva, Switzerland, as a prelude to the 1992 Earth Summit (also known as the United Nations Conference on Environment and Development), held in Rio de Janeiro. Part I explores the nature and scope of women, poverty, and development issues and examines women as managers, protectors, and victims of the environment. Part II looks at unsustainable development, including issues of hunger and malnutrition, problems of environmental degradation and poverty, consumption patterns of developed countries and their impact on developing countries, and women's roles, population issues, poverty, and environmental degradation. Managers and conservers of natural resources are the focus of Part III, examining African women's indigenous knowledge in managing natural resources, case studies of African women, and the importance of water and water policies in preserving life. Part IV discusses environmental degradation and poverty and includes chapters on women migrant workers; women, children, and childhood diarrhea in an Egyptian village; and leather tanning in India. Problems of development and environmental security are presented in Part V, and Part VI discusses the fate of children. Part VII examines actions taken by women and children to improve their lives and their environment, including the energy crisis, ensuring access to clean water, and case studies from Costa Rica concerning population and natural resources. Finally, Part VIII presents recommendations that came out of the symposium and the 1992 Earth Summit.

Tinker, Irene, ed. 1990. *Persistent Inequalities: Women and World Development.* New York: Oxford University Press. 302 pages. Bibliography, index. ISBN 0-19-506158-6.

Tinker and her colleagues provide an excellent historical and political overview of the field of women and economic development. Following an introduction, Ester Boserup provides a current examination of economic change and the role of women by summarizing global trends caused by modernization. In an examination of the politics of women in development, chapters in Section I identify the goals and approaches of advocates, practitioners, and scholars in this field; focus on gender and justice in economic development; provide feminist perspectives on women in development; offer gender perspectives on technology and education; and examine why the socioeconomic impact of export industries set up by multinationals in Third World countries has been so great. Section II examines intrahousehold distribution and control, including gender and cooperative conflicts, the impact of the value of women's time on food and nutrition, and the methods by which patriarchal perceptions of obligations and behavior are imposed on women in Asia. The focus of Section III is on challenging patriarchy, and individual chapters examine the sexual division of labor and the subordination of women in India; changing patterns of gender stratification in West Africa; East African women, work, and the articulation of dominance; women's work in the Caribbean; and the demise of patriarchy.

Tomasevski, Katarina. 1993. *Women and Human Rights.* Atlantic Highlands, NJ: Zed Books. 162 pages. List of organizations, bibliography, index. ISBN 1-85649-119-6.

Women and their human rights have been ignored at all levels of government in countries throughout the world. In providing an overview of this problem and what is being done to focus attention on helping women attain equal rights, this book is an excellent educational tool to help women and their organizations apply existing human rights standards and procedures. Tomasevski emphasizes the differences that exist between the women's agenda and the human rights agenda throughout the world. In trying to stimulate activism on the grassroots level, the author provides suggestions for education and action activities and for legally fighting for women's rights. Individual chapters focus on the history of women's rights; education for empowerment; challenging unequal rights; outlawing and eliminating discrimination; redressing inequalities; protecting the most vulnerable, including refugees, those imprisoned, and the disabled; equal rights for all; and guidance for action.

United Nations. 1995. *The World's Women 1995: Trends and Statistics.* New York: United Nations. 188 pages. ISBN 92-1-161372-8.

This is an excellent sourcebook for information on the status of women in the world today. Full of valuable statistics on women in individual countries, regions, and throughout the world, this book offers information on how women contribute to economic life, politics, and families. Individual chapters focus on population, households, and families; population growth, distribution, and environment; health; education and training; work; and power and influence. Annexes provide information on technical notes on the tables and countries, areas, and geographical groupings. Appendixes. Sources of statistical information are listed.

Walker, Alice, and Pratibha Parmar. 1993. *Warrior Marks: Female Genital Mutilation and the Sexual Blinding of Women.* New

York: Harcourt Brace and Company. 373 pages. Selected bibliography, list of organizations. ISBN 0-15-100061-1.

After writing *Possessing the Secret of Joy,* Alice Walker decided that she needed to do more to stop the practice of female genital mutilation. She talked with Pratibha Parmar, a well-known Indian-British filmmaker who has produced several documentaries concerning major social issues, including issues of race, gender, and sexuality, and the two women decided to produce the film *Warrior Marks,* focusing on female genital mutilation. This book describes their efforts in producing that film, from first corresponding with each other to traveling to England, Senegal, Gambia, and Burkina Faso. Interviews, poems by Alice Walker, and photographs vividly portray the lives and struggles of the African women they talked with.

Winslow, Anne, ed. 1995. *Women, Politics, and the United Nations.* Westport, VT: Greenwood Press. 213 pages. Bibliography, index. ISBN 0-313-29522-0.

Winslow examines the origins of the women's movement and its current strength and cohesion. She analyzes the forces that have shaped the women's movement, primarily the United Nations and the organizations within it and affiliated with it. The authors focus on the specific instruments that have been enacted within the United Nations. Topics discussed include the World Conference of International Women's Year, the 1980 Mid-Decade Conference in Copenhagen, the Nairobi Conference in 1985, the Convention on the Elimination of All Forms of Discrimination against Women, the politics of women and development, equality for women within the UN Secretariat, women's international nongovernmental organizations at the UN, and specialized agencies and the World Bank.

Women: A World Report. New York: Oxford University Press, 1985. 376 pages. ISBN 0-19-520490-5.

As an outgrowth of the United Nations Decade for Women (1975–1985), this book describes the status of women as of 1985 and can be used as a benchmark to measure future changes in the status of women. Part 1 provides information on the status of women in the areas of the family, agriculture, work in the non-agricultural sector, health, sex, education, and politics. Part 2 contains the contributions of ten women who write about women in

ten different countries—five of these women were from developing countries and were sent to report on women in richer, developed countries, while the other five women were from developed nations and were sent to developing countries. This
exchange provides a fascinating perspective on women throughout the world. The chapter on women and the family provides a
description of the experiences of Anita Desai in Norway and
Toril Brekke in Kenya; women and work sent Manny Shirazi to
the Soviet Union and Marilyn French traveled to India; women
and education brought Zhang Jie to the United States and sent Jill
Tweedie to Indonesia; women and politics sent Nawal el
Saadawi to the United Kingdom; and women and sex sent Elena
Poniatowska to Australia and Angela Davis to Egypt. The final
section provides statistics concerning women and the family, fertility, household size, labor force, health, life expectancy, child
survival, mortality rates, literacy rates, enrollment rates in primary and postsecondary levels, and politics.

Women's Feature Service. 1992. *The Power to Change: Women in
the Third World Redefine Their Environment.* Atlantic Highlands, NJ: Zed Books. 236 pages. Index. ISBN 1-85649-225-7.

As a worldwide network of women journalists from approximately 60 countries, the Women's Feature Service gathers information and provides the mainstream media with current and re-
alistic portrayals of women and development. This book
provides a look at women in Africa, South Asia, Southeast Asia,
and Latin America—their lives and their accomplishments. The
introduction describes the important role that women play in development activities and their influence in improving their lives
and the lives of their families. The book describes the ways in
which women have organized to fight for a variety of causes, including those that focus on development issues, environmental
issues, and gender-specific issues. The activities described in this
book include women organizing in India against the Union Car-
bide settlement of the Bhopal gas leak; over 600 women's groups
in Kenya coming together to halt deforestation activities by
planting trees; and women in Brazil fighting mass sterilization.
This book provides an effective glimpse into the lives of real
women in several developing nations.

Books, Regional

Adepoju, Aderanti, and Christine Oppong, eds. 1994. *Gender, Work and Population in Sub-Saharan Africa.* Portsmouth, NH: Heinemann. 245 pages. Bibliography, index. ISBN 0-435-08953-6.

The ways in which women's work has been perceived, examined, and recorded by statisticians, economists, and policymakers are explored in this book. The many contributors examine the culturally prescribed roles of women (and men) and the ways in which these roles affect employment and population issues and policies. Economists, statisticians, and policymakers are encouraged to study the role of women in economic development within the context of the family and kinship systems of the country in which they live. Issues discussed include high mortality and fertility rates, migration for employment, agricultural policies and women producers, women's participation in the labor force, women's economic contributions, gender-sensitive statistics, childbearing and child-rearing practices, work and fertility, family planning, breastfeeding and birth spacing, and the grandmother's role in the household.

Afkhami, Mahnaz, ed. 1995. *Faith and Freedom: Women's Human Rights in the Muslim World.* Syracuse, NY: Syracuse University Press. 244 pages. Index. ISBN 0-8156-2667-3.

Afkhami has gathered together a strong, knowledgeable group of scholars and activists to write about issues concerning Muslim women's search and fight for their rights as humans. Many of the contributors participated in the Washington Dialogue, a conference held in Washington, D.C., in 1994 that focused on religion, culture, and women's human rights in the Muslim world. In Part One, contributors focus on the politics of gender in Muslim countries, reflections on Islam as religion and state, the dichotomy between religious and secular discourse in Islamic societies, the muted voices of women interpreters, the role of women's groups in initiating dialogue on women's issues, and rhetorical strategies and official policies on women's rights. Part Two offers selected cases of women and violence in Muslim countries, including the ambiguity of shari'a and the politics of rights in Saudi Arabia, rape and power in Pakistan, Muslim refugee, returnee, and displaced women, the lack of women's human rights in Algeria, and women's human rights on trial in Jordan.

Agarwal, Bina. 1994. *A Field of One's Own: Gender and Land Rights in South Asia.* New York: Cambridge University Press. 572 pages. Definitions, glossary, references, index. ISBN 0-521-41868-2.

Agarwal has spent over 15 years conducting research on rural poverty, agrarian changes, and the political impact of gender and working with peasant women in South Asia who are involved in grassroots activities concerning women's independent land rights. This book grew out of the need for research in the area of gender and land rights. Despite legislation providing women with certain inheritance and property rights, the stark reality is that "few South Asian women inherit landed property, and even fewer control it" (page xvi). This book examines the disparity between legal rights and implementation of these rights and examines many of the factors involved in preventing women from claiming these rights. Specific chapters focus on land rights for women, conceptualizing gender relations, customary rights and associated practices, traditionally matrilineal and bilateral communities, contemporary laws, the gap between law and practice, the gap between ownership and control, tracing cross-regional diversities, struggles over resources, suggestions for the future, and the dilemmas some of these suggestions create.

Berger, Marguerite, and Mayra Buvinic, eds. 1989. *Women's Ventures: Assistance to the Informal Sector in Latin America.* West Hartford, CT: Kumarian Press. 268 pages. Bibliography, index. ISBN 0-931816-79-3.

Women entrepreneurs and their contributions to society are often ignored in many Latin American countries, in part because they are not seen as true entrepreneurs. Many women sell a variety of items on street corners but are not thought of as businesswomen. This book attempts to focus attention on these women and their accomplishments. Broad areas examined include this informal sector of the economy and programs designed to help; training programs and technical assistance activities that are provided; case studies of credit programs; and major gender issues and evaluations of assistance programs. Specific chapters focus on improving women's access to credit, excess labor supply, small-scale commerce, solidarity group programs, training and technical assistance, credit guarantee mechanisms, the rural development fund, credit and development for women, the MUDE (Mujeres en Desarrollo Dominicana) credit program in the Dominican Republic, and the impact of a credit project for women and men in Ecuador.

Bose, Christine E., and Edna Acosta-Belen, eds. 1995. *Women in the Latin American Development Process.* Philadelphia: Temple University Press. 290 pages. Index. ISBN 1-56639-292-6.

The role of development can be best understood with an interdisciplinary approach that uses both a historical and international political economy framework, according to Bose and Acosta-Belen. Contributors to this volume reflect a variety of backgrounds (anthropology, sociology, history, political science, and economics) and provide a multidisciplinary approach to the study of women in development in Latin America. Major topics examined include the role of colonialism, subordination, and empowerment; gender, industrialization, and transnational corporations; the growth of studies concerning women's role in economic development; changing perspectives of women in the global economy; and strategies for empowering women on an individual, household, and collective level.

House-Midamba, Bessie, and Felix K. Ekichi, eds. 1995. *African Market Women and Economic Power: The Role of Women in African Economic Development.* Westport, CT: Greenwood Press. 214 pages. Bibliography, index. ISBN 0-313-29214-0.

Many studies of African women and economic development have focused on women in West Africa, while fewer studies have been conducted on women and economic development activities in east, central, or southern Africa. This book focuses on women's economic activities from a comparative perspective that includes much of sub-Saharan Africa. Examining African market women and economic power, chapters focus on these issues and their relationship to the sexual division of labor in African cultures: competition between men and women concerning certain market areas and items; the nature of available resources; the cultural, social, and economic barriers that limit women's participation in economic activity; the ways that African women are able to exploit economic, social, and political opportunities; the effect of European imperialism on the status of women; and the effects of postcolonialism programs on the participation of women in economic activities.

James, Valentine Udoh, ed. 1995. *Women and Sustainable Development in Africa.* Westport, CT: Praeger. 203 pages. References, index. ISBN 0-275-95308-4.

In the planning process for agricultural projects in developing countries, increasing attention is being paid to the environmental impacts that these projects will have. Without women's participation in project planning, many of these issues are unknown or ignored. The contributors to this book examine these issues within an African context. Topics include sustaining women's efforts in Africa's development, current and future directions for African women farmers, listening to and learning from African women farmers, the design of gender-specific interventions in Zaire, the sociocultural aspects of women's contributions in Ethiopia, women in commercial agriculture, rural women's participation in Malawi's national rural development programs, increasing female head-of-household participation in agricultural extension, agrarian women and the indigenous textile industry in Nigeria, and the economic role of rural African women in production activities.

Jelin, Elizabeth, ed. 1990. *Women and Social Change in Latin America.* Translated by J. Ann Zammit and Marilyn Thomson. Atlantic Highlands, NJ: Zed Books. 226 pages. Bibliography, index. ISBN 0-86232-870-5.

Women organizing for and working toward achieving their rights and their identity in Latin America is the focus of this book. To examine social movements and the institutionalization of legal options for participating in collective action, Jelin has gathered the writings of a variety of researchers. Topics discussed include the activities of women settlers in a poor neighborhood in Lima, Peru; women, daily life, and politics in São Paulo, Brazil; women in the transition to democracy in Argentina; women and unions in Chile; the peasant women's organization in Bolivia; indigenous women and community resistance; and citizenship and identity.

Khoury, Nabil F., and Valentine M. Moghadam, eds. 1995. *Gender and Development in the Arab World: Women's Economic Participation: Patterns and Policies.* Atlantic Highlands, NJ: Zed Books. 203 pages. Bibliography, index. ISBN 1-85649-365-2.

Many researchers believe that women can play an important role in the economic development of their local neighborhoods and their countries. Khoury and Moghadam explore the role of women in development in Arab countries. They document the patterns and policies of female employment and explain the factors that determine whether or not women are allowed to participate in gainful employment. Cultural bias and its role in estimating women's contributions to their families and their countries is examined. The politics of women's participation in the labor force are discussed. Case studies provide profiles of socioeconomic development and cultural values within individual countries.

Lightfoot-Klein, Hanny. 1989. *Prisoners of Ritual: An Odyssey into Female Genital Circumcision in Africa.* Binghampton, NY: Harrington Park Press. 306 pages. Bibliography, index. ISBN 0-918393-68-X.

Lightfoot-Klein reports on three separate studies that she conducted in Sudan between 1979 and 1983 on female circumcision. She provides the reader with a description of the varieties of female genital circumcision, the reasons why this procedure is carried out, and what the people think about this practice. She describes the methods she used to gather information, the current situation in Sudan, conversations she has had with a variety of professionals and family members, and a history of female genital circumcision in the Western world. The practice of male circumcision is described. In Part II, she offers a chapter of images of people she has talked with and descriptions of her experiences traveling throughout Sudan. Two appendices are included: one provides summaries of the interviews she conducted with 27 women and the other provides summaries of interviews with 5 men.

Moghadam, Valentine M. 1993. *Modernizing Women: Gender and Social Change in the Middle East.* Boulder, CO: Lynne Rienner Publishers. 311 pages. Notes, bibliography, index. ISBN 1-55587-354-5.

Moghadam explores the causes, nature, and direction of change in the Middle East, particularly as these factors have affected the status and social positions of women in this region. Individual chapters focus on economic development, state policy, and women's employment; reforms, revolutions, and the woman question; women, patriarchy, and the changing family; Islamist movements and women's responses; women in the Islamic republic of Iran; and women and social change in Afghanistan.

Obermeyer, Carla Makhlouf, ed. 1992. *Family, Gender, and Population in the Middle East: Policies in Context.* Cairo, Egypt: American University in Cairo Press. 260 pages. ISBN 977-424-357-9.

For this book, Obermeyer has gathered together a variety of scholars who review population policies in the Middle East, including those who advocate fertility limitation in order to encourage national development and preserve environmental resources and those whose primary focus is protecting the rights of women. In the first part of the book, authorities describe the political conditions under which population policies are created and implemented, including legal, religious, and symbolic aspects. The second part discusses the constraints that family structures impose on individual behavior and the ways that the distribution of responsibilities within the household affects reproductive choice. Specific chapters focus on fertility policies and reforms in Turkey, Egypt's population policy, fertility transition in the Mashriq and the Maghrib, population policy in Iran, women and reproduction in Morocco, women's autonomy and gender roles in the Egyptian family, changing hierarchies of gender and generation, setting targets in family planning programs, broadening contraceptive choices, and rethinking family planning policy in light of reproductive health research.

Ogundipe-Leslie, Molara. 1994. *Re-Creating Ourselves: African Women and Critical Transformations.* Trenton, NJ: Africa World Press. 262 pages. Index. ISBN 0-86543-411-5.

This book provides an interesting and important selection of writings concerning gender, politics, and social transformation in Africa. Ogundipe-Leslie examines important issues concerning women living on the African continent. The first part of the book focuses on theory concerning African women, culture, and development. Part Two focuses on practice and reflects the author's experiences as a social activist. These practical examples describe Women in Nigeria (WIN), an organization that grew out of the Women in Nigeria Conference in 1982; the rights of the Nigerian woman; sex and gender problems in Nigeria; a message to middle-class women concerning the Women's Decade; the image of women and the role of the media in a new political culture; global women in church and society; decolonization; and feminism within an African context.

Parpart, Jane L., ed. 1989. *Women and Development in Africa: Comparative Perspectives.* New York: University Press of America. 345 pages. ISBN 0-8191-7378-9.

In order to understand the role of women in society and in development activities, Parpart believes that women's roles must be understood within a comparative framework and an international perspective. Part 1 contains an overview of women and development, focusing on theoretical perspectives, women in rural areas, in informal and formal employment, and the methodologies used to conduct research on women. Part 2 compares women and development in several countries and areas of the world, including Canada, the United States, the Caribbean and Latin America, the Middle East and North Africa, and India. Part 3 focuses on women and development in Africa.

Snyder, Margaret C., and Mary Tadesse. 1995. *African Women and Development: A History.* Atlantic Highlands, NJ: Zed Books. 239 pages. ISBN 1-85649-299-0.

Snyder and Tadesse wrote this book as "a testament to the women of Africa, and to their determination to achieve justice and well-being for present and for future generations" (page 1). The pioneering work of the African Training and Research Center for Women (ATRCW) is described. A historical review of African women's contributions as well as their experiences under colonialism are provided to demonstrate that women's contributions to development have a rich history. Chapters focus on development models and women's movements, women in the political economy, development strategies, women's initiatives, the development of policy concepts with women's concerns and ideas at the center, the ATRCW, the United Nations Economic Commission for Africa (ECA), influencing policy, and women and the future of development in Africa. Appendices provide information on women in Africa, including education, health, economic participation, national machineries, political and legal data, science and engineering school enrollment, and households headed by women.

Thorbek, Susanne. 1994. *Gender and Slum Culture in Urban Asia.* Atlantic Highlands, NJ: Zed Books. 233 pages. Bibliography. ISBN 1-85649-127-7.

Life is difficult for many women in the Third World, but especially for poor women. Thorbek explores the lives of poor women in a slum area near Colombo, Sri Lanka, and in the largest slum of Bangkok, Thailand. She vividly describes the environment in which these women live, the lack of food and water, and their daily experiences. She discovers, and then focuses on, the importance of their relationships with other people—their children, husbands, other family members, and friends. Living in an environment in which life is a daily struggle, Thorbek also explains the influences other than poverty on the lives of these women. Men are considered to be stronger and more clever and with authority and control over women, and their work is considered more important because they are paid. Two women tell their own stories, poignantly showing not only the differences in their lives, but also the similarities.

Turshen, Meredith, ed. 1991. *Women and Health in Africa.* Trenton, NJ: Africa World Press. 250 pages. References, index. ISBN 0-86543-180-9.

African women face a multitude of health problems as a result of the work they do and outside forces that affect them, such as war and revolution, the economy, work opportunities, population growth, and demographic controls imposed by governments, health services, and disease control programs. Contributors to this book focus on the general problems women face in their communities. Specific health issues are discussed based on the experiences within each single country. Individual chapters focus on the impact of war on women's health in Mozambique; women working on plantations in Zimbabwe; nurses organizing in South Africa; domestic workers in South Africa; women, work, and nutrition in Nigeria; the sexual politics of women's productive and reproductive labor; Algerian women and conception and contraception; the politics of population control in Namibia; women, children, and health in Côte d'Ivoire; and gender, power, and the risk of AIDS in Zaire. The editor concludes with a discussion concerning the relationship between gender and health and focuses on the social production of women's health care.

Books, Country-Specific

Afkhami, Mahnaz, and Erika Friedl, eds. 1994. *In The Eye of the Storm: Women in Post-Revolutionary Iran.* Syracuse, NY:

Syracuse University Press. 227 pages. Notes, index. ISBN 0-8156-2633-9.

This book was based in part on a conference concerning women in postrevolutionary Iran that was sponsored by the Foundation for Iranian Studies and the Middle East Center of the University of Pennsylvania and held at George Washington University in Washington, D.C. Focusing on the condition of women in Iran, each article, many based on actual presentations at the conference, examines one aspect of life for these women. Many of the authors suggest that current conditions experienced by these women are based on historical Iranian culture. Topics discussed include a feminist perspective on women in postrevolutionary Iran, women's education, the status of women and female children, major women's issues, sexuality as a commodity, female participation in the labor market, temporary marriage, women in the Iranian cinema, sources of female power in Iran, the legal status of women, and excerpts of specific criminal laws as they apply to women.

Angel, Adriana, and Fiona Macintosh. 1987. *The Tiger's Milk: Women of Nicaragua.* New York: Henry Holt and Company. 142 pages. ISBN 0-8050-0638-9.

In 1956, General Anastasio Somoza Debayle took over the leadership of the country of Nicaragua, with the help of the U.S. government. He was supported by the National Guard, whom he considered his own personal army, until he was forced out of the country in June 1979 when the Sandinista National Liberation Front took over the leadership of Nicaragua. This book relates the stories of the peasant farmers, indigenous and ethnic communities, and women as they search for a peace that did not exist before 1979. Their stories of tragedy and triumph, along with black and white photographs, provide the reader with a first-person understanding of many of the problems faced by Nicaraguans during the Somoza regime and after Daniel Ortega took over the government with the Sandinistas. Experiences of the women of Nicaragua are especially poignant.

Bumiller, Elisabeth. 1990. *May You Be the Mother of a Hundred Sons: A Journey among the Women of India.* New York: Fawcett Columbine. 307 pages. Bibliography, index. ISBN 0-449-90614-0.

Bumiller traveled to India with her husband and lived there for almost four years. She explores the lives of women in India, describing in rich detail the lives and experiences of poor women living in small villages, as well as upper-class women in Delhi. She vibrantly describes their lives, their thoughts, their fears— and provides the reader with an understanding of life in India from an Indian perspective. She describes arranged marriages, bride burnings, wives throwing themselves on the funeral pyres of their deceased husbands, female infanticide, and family planning programs. A brief history of the women's movement in India is provided and the life and legacy of Indira Gandhi is described. Bumiller meets women who are actresses, poets, professors, professionals, and housewives and offers the reader an inside look into their thoughts and experiences.

Burgos-Debray, Elisabeth, ed. 1994. *I, Rigoberta Menchú An Indian Woman in Guatemala.* Translated by Ann Wright. London: Verso. 252 pages. Glossary, bibliography (short). ISBN 0-86091-788-6.

Rigoberta Menchú, an Indian woman from Guatemala, is now living in exile in Mexico. She won the Nobel Peace Prize in 1992 for her work in advocating for human rights in Guatemala. This book tells her story—her early childhood in Guatemala, the torture and death of her brother, and then her father, and finally her mother. She describes life in her village, her political activities, and the events that led to her exile in Mexico. She vividly describes the realities of the political struggles of the Indians in Guatemala and the religious and superstitious beliefs that influence people's behaviors. Her narrative poignantly illuminates her personality and passionate sense of justice.

Calman, Leslie J. 1992. *Toward Empowerment: Women and Movement Politics in India.* Boulder, CO: Westview Press. 230 pages. Bibliography, index. ISBN 0-8133-8103-7.

Calman describes the women's movement in India as having a rich and varied history and as a vital, dynamic movement. The first part of the book describes the political and structural crises in Indian history that inspired women to organize their energies and the resources that encouraged and supported them. Part Two examines the movement's accomplishments and failures and describes what the future may bring for the women's movement in India.

Chant, Sylvia. 1991. *Women and Survival in Mexican Cities: Perspectives on Gender, Labour Markets and Low-Income House-*

holds. New York: St. Martin's Press. 270 pages. Bibliography, index. ISBN 0-7190-3443-4.

Based on a study of three Mexican cities (Querétaro, León, and Puerto Vallarta), Chant examines the relationships among women, employment, and household survival strategies in contemporary urban Mexico. She explains the primary ideas and hypotheses of this study and offers historical, economic, and demographic information on each of the cities in this study. Labor demands, policies and practices of gender recruitment, factors that influence female labor supply, the relationship between participation in the female labor force and household structure, changes in household structure, and women's employment are described. The "implications of women's work and household structure for the survival and welfare of the poor" (page xi), a summary of the research findings, and conclusions concerning the future prospects for low-income women are presented. Two appendices clarify terms and outline the research methodology used in the study.

Chaudhuri, Maitrayee. 1993. *Indian Women's Movement: Reform and Revival.* Delhi: Radiant Publishers. 210 pages. Bibliography, index. ISBN 81-7027-163-2.

This book traces the history of the women's movement in India, examining the impact of the colonial period and the impact of Hindu and Muslim beliefs concerning the status of women. The growth of women's organizations and their participation in politics from 1914 to 1927 is discussed. From 1927 through 1937, women expanded their influence and saw increased attention paid to their position. The movement toward expanded rights took a radical turn during the years from 1937 to 1947.

Kiribamune, Sirima, and Vidyamali Samarasinghe, eds. 1990. *Women at the Crossroads: A Sri Lankan Perspective.* New Delhi: Vikas Publishing House. 248 pages. Index.

This book is based on a conference and workshop of the same name in Kandy, Sri Lanka, in 1985 organized under the auspices of the International Center for Ethnic Studies in Kandy and the Sri Lanka Federation of University Women. Topics include issues in gender equality in developing countries, women in premodern Sri Lanka, tradition and change, women in parliamentary politics, the education of girls and women, the law and social justice, the status of women in Sri Lankan family law, Sri Lankan domestic aides living in West Asia, women's perceptions of their dual roles as mothers and wage earners, marriage, motherhood, and employment, and the impact of a career on marital and family relationships.

Kumar, Nita, ed. 1994. *Women As Subjects: South Asian Histories.* Charlottesville: University Press of Virginia. 239 pages. Index. ISBN 0-8139-1521-X.

The changing identity and status of women in India is discussed by a variety of anthropologists, sociologists, and historians from India, the United Kingdom, and the United States. Topics include gender, violence, and power; women's speech patterns; the writings of three nineteenth-century Indian Christian women; experiences living in purdah; education and female autonomy; gender and politics; and educational experiences of girls in Banaras.

Minturn, Leigh. 1993. *Sita's Daughters: Coming Out of Purdah.* New York: Oxford University Press. 371 pages. Glossary, bibliography, index. ISBN 0-19-507823-3.

Minturn traveled to Khalapur, a small village in India located approximately 100 miles north of Delhi, in 1954 to conduct research on socialization practices and children's behavior. Socialization practices in six countries were examined; other sites included Kenya, Okinawa, the Philippines, Mexico, and New England. In 1974, Minturn returned to Khalapur to examine the changes that occurred in the status of women between 1954/1955 and 1974/1975, supported by the Ford Foundation and a Fulbright fellowship. This book examines the changes that she observed. She covers a variety of areas, including an overview of the caste system and how this affected the women she talked with, marriage customs in Khalapur, family relations such as purdah and the practice of women wearing veils, land and the use of dowry, the role of women in the local economy, and ritual and recreation practices. She examines women's nature and the ways Indian men honored their women, the role and expectations of widows, health and family planning, socialization, and education. She concludes the book with a discussion of the changes she has observed over the 20-year period and discusses the future possibilities for women in India.

Mumtaz, Khawar, and Farida Shaheed. 1987. *Women of Pakistan: Two Steps Forward, One Step Back?* Atlantic Highlands,

NJ: Zed Books. 196 pages. Bibliography, index. ISBN 0-86232-280-4.

Many stories have come out of Pakistan concerning the status of women in that country. This book is a good resource on the beginning of the women's movement in Pakistan. The authors provide historical background on Pakistani history, including the evolution of Islam in politics, colonization activities from 1896 to 1947, and the period following independence. A profile of Pakistani women is presented and women's rights and organizations are described. The creation of the Women's Action Forum is described. General Zia-ul-Haq came to power in a coup and then decided to have the country closely follow Islamic guidelines. He began to take away the rights that women had under Prime Minister Zulfiqar Ali Bhutto. Women formed the Women's Action Forum to fight for these rights. The birth of this organization is described, along with the veiling and seclusion of women and the legal reduction of women's status. The future of Pakistani women is discussed.

Patai, Daphne. 1988. *Brazilian Women Speak: Contemporary Life Stories.* New Brunswick, NJ: Rutgers University Press. 398 pages. Notes, index. ISBN 0-8135-1301-4.

Twenty Brazilian women talk about their lives, their struggles, and the opportunities that life has given them in this provocative book based on interviews conducted by Patai. These women, from all economic backgrounds and from rural as well as urban areas, describe their lives and provide the reader with an inside, intimate understanding of what it is like to be a woman in Brazil. The book is divided into six parts. Part One includes the stories of four women who, each in her own way, feel deeply committed to some type of cause; these include a nun, a woman who helps anyone who needs help, a mother, and a woman involved in spiritualism. Part Two includes the stories of two sisters and their mother. The stories of six women involved in traditionally female occupations are told in Part Three, while political activists are the focus of Part Four. A young schoolgirl and a young prostitute tell their stories in Part Five. Part Six provides the stories of three wealthy women entrepreneurs—two of these women inherited their businesses from their families, while the third woman built her business from scratch.

Russell, Diana E. H. 1989. *Lives of Courage: Women for a New South Africa.* New York: Basic Books. 375 pages. Glossary, references, index. ISBN 0-465-04139-6.

Russell returned to South Africa, where she was born, from the United States and interviewed 24 women activists there. These women include world-famous leaders, trade unionists, members of radical organizations, and student activists who are white, black, Indian, or colored. This extraordinary book is the result of these interviews. Russell divides the book into four parts: women in South African prisons, the anti-apartheid movement, trade-union women fighting for workers' rights, women organizing with women, and the many faces of anti-apartheid activism. She lets each woman tell her own story, which adds to the emotional strength of the book. Women who were interviewed include Winnie Mandela and Nontsikelelo Albertina Sisulu, whose husbands, Nelson Mandela and Walter Sisulu, were leaders of the African National Congress and spent many years in prison; Helen Joseph, a white woman who became the first person to be subjected to house arrest (in 1962) and who became a leader in the anti-apartheid movement; and the granddaughter of Mahatma Gandhi, Ela Ramgobin.

Sasson, Jean. 1994. *Princess Sultana's Daughters.* New York: Doubleday. 229 pages. Glossary, index. ISBN 0-385-47444-X.

As a follow-up to her first book about Princess Sultana (see below), Jean Sasson describes Sultana, what happens to her when her father discovers that she has written about the royal family of Saudi Arabia, and about her married life with her husband and three children. Even though the names had been changed in the first book to protect Sultana and her family, her brother and father discovered that she was indeed guilty of writing the first book, with the help of Sasson. In this book, she continues her life story, revealing the pain and joy that she experiences as a privileged member of the Saudi royal family. She describes the limitations that all Saudi women face: they are not allowed to drive cars, they cannot travel without the permission of their husbands or fathers, and they are not allowed to be seen in public without covering their bodies and their faces. The book reads like a fictional adventure; but the harsh reality is that it is a true glimpse of what life is like today for the women who live in Saudi Arabia.

———. 1992. *Princess: A True Story of Life behind the Veil in Saudi Arabia.* New York: William Morrow and Company. 288 pages. Index. ISBN 0-688-11675-2.

Sultana, a princess in Saudi Arabia, has four mansions on three continents, a private jet, and many other possessions common to wealthy Saudi Arabians, but she is unhappy because she realizes the low position of women in her country. She realizes that she has no real freedom and no control over her own life and decides to write this book about her experiences. Working with Jean Sasson, she tells the story of her life, anonymously, because the men in her family as well as the religious establishment in Saudi Arabia could easily call for her death if they discovered that she was revealing things best left untold (according to the religious establishment). She describes her childhood, her arranged marriage, the lives of her sisters, and reveals the incredible restrictions that women face in her country.

White, Sarah C. 1992. *Arguing with the Crocodile: Gender and Class in Bangladesh.* Atlantic Highlands, NJ: Zed Books. 186 pages. Bibliography, index. ISBN 1-85649-085-8.

White lived in Kumirpur, a small village in Bangladesh, from October 1985 to July 1986. Her original aim was to study the impact of agricultural development on village women. This book discusses her study, what she found, and what she learned about the people she met. Topics include research on women in Bangladesh, land ownership, sharecropping, agricultural labor, credit, small business, women in the market, arranged marriages, marriage payments, household structure, land and property, and women's personal assets and income.

Journals

The journals listed below often contain articles that focus on some subject of concern to women in the Third World and may lead the reader to additional resources on this topic.

African Population Studies
Asian and Pacific Population Forum
Biology and Society
Comparative Education Review
Demography
Development
Development and Change
Economic Development and Cultural Change
Family Planning Perspectives
Feminist Studies

Food and Nutrition Bulletin
Gender and Society
Geoforum
Health Policy and Education
Health Transition Review
Human Rights Quarterly
International Family Planning Perspectives
International Journal of Health Services
International Journal of Middle East Studies
Journal of Biosocial Science
Journal of Comparative Family Studies
Journal of Developing Areas
Journal of Family Welfare
Journal of Population and Social Studies
Population and Development Review
Population Studies
Signs: Journal of Women in Culture and Society
Social Science and Medicine
Studies in Family Planning
Women and Health
Women Envision
Women's Studies International Forum
World Development
World Health Forum
World Health Statistics Quarterly
World Views

Bibliographies

Many bibliographies exist that provide additional sources of information on women in the Third World. Because this chapter focuses on books published since 1990, the resources listed below will lead the reader to the many other resources published earlier.

Bindocci, Cynthia Gay. 1993. **Women and Technology: An Annotated Bibliography.** New York: Garland Publishing.

Bullwinkle, Davis A. 1989. **Women of Northern, Western, and Central Africa: A Bibliography, 1976–1985.** New York: Greenwood Press. 603 pages. ISBN 0-313-26609-3.

Byrne, Pamela, and Suzanne R. Ontiveros, eds. 1986. *Women in the Third World: A Historical Bibliography.* Santa Barbara: ABC-CLIO.

Coles, Catherine M., and Barbara Entwisle. 1986. *Nigerian Women in Development: A Research Bibliography.* Atlanta, GA: African Studies Association.

Danforth, Sandra C. 1982. *Women and National Development.* Monticello, IL: Vance Bibliographies. 35 pages.

Falk, Nancy Auer. 1994. *Women and Religion in India: An Annotated Bibliography of Sources in English, 1975–1992.* Kalamazoo, MI: New Issues Press. 295 pages.

Faris, Mohamed A., and Mahmood H. Khan. 1994. *Egyptian Women in Agricultural Development: An Annotated Bibliography.* Boulder, CO: Lynne Rienner Publishers.

Fenton, Thomas, and Mary J. Heffron, eds. 1987. *Women in the Third World: A Directory of Resources.* Maryknoll, NY: Orbis.

Fister, Barbara. 1995. *Third World Women's Literatures: A Dictionary and Guide to Materials in English.* Westport, CT: Greenwood.

Ghorayshi, Parvin. 1994. *Women and Work in Developing Countries: An Annotated Bibliography.* Westport, CT: Greenwood.

International Labor Organization. 1995. *Women Workers: An Annotated Bibliography, 1983–1994.* New York: International Labor Organization.

Kelly, David H., and Gail P. Kelly. 1989. *Women's Education in the Third World: An Annotated Bibliography.* New York: Garland.

Oshana, Maryann. 1984. *Women of Color: A Filmography of Minority and Third World Women.* New York: Garland.

Radcliffe, Sarah A. 1988. *Gender in the Third World: A Geographical Bibliography of Recent Work.* Sussex: Institute of Development Studies. 90 pages. ISBN 0-903-35481-0.

Saulniers, Suzanne Smith, and Cathy A. Rakowski. 1977. *Women in the Development Process: A Select Bibliography on Women in Sub-Saharan Africa and Latin America.* Austin: Institute of Latin American Studies, University of Texas. 287 pages. ISBN 0-292-79010-4.

Seager, Joni, and Ann Olson. *Women in the World: An International Atlas.* New York: Simon and Schuster.

Townsend, Janet G. 1988. *Women in Developing Countries: A Selected, Annotated Bibliography for Development Organizations.* Sussex: Institute of Development Studies. 188 pages.

UN High Commissioner for Refugees. 1989. *Refugee Women: A Selected and Annotated Bibliography.* Geneva: UNHCR, Centre for Documentation on Refugees.

Selected Nonprint Resources

7

This chapter provides annotated descriptions of videos and films that focus on women in the Third World and sources of information that can be found on the Internet.

Video Sources

Algeria: Women at War

Type:	VHS
Length:	52 minutes
Date:	1992
Cost:	Purchase: $295; rental: $75
Source:	Women Make Movies
	462 Broadway, Suite 500D
	New York, NY 10013
	(212) 925-0606
	Fax: (212) 925-2052
	e-mail: distdept@wmm.com

This video provides a rare glimpse into the role that Algerian women played in the country's liberation struggle from the French over 30 years ago and their role in current politics. Using a combination of interviews and archival footage, the video examines the position of women in Algeria, the rise of Islam, and increasing levels of political violence. Critical questions are raised concerning the balance between women's rights and national liberation struggles.

All Dressed in White
Type: VHS
Length: 18 minutes
Date: 1994
Cost: Purchase: $150; rental: $50
Source: University of California Extension
Center for Media and Independent Learning
2000 Center Street, Fourth Floor
Berkeley, CA 94704
(510) 642-0460
Fax: (510) 643-9271

The complex relationships among religion, ethnicity, and gender are explored in this documentary that chronicles the experiences of four women and their wedding dresses. The travels of four Catholic women from three generations are examined as they migrated from Goa, India, to Singapore, and then to California. Each of the women married at a different time and place, and each wedding created different dilemmas for the women in defining their own cultural identities. By examining the personal lives of each of these women, the film illustrates that the decisions they made have had great significance for the identity of an entire ethnic group.

As Women See It (five videos)
Type: VHS
Length: 30 minutes each
Date: 1983
Cost: Purchase: $495 for all; rental: $60 each
Source: Women Make Movies
Distribution Service
462 Broadway, Suite 500D
New York, NY 10013
(212) 925-0606
Fax: (212) 925-2052
e-mail: distdept@wmm.com

This series of five videos is by women and about women in developing countries. *Sudesha* describes the life of one woman involved in the Chipko environmental movement in India. *Selbe* provides a glimpse into the daily life of women in Senegal. *Bread and Dignity* intermingles historic newsreel footage with contemporary interviews to review the role that women have played in the political struggles in Nicaragua. In *Women of El Planeta,* two women encourage other women in Peru to solve their community's problems. *Permissible Dreams* offers a look at life for Egyptian women.

Birth and Belief in the Andes of Ecuador
Type: VHS
Length: 28 minutes
Date: 1995
Cost: Purchase: $175; rental: $50
Source: University of California Extension
             Center for Media and Independent Learning
             2000 Center Street, Fourth Floor
             Berkeley, CA 94704
             (510) 642-0460
             Fax: (510) 643-9271

An intimate portrait of women living in four communities in the Andes is presented in this video. They discuss their beliefs and practices concerning childbirth and infant care. Because modern medical care has only recently penetrated into the rural Andes, many of these women have relied on ethnomedicine to manage their reproductive practices. These practices include ideas about conception, whether human or supernatural, postpartum seclusion, and perceived gender differences about the needs and personalities of infant girls and boys. The film shows that even though their folk medicine is based on several magical premises, the women receive real physical and emotional benefits. The film is in Spanish, with English subtitles and innovative side titles.

Celso and Cora
Type: VHS, 16mm
Length: 109 minutes
Date: 1983
Cost: Video purchase: $490; 16mm purchase: $1,395;
             16mm rental, $125
Source: First Run/Icarus Films
             153 Waverly Place, Sixth Floor
             New York, NY 10014
             (212) 727-1711; (800) 876-1710
             Fax: (212) 989-7649
             e-mail: FRIF@echonyc.com

Celso and Cora is a documentary about a young couple and their two children living in a squatter settlement in Manila, the Philippines. Celso and Cora sell cigarettes outside of a downtown hotel, which is against city regulations. Over a three-month period, filmmakers follow this family, starting with the attempts of Cora to find a new place for the family to live after being evicted. The stresses of surviving in this world put a real strain on their marriage.

Dadi's Family

Type:	VHS, 16mm
Length:	59 minutes
Date:	1980
Cost:	VHS purchase: $145; VHS rental: $40; 16mm purchase: $750; 16mm rental: $70
Source:	Documentary Educational Resources
	101 Morse Street
	Watertown, MA 01272
	(617) 926-0491
	Fax: (617) 926-9519

As the grandmother and mother-in-law, Dadi explains that she is the "manager " of her extended family in the Haryana region of northern India. In this area, women leave the villages in which they were born and come as strangers to the households of their husbands' mothers. Through the women in Dadi's family, this video explores the relationships among family members and the problems that can occur. The women talk about the tensions created by Dadi's authority, the loneliness of veiled daughters-in-law who are always seen as outsiders, and husbands' expectations that wives will perform multiple tasks. These tasks include working in the fields, gathering water and cow dung for fuel, and having food and water waiting at home whenever the husbands want to eat or drink. Social and economic changes occurring outside the home also put pressure on the stability and cohesion of the family.

Daughters of the Nile

Type:	VHS
Length:	46 minutes
Date:	1993
Cost:	Purchase: $395; rental: $65
Source:	Filmakers Library
	124 East 40th Street

New York, NY 10016
(212) 808-4980
Fax: (212) 808 4983
e-mail: info@filmakers.com

This video captures the essence of Egyptian women and their subordinate lives under the Islamic code. Men and women speak about their traditions, expectations, and patterns of life. Articulate women with little schooling are interviewed; their lives are focused on childbearing and tough physical work. Choices in life are limited, and they accept without question circumcision, arranged marriages, large families, and polygamous husbands. Through their participation in this video, the women begin to question some of the beliefs that they have taken for granted in their lives.

Defying the Odds: Women around the World Create New Roles
Type: VHS
Length: 29 minutes
Date: 1997
Cost: Purchase: $295; rental: $55
Source: Filmakers Library
             124 East 40th Street
             New York, NY 10016
             (212) 808-4980
             Fax: (212) 808 4983
             e-mail: info@filmakers.com

Produced for the Fourth World Conference on Women in Beijing in 1996, this video focuses on the lives of four women of varying ages and backgrounds who have broken ground in new fields. They question many traditions as they create promising careers for themselves. Asthma Jahangir, a well-known lawyer from Pakistan, criticizes the barriers that she faced in becoming a lawyer. In Guatemala, Sandra Gonzalez is a single parent and a labor organizer at her employer's textile factory, where she has urged her co-workers to unionize. In Latvia, Mara Kimele is a theater director. Tam Goossen, formerly from Hong Kong, raises her daughter, cares for her ailing mother, and wins an election in her newly adopted homeland.

Faces of Change
Type: VHS
Length: 5 videos, 17 minutes each

Date: 1975–1976
Cost: Purchase: $145 each; rental: $40 each
Source: Documentary Educational Resources
101 Morse Street
Watertown, MA 01272
(617) 926-0491; (800) 569-6621
Fax: (617) 926-9519

This series of five videos focuses on women in five different countries: Bolivia, Kenya, Afghanistan, Taiwan, and the Soko Islands off the coast of China. The women's lifestyles are seen through their daily routines and by their attitudes, provided through interviews with them. The economic, political, religious, and educational status of women are explored as well as their legal and customary rights and the degree of changes in their actual and perceived roles.

Fire Eyes: Female Circumcision
Type: VHS
Length: 60 minutes
Date: 1995
Cost: Purchase: $445; rental: $85
Source: Filmakers Library
124 East 40th Street
New York, NY 10016
(212) 808-4980
Fax: (212) 808 4983
e-mail: info@filmakers.com

This video is one of the few in existence to present an African viewpoint concerning the culturally sanctioned practice of female genital circumcision. Soraya Mire, a filmmaker from Somalia, created this video, based on her experience with this practice when she was 13 years old. The video explores the socioeconomic, psychological, and medical consequences of this ancient custom. Several women who have experienced this practice speak out, describing their experiences. Many mothers agree with the practice and insist that their daughters also undergo the circumcision, even though they know the damage that will result. They continue to practice this custom in order to conform to the male expectation for a chaste wife. Doctors describe the various forms of female circumcision and the many physical problems that result from it.

Five Centuries Later
Type: VHS
Length: 54 minutes
Date: 1992
Cost: Purchase: $390; rental, $75
Source: First Run/Icarus Films
153 Waverly Place, Sixth Floor
New York, NY 10014
(212) 727-1711; (800) 876-1710
Fax: (212) 989-7649
e-mail: FRIF@echonyc.com

Rigoberta Menchú (see Chapter 3), a Guatemalan Indian and fighter for human rights, is featured in this video. The current status of Central American indigenous peoples is examined. In countries such as Guatemala and Bolivia the indigenous people have no power and no rights; they are usually exceptionally poor, allowed to work only the most menial jobs. Since the time that Europeans appeared on their land, these people have struggled to preserve their traditions and their life styles. As traditionally agrarian communities, indigenous families are facing the loss of their land. This video examines the future of these people.

Focus on Women
Type: VHS
Length: 28 minutes
Date: 1980
Cost: $50
Source: United Nations
Audio-Visual Promotion and Distribution Unit
Media Division, Department of Public Information
Room S-805B
New York, NY 10017
(212) 963-6939
Fax: (212) 963-6869
e-mail: Sue-Ting-Len@un.org

Developed during the middle of the United Nations Decade for Women, this video examines the traditional image of women as they are portrayed in the world's visual media. The part that women play in determining that image is examined. The dependent, submissive heroine of the Indian cinema shows signs of becoming more independent as young Indian women technicians challenge the male-dominated film industry in India. In Egypt, women actually are in the majority of the professional staff at Egyptian Radio and Television. However, this has had a limited effect on changing the status of women. In contrast, a low-budget television show in the Dominican Republic stresses the achievements of low-income and rural women whose actions affect the future of their communities. This video is available in English, French, and Spanish.

The Hamar Trilogy

Type:	VHS
Length:	50 minutes each
Date:	1996
Cost:	Purchase: $445 each; rental $75 each
Source:	Filmakers Library
	124 East 40th Street
	New York, NY 10016
	(212) 808-4980
	Fax: (212) 808 4983
	e-mail: info@filmakers.com

This series of three videos focuses on the Hamar, an isolated people living in southwestern Ethiopia whose traditional lifestyle has not been impacted by the war and famine in northern Ethiopia. The Hamar women are strong and outspoken. The first video, *The Women Who Smile,* centers on Duka, a young single girl who learns what to expect from life from the older women in the village. Their conversations range from teenage pregnancy and relationships with men to growing old. Although men are dominant in this society, the women can hold their own and sometimes mock the posturing of the men. The second video, *Two Girls Go Hunting,* tells the story of Duka and Gardi, two girls who are preparing to marry men they have never met. The third video, *Our Way of Loving,* shows Duka as a mother with two children. She spends most of her time caring for her children and her husband. While their marriage seems affectionate, her husband beats her when he is provoked. She accepts this as part of the widespread belief that this is a man's way of loving.

Hidden Faces

Type:	VHS, 16mm
Length:	52 minutes
Date:	1990

Cost: VHS purchase: $295; VHS rental: $90;
           16mm rental: $155
Source: Women Make Movies
           Distribution Service
           462 Broadway, Suite 500D
           New York, NY 10013
           (212) 925-0606
           Fax: (212) 925-2052
           e-mail: distdept@wmm.com

This video was originally intended as a documentary about the life of Nawal el Saadawi (see Chapter 3), a renowned feminist writer from Egypt. However, it developed into a broader examination of the life of women living in a Muslim society. Safaa Fathay, a young Egyptian woman living in Paris, returns home to interview Nawal el Saadawi but becomes disillusioned with her. Taking passages from el Saadawi's writings, Fathay travels to her family home and discovers similar conflicts between the traditional and modern ways facing women today. Fathay's mother's decision to return to wearing the veil and the genital circumcision of her female cousins bring home the realization that the country is renewing their beliefs in fundamentalism. Fathay examines the contradictions of feminism in a Muslim environment, providing an unforgettable picture of contemporary life for women in the Arab world.

I Have a Problem, Madam

Type: VHS
Length: 59 minutes
Date: 1995
Cost: Purchase: $390; rental, $75
Source: First Run/Icarus Films
           153 Waverly Place, Sixth Floor
           New York, NY 10014
           (212) 727-1711; (800) 876-1710
           Fax: (212) 989-7649
           e-mail: FRIF@echonyc.com

In this video, Vanessa comes to the legal aid clinic in Uganda because she and her children are left homeless by her husband, who has sent her away after 30 years of marriage and brought a new woman into his house. In Uganda, tradition dictates that a man can have as many wives as he can afford; women have no possessions and depend totally on their husbands for everything.

Western influences are slowly changing attitudes. Several legal aid centers have been opened for women, run by female lawyers who provide information and advice for women in trouble. A weekly radio show advertises the centers'services. This film visits one of these centers in Mbale, where lawyers try to mediate between husbands and wives. Proceedings of the High Court are shown, where one woman is on trial for murdering her husband with an ax after having been beaten all day by him. This video was a Golden Calf Award winner at the Dutch Film Festival in 1995.

The Impossible Dream
Type: 16mm
Length: 35 minutes
Date: 1983
Cost: $50
Source: United Nations
             Audio-Visual Promotion and Distribution Unit
             Media Division, Department of Public Information
             Room S-805B
             New York, NY 10017
             (212) 963-6939
             Fax: (212) 963-6869
             e-mail: Sue-Ting-Len@un.org

This animated film takes a wry, humorous look at a problem that women everywhere face—the double workload of a full-time job and responsibility for the family and all household chores. An average family with a baby and two school-age children is shown, with both parents working outside the home. The woman puts in identical hours to the man but earns less money. She is also responsible for caring for the children and taking care of all household chores. The video is available in Arabic, English, French, and Spanish.

In Danku the Soup Is Sweeter:
Women and Development in Ghana
Type: VHS
Length: 30 minutes
Date: 1993
Cost: Purchase: $295; rental: $55
Source: Filmakers Library
             124 East 40th Street

New York, NY 10016
(212) 808-4980
Fax: (212) 808 4983
e-mail: info@filmakers.com

Life in the village of Danku in northern Ghana is a struggle. The women bear the largest burden of caring for the children, raising food, and trying to improve the lives of their families. The Canadian International Development Agency has supported a project to provide access to credit for the women in the village. The film chronicles the experiences of two women who take advantage of this program. They borrow a small amount of money for start-up expenses and work hard to pay back the loans. They sell their products from door to door and at the market near their village. They begin to make some money and are able to improve the lives of their families.

In the Name of God: Helping Circumcised Women
Type: VHS
Length: 29 minutes
Date: 1997
Cost: Purchase: $295; rental: $55
Source: Filmakers Library
124 East 40th Street
New York, NY 10016
(212) 808-4980
Fax: (212) 808 4983
e-mail: info@filmakers.com

Today, the number of women who are genitally circumcised is estimated to be close to 115 million. Instruments used during the circumcision include razors, scissors, or other, more primitive tools. This video takes the viewer to Addis Ababa, Ethiopia, to the Fistula Hospital, one of the few places where women who have been circumcised receive treatment. Many recovered patients now help doctors treat these women and repair their injuries. An increasing number of Ethiopian women have started to protest this practice, but change is slow.

Iraqi Women: Voices from Exile
Type: VHS
Length: 54 minutes
Date: 1994
Cost: Purchase: $250; rental: $75

Source: Women Make Movies
Distribution Service
462 Broadway, Suite 500D
New York, NY 10013
(212) 925-0606
Fax: (212) 925-2052
e-mail: distdept@wmm.com

This emotional video presents a fascinating and rare look at the recent history of Iraq through the eyes of Iraqi women currently living in exile in Britain. Males are usually the only ones allowed to speak to the outside world in Iraq—most of the time women's voices are not heard at all. This documentary offers meaningful, vivid interviews with women concerning their lives in Iraq before Saddam Hussein came to power, during his repressive regime, and during the Gulf War in 1991.

Islam and Feminism
Type: VHS
Length: 25 minutes
Date: 1991
Cost: Purchase: $190; rental, $45
Source: First Run/Icarus Films
153 Waverly Place, Sixth Floor
New York, NY 10014
(212) 727-1711; (800) 876-1710
Fax: (212) 989-7649
e-mail: FRIF@echonyc.com

In Pakistan, Nafisa Hoodbhoy, a journalist, investigated the rapes of three nurses in a hospital; one nurse was jailed, but the attackers were never charged. Pakistan's Islamic law does not differentiate between rape, adultery, and fornication. This video examines these laws and the effects that they have on women in Pakistan. Under this law, a woman and a man arrested for fornication are sentenced to 100 lashes and death by stoning. Pakistani courts value the testimony of two women equal to the testimony of one man. A woman who has been raped can be charged with having extramarital sex under Pakistani law. This video examines the contradictions in this law and describes the efforts of several organizations, such as the Women's Action Forum, to protect women against this type of discrimination.

Kamala and Raji
Type: VHS
Length: 46 minutes
Date: 1996
Cost: Purchase: $195; rental: $45
Source: Documentary Educational Resources
             101 Morse Street
             Watertown, MA 01272
             (617) 926-0491
             Fax: (617) 926-9519

Two women, Kamala and Raji, tell their stories in this poignant video about their lives in Ahmedabad, India. The city is bustling with activity, poverty is evident, but the mood is vibrant. These two working women are struggling to improve their lives, and sometimes they find it necessary to defy their husbands, the police, and a rich tradition in which women are considered second-class citizens. Kamala, an organizer for the Self-Employed Women's Association (SEWA), is a young mother. Her husband sometimes abuses her, and the burden of feeding her children and maintaining the home falls on her shoulders. Raji sells vegetables, is a SEWA representative, and is happily married. The two women tell their own stories, discussing marriage, men, women's rights, justice, and their own personal successes and failures.

Key to Freedom: Women and Literacy
Type: VHS
Length: 28 minutes
Date: 1990
Cost: $50
Source: United Nations
             Audio-Visual Promotion and Distribution Unit
             Media Division, Department of Public Information
             Room S-805B
             New York, NY 10017
             (212) 963-6939
             Fax: (212) 963-6869
             e-mail: Sue-Ting-Len@un.org

The typical citizen of the world is young, poor, female, and often illiterate. This illuminating documentary, narrated by Germaine Greer, features women in Mail, Thailand, Costa Rica, and New York. These women were illiterate but have learned to read and write, which has dramatically altered their lives. Several projects that advance literacy for women while being responsive to their immediate needs are examined. The video is available in English, French, and Spanish.

Lady Marshall

Type:	VHS
Length:	21 minutes
Date:	1990
Cost:	Purchase: $250; rental: $60
Source:	Women Make Movies
	462 Broadway, Suite 500D
	New York, NY 10013
	(212) 925-0606
	Fax: (212) 925-2052
	e-mail: distdept@wmm.com

An excellent case study, this video focuses on Marshall Point, a small fishing village on the Nicaraguan coast, and the Afro-Caribbean women there who have built up a successful business—a successful boating operation and the only one run by women in the area. The video follows the women as they gain economic independence, gain pride in accomplishment, and play a crucial role in the functioning of their community.

Las Madres: The Mothers of Plaza de Mayo

Type:	VHS
Length:	64 minutes
Date:	1985
Cost:	Purchase: $250; rental: $90
Source:	Women Make Movies
	462 Broadway, Suite 500D
	New York, NY 10013
	(212) 925-0606
	Fax: (212) 925-2052
	e-mail: distdept@wmm.com

This is an excellent video describing the efforts of Argentinian mothers who demanded that the government provide information concerning the fate of their 30,000 sons and daughters who disappeared from sight. A history of Argentina during the 1970s and 1980s is provided, along with an examination of the ways that women became empowered in a society that expected women to remain silent.

Making Their Way
Type:	VHS
Length:	27 minutes
Date:	1990
Cost:	$50
Source:	United Nations
	Audio-Visual Promotion and Distribution Unit
	Media Division, Department of Public Information
	Room S-805B
	New York, NY 10017
	(212) 963-6939
	Fax: (212) 963-6869
	e-mail: Sue-Ting-Len@un.org

Even though women have made some progress in recent years, many women still face discrimination in the workplace in areas ranging from unequal pay to restrictive customs and traditions. This video was filmed in five countries—Czechoslovakia, Ecuador, Lesotho, Norway, and Singapore. Women from different economic and social levels are shown as they work in a variety of jobs. Their need for equality in career opportunities and advancement is emphasized. The video is available in English, French, and Spanish.

Mama Benz
Type:	VHS
Length:	48 minutes
Date:	1994
Cost:	Purchase: $350; rental: $65
Source:	Filmakers Library
	124 East 40th Street
	New York, NY 10016
	(212) 808-4980
	Fax: (212) 808 4983
	e-mail: info@filmakers.com

Strong older women often dominate the colorful markets throughout Africa. They rule the market, are treated with deference, control prices, and decide who can buy their goods. Many have become wealthy as a result of their good business sense. Most people refer to these women affectionately as Mama Benz, because each of these women has a Mercedes Benz as her trademark. This video profiles one of these women; a richly dressed woman with a staffed mansion and a Mercedes Benz that she drives throughout the rural area as she presides over the cloth market in Lome, Togo. She comes to the market every day, sitting in her stall surrounded by her colorful cloth and haggling with her customers over the price of her goods.

Maria and Many Others
Type: VHS
Length: 22 minutes
Date: 1993
Cost: Purchase: $175; rental, $45
Source: First Run/Icarus Films
153 Waverly Place, Sixth Floor
New York, NY 10014
(212) 727-1711; (800) 876-1710
Fax: (212) 989-7649
e-mail: FRIF@echonyc.com

Maria is 13 years old and the oldest of 9 children in her family in Ecuador. The video shows her helping her mother with household tasks and the other tasks that are required to run their small farm. Her father, like 70 percent of the men in Ecuador, must travel away from home to earn a living. Many girls are married by the time they are 15 years old, and while Maria can run the household, she has never known what it is like to play and to be a child.

My Home, My Prison
Type: VHS, 16mm
Length: 66 minutes
Date: 1992
Cost: VHS purchase: $295; VHS rental: $90; 16mm rental: $160
Source: Women Make Movies
Distribution Service
462 Broadway, Suite 500D
New York, NY 10013
(212) 925-0606
Fax: (212) 925-2052
e-mail: distdept@wmm.com

This moving video is based on the autobiography of Raymonda Hawa Tawil, a Palestinian peace activist and journalist. Set against the last 50 years of Israeli-Palestinian conflict, the viewer is provided with an understanding of many of the challenges that face those attempting to bring peace to the Middle East. Tawil and other Palestinians from universities and refugee camps are interviewed and provide an inside look at the major issues they face.

My Husband Doesn't Mind if I Disco
Type: VHS
Length: 28 minutes
Date: 1995
Cost: Purchase: $175; rental: $50
Source: University of California Extension
Center for Media and Independent Learning
2000 Center Street, Fourth Floor
Berkeley, CA 94704
(510) 642-0460
Fax: (510) 643-9271

Western media often portray Tibet as a land of mystics suffering under the rule of Chinese communists. However, following 40 years of living under the political and economic changes introduced by the Chinese, many Tibetans survive by drawing from both traditional Tibetan values and newer state ideologies. This documentary explores the ways that women in one community in eastern Tibet have survived the many political and social changes that have affected them. The effects on the women of their exposure to feminism while under Marxist rule are examined, as well as the traditional cultural attitudes toward women and their relations with men.

Ndebele Women: The Rituals of Rebellion
Type: VHS
Length: 52 minutes
Date: 1997
Cost: Purchase: $395; rental: $75
Source: Filmakers Library
124 East 40th Street
New York, NY 10016
(212) 808-4980
Fax: (212) 808 4983
e-mail: info@filmakers.com

This film explores the rituals of the Ndebele women who are known throughout the world for their use of vividly colored art forms, especially their colorful houses and clothes. Called the "rainbow people " by Nelson Mandela, the Ndebele have a history of racial oppression, forced removal from their ancestral land, and poverty. Their fertility rites are celebrated to bind them to their ancestral traditions. The performance art shows how traditional forms of expression can be transformed into a means for political empowerment.

No Longer Silent
Type: VHS
Length: 57 minutes
Date: 1987
Cost: $199
Source: International Film Bureau
332 South Michigan Avenue
Chicago, IL 60604-4382
(312) 427-4545

This video illustrates what it is like to be a woman in India. Kamla Bhasin is an Indian woman who works with the United Nations in rural development activities. She is shown conducting workshops, leading a demonstration, preparing for a march in celebration of International Women's Day, and discussing her feelings about many aspects of life in India for a woman. She helps Indians in rural areas organize themselves to fight for their rights. This documentary is useful in discussions of many issues that face women in the world today—the social, political, and cultural alienation of women living in the Third World, inequalities in the criminal justice system, raising the consciousness of poor women, sex roles, deviance, mass media, social change, and social movements. Topics specific to India include abortion, the sex ratio, health care, nutrition, bride burning, and the depiction of women in the media in India.

Not without my Veil: Amongst the Women of Oman
Type: VHS
Length: 29 minutes
Date: 1995
Cost: Purchase: $295; rental: $55
Source: Filmakers Library
124 East 40th Street
New York, NY 10016
(212) 808-4980
Fax: (212) 808 4983
e-mail: info@filmakers.com

This video introduces the viewer to the women of Oman—educated, independent women who dress in the traditional way even though they are moving into new areas of access for women. The story of Dagmar Taylor-Al Busaidy is told in this video. She spent her early years in England and then returned to Oman in 1976 when the new sultan was introducing many changes in her country. When she dressed in Western clothes in Oman many people stared, she was an object of curiosity, and had trouble pursuing her goals. When she decided to wear the veil, she was able to pursue her vocational interests. Other women shown in the video have succeeded in careers as heads of banks, pilots, and doctors. Even though they wear the veil—as a symbol of their history and origins—their strength is not compromised.

Nyamakuta—The One Who Receives: An African Midwife
Type: VHS
Length: 32 minutes
Date: 1989
Cost: Purchase: $295; rental: $55
Source: Filmakers Library
             124 East 40th Street
             New York, NY 10016
             (212) 808-4980
             Fax: (212) 808 4983
             e-mail: info@filmakers.com

As a nyamakuta, a traditional midwife, Mai Mafuta helps women in Zimbabwe deliver their babies. Many women in developing countries rely on midwives to help them with childbirth, and Mai Mafuta is a skillful, compassionate midwife following in her grandmother's tradition. More than 80 countries have started training traditional midwives in modern medical methods to help protect the lives of mothers and infants. Several years earlier, Mafuta had been unable to save the life of her own daughter who died while giving birth. Following this experience, she enrolled in one of these training programs. She narrates her own story and helps the viewer understand the problems that many women face in the Third World.

Once This Land Was Ours
Type: VHS
Length: 19 minutes

Date: 1991
Cost: Purchase: $250; rental: $60
Source: Women Make Movies
          462 Broadway, Suite 500D
          New York, NY 10013
          (212) 925-0606
          Fax: (212) 925-2052
          e-mail: distdept@wmm.com

This documentary focuses on women agriculture workers in India and their attempts to provide for and support their families. These women work to produce food for others but have difficulty providing food for their own children. Using testimonies of these women and images of them at work, the video examines the feminization of poverty in rural parts of India.

A Peruvian Equation
Type: VHS
Length: 10 minutes
Date: 1992
Cost: Purchase: $125; rental, $30
Source: First Run/Icarus Films
          153 Waverly Place, Sixth Floor
          New York, NY 10014
          (212) 727-1711; (800) 876-1710
          Fax: (212) 989-7649
          e-mail: FRIF@echonyc.com

Part of a series that captures the poignancy of the human experience, this short video documents the daily life of a Quecha Indian family struggling to survive in the shantytowns outside the Peruvian capital of Lima. Perdita, the mother of nine children, describes her life as filled with conflict and suffering. The threat of military brutality is a part of their lives; the rebellious Shining Path group controls the shantytown. The film's use of subtitles provides statistics that place Perdita's life in the broader context of Peruvian poverty.

Rights of Passage
Type: VHS
Length: 30 minutes
Date: 1996
Cost: Purchase: $295; rental: $55
Source: Filmakers Library

124 East 40th Street
New York, NY 10016
(212) 808-4980
Fax: (212) 808 4983
e-mail: info@filmakers.com

For young women around the world, puberty is a time of transition and the most vulnerable time in their lives. In many countries where young girls have little value, puberty marks the beginning of a life of abuse and the possibility of early death. The stories of four young women in different parts of the world are presented here, examining the personal cost of this transition in life. The adolescent girls in this video are from Nicaragua, India, Jamaica, and Burkina Faso. Aleyda from Nicaragua sniffs glue and is heading into a life of prostitution. In India, Tarranum's parents have taken her out of school and are waiting to marry her off. Fourteen-year-old Natalyn is seven months pregnant in Jamaica. Adjara from Burkina Faso faces the terror of female genital mutilation.

Rites

Type: VHS
Length: 52 minutes
Date: 1991
Cost: Purchase: $445; rental: $75
Source: Filmakers Library
             124 East 40th Street
             New York, NY 10016
             (212) 808-4980
             Fax: (212) 808 4983
             e-mail: info@filmakers.com

This video explores the custom of female genital circumcision and describes the efforts of women throughout the world to stop this painful practice. Three major contexts in which circumcision occurs are explored, cosmetic, punitive, and as a rite of passage. Dr. Ornella Moscurri describes the ways in which women in the late nineteenth century were subjected to circumcision if they behaved in ways that their husbands did not approve of.

Rosalina

Type: VHS, 16mm
Length: 23 minutes
Date: 1987

Cost: VHS purchase: $190; 16mm purchase: $475;
             16mm rental: $50
Source: First Run/Icarus Films
             153 Waverly Place, Sixth Floor
             New York, NY 10014
             (212) 727-1711; (800) 876-1710
             Fax: (212) 989-7649
             e-mail: FRIF@echonyc.com

This touching story chronicles the life of Rosalina, a 12-year-old girl whose family's home was set on fire during the civil war in El Salvador. The family has sought refuge in a camp in Honduras. Rosalina attends school, helps her mother with household tasks, plays games with her friends, and dreams of returning to her home in El Salvador.

Sidet: Forced Exile
Type: VHS
Length: 60 minutes
Date: 1991
Cost: Purchase: $295; rental: $75
Source: Women Make Movies
             462 Broadway, Suite 500D
             New York, NY 10013
             (212) 925-0606
             Fax: (212) 925-2052
             e-mail: distdept@wmm.com

Over two million refugees have left Ethiopia during the past two decades, due to famine, poverty, political strife, and religious persecution. This poignant video presents the life stories of three women refugees settled in neighboring Sudan. The women's attempts to survive displacement, resettlement camps, and ineffectual bureaucracy are examined. This video provides a good analysis of this social and economic crisis from the perspective of Third World women.

Something Like a War
Type: VHS
Length: 52 minutes
Date: 1991
Cost: Purchase: $295; rental: $90
Source: Women Make Movies
             462 Broadway, Suite 500D

New York, NY 10013
(212) 925-0606
Fax: (212) 925-2052
e-mail: distdept@wmm.com

This chilling video examines India's family planning program from the viewpoint of the women who are targeted for services. Tracing the history of the family planning program in India, the cynicism, corruption, and brutality of its implementation are described. The women who were its targets discuss their status, sexuality, fertility control, and health. Their perceptions of the program are vividly different from the views of the program organizers and proponents. This video is a great resource for the study of international development and aid, population control, reproductive rights, health, and women.

Song of Umm Dalaila: The Story of the Sahrawis
Type: VHS
Length: 30 minutes
Date: 1993
Cost: Purchase: $195, rental: $40
Source: Documentary Educational Resources
             101 Morse Street
             Watertown, MA 01272
             (617) 926-0491; (800) 569-6621
             Fax: (617) 926-9519

The experiences of Sahwari women, who make up 80 percent of the adults living in refugee camps in southwest Nigeria, are detailed in this documentary. The Sahrawis became refugees in 1975 when Morocco invaded and occupied their homeland, the former Spanish colony of Western Sahara in northwest Africa. The women tell their own stories, revealing how they have become responsible for the safety and survival of their families and of their culture.

Spear and Sword: A Payment of Bridewealth on the Island of Roti
Type: VHS, 16mm
Length: 25 minutes
Date: 1990
Cost: VHS purchase: $195; VHS rental: $35;
             16mm purchase: $550; 16mm rental: $65
Source: Documentary Educational Resources

101 Morse Street
Watertown, MA 01272
(617) 926-0491
Fax: (617) 926-9519

This documentary focuses on the negotiations that take place between two families during a payment of bridewealth. The practice of bridewealth is explained, including images of the bride's representative collecting money and animals and discussing problems that might arise during negotiations. The men and women chosen to represent the groom walk the three miles to the bride's family home in silence. Discussions that accompany the transfer of money and animals to the groom's representatives are chronicled.

These Girls Are Missing: The Gender Gap in Africa's Schools

Type: VHS
Length: 60 minutes
Date: 1996
Cost: Purchase: $295; rental: $75
Source: Filmakers Library
124 East 40th Street
New York, NY 10016
(212) 808-4980
Fax: (212) 808 4983
e-mail: info@filmakers.com

Across Africa, many girls do not receive an education. This video provides the stories of several girls throughout Africa and their experiences. These girls include Nadouba and Bintu in the small West African village, Taz; Patricia from the elite St. Mary's Secondary School in Malawi; and Ethel and her mother who have conflicting feelings about life in their small village and the advantages of the modern world. The video also contains a conversation with a group of Malinke elders. The viewer begins to understand the cultural attitudes that undermine the future of Africa's young girls.

Time of Women

Type: VHS
Length: 20 minutes
Date: 1988
Cost: Purchase: $225; rental: $60
Source: Women Make Movies

462 Broadway, Suite 500D
New York, NY 10013
(212) 925-0606
Fax: (212) 925-2052
e-mail: distdept@wmm.com

This documentary provides a moving portrait of life in an Ecuadorian village that is populated primarily by women and children. Many of the village's men have left to find work in other areas; sometimes they are gone for years at a time. This video explains the situation that exists in many Third World countries, where the men are forced to seek work away from home, leaving the women to care for the children, the home, and themselves. Focusing on the strengths of these women, as well as the sadness in their lives, this video provides a personal look at the impact of national economic policies on those most affected by these policies.

To Empower Women: The Beijing Platform for Action

Type: VHS
Length: 28 minutes
Date: 1996
Cost: $15, individuals; $50, institutions
Source: Off Center Video
1300 Shattuck Avenue, Suite A
Berkeley, CA 94709
(510) 486-8010
Fax: (510) 644-2139
e-mail: margots999@aol.com

The Platform for Action was signed by 189 nations during the Fourth World Conference on Women held in Beijing in 1995. This document is the strongest statement of consensus on women's equality, empowerment, and justice ever produced. Narrated by Bella Abzug, this video shows women who attended the conference as they movingly describe their experiences in working to improve the conditions of women in their countries. Five planks of the platform are illustrated; these include poverty, education, economics, human rights, and armed conflict.

Tobelo Marriage

Type: VHS
Length: 106 minutes
Date: 1990

Cost: Purchase: $225; rental: $75
Source: University of California Extension
Center for Media and Independent Learning
2000 Center Street, Fourth Floor
Berkeley, CA 94704
(510) 642-0460
Fax: (510) 643-9271

This documentary portrays a remarkable marriage ritual on a Moluccan island of eastern Indonesia. A large-scale exchange of valuable items is included; this exchange requires high-level negotiation skills, many ceremonies, and long-term activities in preparation for the negotiations. Unexpected complications arise because the bride and groom elope before all arrangements are made. The video has won Margaret Mead Film Festival honors and is an American Anthropological Association selection.

To Hold Our Ground
Type: VHS, 16mm
Length: 51 minutes
Date: 1991
Cost: VHS purchase: $199; 16mm purchase: $975;
VHS or 16mm rental: $75
Source: International Film Bureau
332 South Michigan Avenue
Chicago, IL 60604-4382
(312) 427-4545

A moving story of women and children in the Philippines, this video describes their work in organizing themselves to improve the quality of their lives. These women have been evicted from their homes, are often in debt, and have trouble supporting and protecting their families. They are squatters living in makeshift bamboo huts outside Cebu, the second largest city in the Philippines. The women work as sidewalk vendors, trying to support their families. Tessie Fernandez, a dynamic community organizer, pulls together these women into an organized group working for their rights. The video examines the efforts of women to organize for social change, the strength and resourcefulness of these women, and the desperate situation of abandoned children.

Tomorrow's World
Type: VHS
Length: 24 minutes

Date: 1984
Cost: $50
Source: United Nations
Audio-Visual Promotion and Distribution Unit
Media Division, Department of Public Information
Room S-805B
New York, NY 10017
(212) 963-6939
Fax: (212) 963-6869
e-mail: Sue-Ting-Len@un.org

The world's population is anticipated to be six billion by the year 2000. The rate of increase in population has been declining since the World Population Plan of Action was adopted in 1974. This film documents three success stories. In Tunisia the age of marriage has been raised, along with the outlawing of polygamy and other legislation that has given women more control over their families' destinies. In Thailand, good humor and innovation are at the heart of the family planning program. In Mexico, family planning is integrated into general health programs that emphasize mother and child care. The video is available in English, French, and Spanish.

Two Dollars with or without a Condom
Type: VHS
Length: 40 minutes
Date: 1997
Cost: Purchase: $295; rental: $55
Source: Filmakers Library
124 East 40th Street
New York, NY 10016
(212) 808-4980
e-mail: info@filmakers.com

Ethiopia has become a haven for prostitution in the Middle East. In one area of Addis Ababa, over 130,000 girls, many of them under the age of 18 years, support themselves by selling their bodies. This documentary introduces the viewer to the girls involved in this business; many are orphaned, have been kicked out of their homes, or are seeking a better life for themselves. But the younger girls hardly earn enough money to buy food. The older ones earn about $2 a night but want to work their way up to working the luxury hotels as high-class prostitutes. Most of these young women are HIV positive; customers seek out young girls in the belief that they are not yet infected with HIV. Some agencies try to help these girls, but the need is overwhelming and the girls find that prostitution is the only way to survive.

The Veiled Hope: Women of Palestine
Type: VHS
Length: 55 minutes
Date: 1994
Cost: Purchase: $250; rental: $75
Source: Women Make Movies
Distribution Service
462 Broadway, Suite 500D
New York, NY 10013
(212) 925-0606
Fax: (212) 925-2052
e-mail: distdept@wmm.com

The challenges facing Palestinian women are explored in this documentary, which offers a series of portraits of women living on the Gaza and West Bank. The women describe their daily lives as doctors, schoolteachers, and activists and discuss their activities to rebuild Palestinian cultural identity. They provide the viewer with an intimate view of the complex feelings that women have concerning the emergence of political Islamic movements. These women believe in the national liberation struggle but also the struggle for women's rights.

The Vienna Tribunal
Type: VHS
Length: 48 minutes
Date: 1994
Cost: Purchase: $195; rental: $60
Source: Women Make Movies
Distribution Service
462 Broadway, Suite 500D
New York, NY 10013
(212) 925-0606
Fax: (212) 925-2052
e-mail: distdept@wmm.com

This video provides highlights of the moving personal testimonies at the Global Tribunal on Violations of Women's Rights, held in conjunction with the United Nations World Conference on Human Rights in Vienna in 1993. Developed in conjunction with the Center for Women's Global Leadership, this video offers a thought-provoking analysis of the abuses that women suffer throughout the world.

Warrior Marks

Type: VHS, 16mm
Length: 54 minutes
Date: 1993
Cost: VHS purchase: $295; VHS rental: $85; 16mm rental: $85
Source: Women Make Movies
            462 Broadway, Suite 500D
            New York, NY 10013
            (212) 925-0606
            Fax: (212) 925-2052
            e-mail: distdept@wmm.com

Alice Walker is the executive producer of this excellent video that focuses on female genital circumcision, or mutilation, as it is referred to in the film. One hundred million women are estimated to be affected by this surgery, and this powerful video explores some of the cultural and political complexities surrounding this issue. Interviews are conducted with women from Senegal, Gambia, Burkino Faso, the United States, and England who are affected by and concerned with genital mutilation. Walker, Pulitzer Prize–winning author of *The Color Purple* and *Possessing the Secret of Joy,* provides her personal reflections on this volatile subject. Walker and Pratibha Parmar describe their experiences of making this film in their book, *Warrior Marks: Female Genital Mutilation and the Sexual Blinding of Women.*

Water for Tonoumassé

Type: VHS
Length: 28 minutes
Date: 1990
Cost: Purchase: $295; rental: $55
Source: Filmakers Library
            124 East 40th Street
            New York, NY 10016
            (212) 808-4980
            Fax: (212) 808-4983
            e-mail: info@filmakers.com

In southern Togo, in West Africa, the long dry season creates problems for women collecting water for cooking and bathing. In this video, one woman makes an eight-hour trek, leaving home at 1:00 A.M., to gather water. However, the water she gathers is contaminated. A group of villagers decides that they must have a new source of water, so they work together to have a well drilled near the village. This video chronicles the efforts of the villagers, primarily women, who worked to have the well drilled. Many of the village men are surprised that the women are capable of making decisions, handling money, and learning how to keep the pump working. This vivid example of a successful development project shows how women are transformed and their daily lives are improved when they take action themselves.

Weavers in Ahuiran
Type: VHS, Beta, 3/4U
Length: 54 minutes
Date: 1990
Cost: $225
Source: University of California Extension
            Center for Media and Independent Learning
            2000 Center Street, 4th Floor
            Berkeley, CA 94704
            (510) 642-0460
            Fax: (510) 643-9271

This German documentary profiles the weaving techniques, social organization, and economic situation of the women weavers in a weaving village in Michoacan, Mexico. The changes that have occurred in weaving techniques over the years, work organization caused by difficult economic conditions, and how the weaving methods are passed down through the generations are examined. The changes caused by the long absences of the women's husbands as they become migrant farm workers in the United States are shown.

Weaving the Future: Women of Guatemala
Type: VHS, Beta, 3/4U
Length: 28 minutes
Date: 1988
Cost: $225
Source: Women Making Movies
            462 Broadway, Suite 501
            New York, NY 10013
            (212) 925-0606

This fast-paced documentary explores the pivotal role women play in building a strong and fair society. Their efforts are shown in the context of terrorism, political strife, and poverty.

With These Hands

Type:	VHS
Length:	33 minutes
Date:	1987
Cost:	Purchase: $350; rental: $55
Source:	Filmakers Library
	124 East 40th Street
	New York, NY 10016
	(212) 808-4980
	Fax: (212) 808 4983
	e-mail: info@filmakers.com

The stories of three women from three different African countries—Kenya, Burkina Faso, and Zimbabwe—are told in this video. The women explain the troubles they have trying to feed and support their families. Women are responsible for growing most of the food, about 75 percent of all food, throughout Africa. They are constantly frustrated by the men in their villages as well as by outside business interests. Most husbands do not help their wives because they believe farm work is demeaning and meant only for women. This video demonstrates the strength of women in Africa and their attempts to challenge traditional male authority.

Women at Risk

Type:	VHS
Length:	56 minutes
Date:	1991
Cost:	Purchase: $295; rental: $75
Source:	Filmakers Library
	124 East 40th Street
	New York, NY 10016
	(212) 808-4980
	Fax: (212) 808 4983
	e-mail: info@filmakers.com

Most of the 15 million refugees around the world are women and young girls. Three female refugees are profiled in this video. Mai-Lien, a 13-year-old Vietnamese girl, came with her 10-year-old brother to a refugee camp in Malaysia. Because she is alone, except for her brother, she is unprotected and vulnerable to all types of threats to her health and life. Pheria, a 40-year-old mother of four, lives in a refugee camp in Zambia. During the civil war in Mozambique, her husband disappeared and she was left to protect and support her family after fleeing to Zambia. Juana, a 28-year-old Salvadoran and mother of three children, is pregnant and living in Costa Rica. She attempted to seek refuge in a more welcoming country but was denied. Now she is unsure how she and her family will survive.

Women, Children and War
Type: VHS, Beta, 3/4U
Length: 15 minutes
Date: 1975
Cost: Call for current prices
Source: Alden Films
P.O. Box 449
Clarksburg, NY 08510
(908) 462-3522

This video examines the impact of the Yom Kippur War on the lives of wives, mothers, and children in Israel. For junior high, senior high, college, and adult audiences.

Women in Bangladesh
Type: VHS
Length: 23 minutes
Date: 1996
Cost: Purchase: $250; rental: $55
Source: Filmakers Library
124 E. 40th Street
New York, NY 10016
(212) 808-4980; (800) 555-9815
e-mail: info@filmakers.com

Taslina Nasreen, a writer from Bangladesh, is profiled in this video. She gained international attention when Islamic leaders issued a fatwa calling for her death. The leaders offered a large reward for the person who was able to kill her. One of the few women to call for more freedom for the women of Bangladesh, Nasreen is interviewed in this video from her hiding place outside the country. Her story is placed in the context of the condition suffered by women throughout Bangladesh. Also presented in this video is a message from Begum Zia, the female prime minister of Bangladesh.

Women in Nicaragua
Type: VHS
Length: 28 minutes
Date: 1982
Cost: Purchase: $280; rental: $55
Source: First Run Features/Icarus Films
153 Waverly Place, Sixth Floor
New York, NY 10014
(212) 727-1711; (800) 876-1710
Fax: (212) 989-7649
e-mail: FRIF@echonyc.com

Women in Nicaragua have struggled for many years to gain equality with men in their country. This documentary features Gladys Baez, the first woman to join the Sandinista guerrilla forces in the early 1960s. Made for junior high, senior high, college, and adult audiences.

Women in the Middle East
Type: VHS, 16mm
Length: 4 videos, 26 minutes each
Date: 1982
Cost: VHS purchase: $280 each; 16mm purchase: $470 each; 16mm rental: $55 each
Source: First Run/Icarus Films
153 Waverly Place, Sixth Floor
New York, NY 10014
(212) 727-1711; (800) 876-1710
Fax: (212) 989-7649
e-mail: FRIF@echonyc.com

This series consists of four videos that describe the changing role of women in the Middle East, including how they cope with the religious, political, and economic upheavals occurring throughout the region. The first video, *A Veiled Revolution,* considers the possible reasons for the resurgence of Islamic fundamentalism and the rejection of Western values. Egyptian women are returning to the practice of wearing a veil whenever they are in public, after their grandmothers fought for the right to not wear them. Another video, *The Price of Change,* examines the effects of women working outside the home in Egypt. Five women, including a factory worker, a doctor, and an opposition member of Egypt's Parliament, tell their stories. *Women under Siege* describes the activities of six women who played crucial roles in a Palestinian community constantly under siege by the Israeli military. The women are mothers, teachers, organizers, laborers, and sometimes fighters protecting their lives and their families. The final film, *Saints and Spirits,* explores three religious events in Morocco through the eyes of Aisha bint Muhammad. These events include the festive annual renewal of contact with spirits in Marrakech, the pilgrimage to the shrine in the Atlas Mountains, and the veneration of a new saint's shrine.

Women in War: Voices from the Front Lines
Type: VHS
Length: 2 videos, 48 minutes each
Date: 1991
Cost: Purchase: $445 for both; rental: $90 for both
Source: Filmakers Library
         124 East 40th Street
         New York, NY 10016
         (212) 808-4980
         Fax: (212) 808 4983
         e-mail: info@filmakers.com

The two videos in this series profile women living in war-torn areas of the world and facing day-to-day problems. The first video shows Israeli and Palestinian women in Israel willing to bear arms; at the same time they are involved in the peacemaking process. Then, the efforts of Nobel Peace Prize–winner Mairead Corrigan and Betty Williams to form Peace People, a movement to end the violence in Northern Ireland, are described. The second video, dedicated to the women of the Americas, shows women in El Salvador assuming leadership positions in the popular front movement and women in Boston, New York, Washington, and Los Angeles fighting to rid their neighborhoods of crime.

The Women Next Door
Type: VHS, 16mm
Length: 80 minutes
Date: VHS purchase: $295; VHS rental: $90;
         16mm rental: $175
Source: Women Make Movies

Distribution Service
462 Broadway, Suite 500D
New York, NY 10013
(212) 925-0606
Fax: (212) 925-2052
e-mail: distdept@wmm.com

A thoughtful and emotional documentary about women in the Palestinian-Israeli conflict, this video provides the viewer with insight into some of the difficult problems of the peace process and future problems. *The Women Next Door* describes the ways that the Israeli occupation has affected women on both sides of the conflict.

Women of Niger
Type: VHS
Length: 26 minutes
Date: 1993
Cost: Purchase: $250; rental: $60
Source: Women Make Movies
           Distribution Service
           462 Broadway, Suite 500D
           New York, NY 10013
           (212) 925-0606
           Fax: (212) 925-2052
           e-mail: distdept@wmm.com

As a traditionally Islamic country, Niger finds itself in a clash between Muslim fundamentalism and the struggle for democracy. In the elections of 1993, men voted by proxy for their wives and daughters. Polygamy is authorized by law. Women who speak out for their rights have been physically attacked. This video examines women working together to defend democracy, in the hope that they will receive equal rights in a democratic country.

Women of the Sahel
Type: VHS
Length: 52 minutes
Date: 1995
Cost: Purchase: $390; rental, $75
Source: First Run/Icarus Films
           153 Waverly Place, Sixth Floor
           New York, NY 10014
           (212) 727-1711; (800) 876-1710

Fax: (212) 989-7649
e-mail: FRIF@echonyc.com

In Niger, only 5,000 of approximately 9 million residents are salaried workers. The work that is done in the informal sector, where most women work, is essential to the survival of many families in Niger. This informal sector accounts for more than half of the country's economic activity. The filmmakers visit with several women who work in the informal sector—making peanut oil, extracting salt from the earth, and turning gypsum into plaster. Craftswomen who make and decorate pottery, weave straw mats, and do intricate leather work are portrayed. This film introduces some of the cooperative organizations that the women have organized to provide loans or to sell products to wholesalers and importers and clearly demonstrates the hidden economic infrastructure that is so important for the survival of many families in developing countries.

Women of the Toubou
Type: 16mm
Length: 25 minutes
Date: 1974
Cost: Purchase: $425; rental: $40
Source: Phoenix/BFA Films
             2349 Chaffee Drive
             St. Louis, MO 63146
             (314) 569-0211; (800) 221-1274
             Fax: (314) 569-2834

The Toubou is a nomadic tribe living in the Sahara flatlands and in the mountains. The Toubou society is matriarchal and women are treated as equals by the men. The video provides a glimpse of the life that the women of the Toubou lead. The tribe has resisted all efforts of the Turks, French, and the government of Chad to control them. This video is for senior high, college, and adult audiences.

Women of the World
Type: VHS, Beta, 3/4U
Length: 60 minutes
Date: 1989
Cost: $59.95
Source: PBS Home Video
             Catalog Fulfillment Center

P.O. Box 4030
Santa Monica, CA 90411
(800) 531-4727; (800) 645-4PBS

This video profiles the lives of outstanding women who have faced a variety of challenges. For junior high, senior high, college, and adult audiences.

Women Writing around the World
Type: VHS
Length: 36 minutes
Cost: $119
Source: University of Toronto
Information Commons
130 St. George Street
Toronto, ON, Canada M5S 1A1

This video provides footage from an international colloquium organized by the University of Toronto on the problems that women face around the world. Discussions on censorship, poverty, and politics are shown. Insights are provided from Dorothy Livesay, Canadian poet and essayist; Lakshmi Kannan, poetry writer who lives in New Delhi; Makeda Silvera, Jamaican-born writer; Miriam Tlali, writer from Soweto; and Flora Nwapa, novelist and short story writer from Nigeria. For senior high, college, and adult audiences.

Women's Lives and Choices
Type: VHS
Length: 3 videos, 28 minutes each
Date: 1995
Cost: Purchase: $295; rental: $90
Source: Women Make Movies
Distribution Service
462 Broadway, Suite 500D
New York, NY 10013
(212) 925-0606
Fax: (212) 925-2052
e-mail: distdept@wmm.com

This series of videos focuses on women's health and the social, cultural, and economic factors that influence reproductive choice. *Ventre Livre* provides a dismal picture of life for women living in Brazil where sterilization and abortion are often the only forms of birth control available. *Rishte* examines the practice of male sex preference in India and its effect on women and follows the life of Lali Devi, a mother of five daughters who poisoned herself and two of her daughters. *Desired Number* demonstrates how family planning issues often interfere with traditional family values, using the Ibu Eze ceremony in Nigeria to examine these issues.

Women's Olamal: The Organization of a Maasai Fertility Ceremony

Type:	VHS, Beta, 3/4U
Length:	110 minutes
Date:	1985
Cost:	Call for current prices
Source:	Documentary Educational Resources
	101 Morse Street
	Watertown, MA 02172
	(617) 926-0491; (800) 569-6621

Following the events that preceded a controversial ceremony in Loita, Kenya, to bless the women and to increase their ability to have children, this video explores women's attitudes toward childbirth and fertility. Some of the tensions between women and men are depicted, including the differences of beliefs and opinions between men and women concerning fertility. The women are interviewed and provide explanation and insight into the ceremony and their beliefs. For junior high, senior high, college, and adult audiences.

A Zenana: Scenes and Recollections

Type:	VHS, 16mm
Length:	36 minutes
Date:	1982
Cost:	VHS purchase: $195; VHS rental: $35;
	16mm purchase: $550; 16mm rental: $65
Source:	Documentary Educational Resources
	101 Morse Street
	Watertown, MA 01272
	(617) 926-0491
	Fax: (617) 926-9519

In India, the women's quarters, or zenana, are the most secluded section of the palace. Until recently, palace women lived behind protective walls and doors that kept them securely within the palace walls. This video provides a glimpse into the lives of women in the zenana at Dhrangadra in northern India. This was the seat of power for the Jhala Rajputs from the eleventh century until 1947. The experiences of several of the palace women are told through songs, dances, and stories. The Maharani, wife of the Maharaja, is the mother of one of the filmmakers. She and the other women discuss the traditional roles of women in their position, the strict guidelines of their former seclusion, and the ideals of women's purity and inner strength.

Online/Internet Resources

There are many sites on the Internet that focus on women in the Third World. The following sites provide the reader with an idea of the type of sites that are available. Many of these sites provide links to other sites of related interest.

Amnesty International
http://www.io.org/amnesty/overview.html

This site provides information on Amnesty International and its human rights activities throughout the world.

The Arab Women's Home Page
http://www.usnet/arabwomen

This site provides Arab women worldwide with an open forum to share their experiences. It creates a connection among Arab women as well as women from other cultures. Links are provided to related pages.

Association for Middle East Women's Studies
http://humanities.ucsb.edu/~gallaghe/amews.html

The Association for Middle East Women's Studies (AMEWS) is an affiliated organization of the Middle East Association of North America. This association was founded more than ten years ago by scholars interested in promoting research in the field of Middle East women's studies.

AVSC International
http://www.igc.apc.org/avsc

AVSC International works to provide access to family planning services to women and men throughout the world.

Contact Center Network
http://www.contact.org

This site contains a global directory of nonprofit websites, with links to over 9,000 sites in 100 countries. Many of these sites focus on women in the Third World.

DIANA
http://www.law.uc.edu:81/Diana

Many documents, including bibliographies, concerning human rights are located at this site, based at the Center for Electronic Text in the Law at the University of Cincinnati College of Law. Much of this information concerns women's human rights. Links are provided to other related sites.

Directory/Anthology about Iranian Women
http://www.zan.org

A site that provides arts and ideas concerning Iranian women, this page encourages participation of all women in an atmosphere that is free from any political or religious affiliations. The authors are trying to break down stereotypes of Iranian women and provide a networking opportunity that connects all Iranian women, no matter where they live.

Female Genital Mutilation
http://www.hollyfield.org/org.fgm

This site includes reference material, efforts on eradicating this practice, legislation (both national and international), links to other pages on female genital mutilation, and discussion forums.

Global Center News
gopher://gopher.igc.apc.org:70/11/orgs/cwgl/pub

The Center for Women's Global Leadership (see Chapter 5) operates this site, which provides information on the center's activities as well as links to other sources of information.

Human Rights Country Reports
gopher://cyfer.esusda.gov/11/ace/state/hrcr

Reports on human rights conditions in many countries are found at this gopher site.

The Informal Credit Homepage
http://titsoc.titech.ac.jp/titsoc/higuchi-lab/icm/icm-people-banks.html

Links to many sources of women's credit are provided here, including Bangladesh's Grameen Bank and India's Self-Employed Women's Association (SEWA). A rich source of information concerning sources of credit for women in the Third World.

JHPIEGO Corporation
http://www.jhpiego.jhu.edu

JHPIEGO Corporation is a nonprofit organization dedicated to improving the health of women and families throughout the world. The program's goal is to increase the availability of high quality reproductive health services.

Novartis: Foundation for Sustainable Development
http://foundation.novartis.com

Established in December 1996, this site was previously known as the Ciba-Geigy Foundation for Cooperation with Developing Countries. The foundation works to create an environment in which dignified human development can take place in the Third World. Projects funded focus on agriculture, health care, and social development. This site provides information about the foundation and its projects.

One World
http://www.oneworld.org

A community of over 120 leading global justice organizations is contained at this site, which provides news services and links to related sources of information. Current news, by country and by theme, from agriculture, civil rights, freedom of expression, human rights, and poverty to women's rights is provided. Related pages provide information on radio, guides, a think tank, and a gallery. This site is a good source of current information concerning women in the Third World.

Population Council
http://www.popcouncil.com

The Population Council is a nonprofit, nongovernmental research organization devoted to improving the reproductive health and well-being of women and men throughout the world. The council studies population issues and trends, conducts social and reproductive sciences research, and works with government and private organizations to improve family planning and related health services.

Population Institute
http://www.populationinstitute.org

As a population advocacy organization, the Population Institute provides leadership in creating national and international awareness of the social, economic, and environmental implications of rapid population growth. Dedicated to bringing about global population stabilization, the institute has members in 160 countries.

Population Reference Bureau
http://www.prb.org/prb

The Population Reference Bureau works with public and private sector partners to increase the amount, accuracy, and usefulness of information concerning changes in population and the impact these changes may have on society.

Program for Appropriate Technology in Health
http://www.path.org

The Program for Appropriate Technology in Health focuses on improving health, especially the health of women and children.

SolidAfrica
http://humanism.org/SolidAfrica

SolidAfrica encourages the economic empowerment of women in the areas of socioeconomic crisis and hardship. Women who have already started businesses are aided in their attempts to gain access to credit, new technologies, marketing activities, management, and training opportunities. Practical information is exchanged with universities, nonprofit organizations, international development agencies, foundations, and corporations. Links to related organizations are provided.

South Asian Women's Network
http://www.uniacs.umd.edu/users/sawweb/sawnet

Full of practical information, this site offers a forum for people interested in issues concerning women in South Asia. South Asian women's organizations, books, children's books, cinema reviews and literature, domestic violence, news about South Asian women, articles of interest, charities and political organizations, health information, careers, grants and funding, electronic resources, and homepages of South Asian Women's Network (SAWNET) members are provided by this page.

Third World Organization for Women in Science
http://www.ictp.trieste.it/%7Etwas/TWOWS.html

The Third World Organization for Women in Science (TWOWS) is the first international forum to unite eminent women scientists from Third World countries with the objective of strengthening their role in the development process and promoting their representation in scientific and technological leadership. Members include over 1,500 individual and 25 full institutional members from 82 developing countries.

Tibetan Women's Association
http://www.grannyg.bc.ca./tibet/tibet/.html

This NGO is headquartered in Dharmasala, India, with over 37 branches worldwide and focuses on violations of women's rights in Tibet.

United Nations Department of Public Information
http://www.un.org

This site provides information concerning the United Nations, its programs, activities, and publications.

United Nations Development Fund for Women
http://www.ingenia/com.unifem

This site offers information about the United Nations Development Fund for Women (UNIFEM) and its programs and publications and links to other sites related to women in development.

Women in Development Network
http://focusintl.com/widnet.htm

This is the site for the Women in Development Network (WIDNET).

Women of Africa Resources
http://www.lawrence.edu/~bradleyc/war.html

Operated by Lawrence University, this site offers general information, bibliographies, syllabi, and links to other resources on African women. Annotated bibliographies focus on women in west Africa, South Africa, and east Africa. Online articles provide information by and about African women.

Women's Endowment and
Development Organization Newsletter
gopher://igc.apc.org:70/11/orgs/wedo/news

The Women's Endowment and Development Organization (WEDO) Newsletter provides a wide range of information concerning women in development as well as links to additional information.

Women's Feature Service
http://www.womensnet.org/wfs

The Women's Feature Service is an international organization that disseminates information on women's development and works to change discrimination in the media's portrayal of women.

WomensNet
http://gopher:igc.apc.org:70/00/women/WN

This site is for serious researchers and organizations interested in issues of interest to women throughout the world. WomensNet is part of the Institute for Global Communications (IGC), a nonprofit computer system that focuses on peace, social justice, and human rights. Networking and information resources are provided. There is a charge to join this network.

World Health Organization/UNICEF
http://www.oneworld.cug/unicef/progress/summary

A summary of the progress that nations have made concerning many health issues of interest to women is found at this site.

The World's Women On-Line
http://wwol.inre.asu.edu/wwol.html

Set up in conjunction with the United Nations Fourth World

Conference on Women, this site is an electronic art networking project that uses the Internet as a global exhibition format.

Zonta International

http://www.grannyg.bc.ca/zonta.html

Zonta is a worldwide service organization composed of executives in business and the professions who work together to advance the status of women throughout the world. There are approximately 35,000 members in over 1,100 clubs in 68 countries.

Appendix:
Third World
Countries

Afghanistan	Ecuador
Algeria	Egypt
Angola	El Salvador
Antigua	Equatorial Guinea
Argentina	Ethiopia
Bahamas	Fiji
Bahrain	Gabon
Bangladesh	Ghana
Barbados	Grenada
Belize	Guatemala
Benin	Guinea
Bhutan	Guyana
Bolivia	Haiti
Botswana	Honduras
Brazil	India
Brunei	Indonesia
Burkina Faso	Iran
Burma	Iraq
Burundi	Ivory Coast
Cameroon	Jamaica
Cape Verde	Jordan
Central African	Kampuchea
Republic	Kenya
Chad	Kiribati
Chile	Korea, Democratic
Colombia	People's Republic
Comoros	(North)
Congo	Korea, Republic of
Costa Rica	(South)
Djibouti	Kuwait
Dominica	Laos
Dominican Republic	Lebanon

Lesotho
Liberia
Libya
Madagascar
Malawi
Malaysia
Maldives
Mali
Mauritania
Mauritius
Mexico
Morocco
Mozambique
Namibia
Nauru
Nepal
Nicaragua
Niger
Nigeria
Oman
Pakistan
Panama
Papua New Guinea
Paraguay
Peru
Philippines
Qatar
Rwanda
St. Kitts and Nevis
St. Lucia
St. Vincent
São Tomé and Principe

Saudi Arabia
Senegal
Seychelles
Sierra Leone
Singapore
Solomon Islands
Somalia
Sri Lanka
Sudan
Suriname
Swaziland
Syria
Tanzania
Togo
Tonga
Trinidad and Tobago
Tunisia
Turkey
Tuvalu
Uganda
United Arab Emirates
Uruguay
Vanuatu
Venezuela
Vietnam
Western Samoa
Yemen Arab Republic
Yemen Democratic Republic
Zaire
Zambia
Zimbabwe

The United Nations divides these countries into the following regions for purposes of study and analysis:

Africa
  Northern Africa
    Algeria
    Egypt
    Libya
    Morocco
    Tunisia
    Western Sahara
  Sub-Saharan Africa
    Angola
    Benin
    Botswana

Burkina Faso
Burundi
Cameroon
Cape Verde
Central African Republic
Chad
Comoros
Congo
Djibouti
Equatorial Guinea
Eritrea
Ethiopia

Gabon
Gambia
Ghana
Guinea
Guinea-Bissau
Ivory Coast
Kenya
Lesotho
Liberia
Madagascar
Malawi
Mali
Mauritania
Mauritius
Mozambique
Namibia
Niger
Nigeria
Rwanda
São Tomé and Principe
Senegal
Seychelles
Sierra Leone
Somalia
South Africa Sudan
Swaziland
Tanzania
Togo
Uganda
Zaire
Zambia
Zimbabwe

**Latin America and
the Caribbean**
Central America
Belize
Costa Rica
El Salvador
Guatemala
Honduras
Mexico
Nicaragua
Panama

South America
Argentina
Bolivia
Brazil
Chile
Colombia
Ecuador
French Guiana
Guyana
Paraguay
Peru
Suriname
Uruguay
Venezuela
Caribbean
Antigua and Barbuda
Bahamas
Barbados
Dominica
Dominican Republic
Grenada
Haiti
Jamaica
St. Kitts and Nevis
St. Lucia
St. Vincent
Trinidad and Tobago

Asia and Pacific
Eastern Asia
Korea, Democratic People's
Republic (North)
Korea, Republic of (South)
Southeastern Asia
Brunei
Indonesia
Malaysia
Myanmar (Burma)
Philippines
Singapore
Thailand
Vietnam

Acronyms

ILO   International Labor Organization

INGO   International nongovernmental organization. These organizations provide development assistance to Third World countries, but their corporate headquarters are located in developed countries.

NCIH   National Council for International Health

NGO   Nongovernmental organization. These organizations provide development, relief, education, and advocacy services throughout the Third World.

UN   United Nations

UNESCO   United Nations Educational, Scientific and Cultural Organization

UNFPA   United Nations Fund for Population Activities

UNHCR   United Nations High Commissioner for Refugees

Index

Karen L. Kinnear holds an M.A. in sociology and is a professional researcher, editor, and writer with over 20 years' experience in sociological, economic, statistical, and financial analysis. She has explored various research topics while studying and traveling in India. As a Peace Corps volunteer in Tonga, she studied women's economic activities and helped with census planning. She has traveled to Ecuador, Western Samoa, Mexico, Morocco, and Nepal and talked with women in each of these countries. Among her previous publications are *Violent Children: A Reference Handbook* and *Childhood Sexual Abuse: A Reference Handbook.*